Water and Power
in Highland Peru

WATER AND POWER IN HIGHLAND PERU

The Cultural Politics of Irrigation and Development

PAUL H. GELLES

RUTGERS UNIVERSITY PRESS
New Brunswick, New Jersey, and London

Library of Congress Cataloging-in-Publication Data

Gelles, Paul H., 1957–
 Water and power in highland Peru : the cultural politics of irrigation
and development / Paul H. Gelles.
  p. cm.
 Includes bibliographical references and index.
 ISBN 0–8135–2806–2 (cloth : alk. paper)—ISBN 0–8135–2807–0
(pbk. : alk. paper)
  1. Quechua Indians—Agriculture—Peru—Cabanaconde. 2. Irrigation—
Social aspects—Peru—Cabanaconde. 3. Cabanaconde (Peru)—Politics and
government. 4. Cabanaconde (Peru)—Ethnic relations. 5. Quechua
Indians—Peru—Ethnic identity. I. Title

 F3429.3.I77 G45 2000
 333.91'3'098532—dc21

                                                                99-049069

British Cataloging-in-Publication data for this book is available from the British
Library

Manufactured in the United States of America

for
my mother, father, brother, and sister
and for
my friends in the Andes and in Lima

Contents

Illustrations

PHOTOGRAPHS

(pages 93 through 97)

1. Cabanaconde and Environs
2. Irrigation Water in Street
3. Irrigation Water Coursing over Terraces
4. Majes Canal
5. Water Mayor Overseeing Irrigation
6. Women and Children
7. Vicuña Fetus and Q'apa
8. Mount Hualca-Hualca
9. Harvest Q'apa (Mother and Daughter)
10. The Two Water Mayors

Preface

> But were the seas made of ink
> And the sky a little white page
> And my fist a tiny paintbrush
> To write this watersong.
> > Hualina from the community of
> > Huachupampa, Huarochirí

In the Peruvian Andes, as in many other parts of the world, irrigation water is a key element of production as well as a source of great meaning and conflict. I believe that to understand irrigation we must understand community. One of the predominant social forms and sites of cultural production in Ecuador, Bolivia, and Peru, the Andean community must be understood as an inherently conflicted entity, as well as one that is constituted, in part, by a cultural orientation that joins local identity and production to sacred landscapes. My analysis insists that Andean irrigation must also be understood in terms of the ways that larger regional, national, and international forces enter the community and in terms of a wide cultural divide that exists in contemporary Peruvian society.

Studying the historical roots, cultural logics, and political forces of state and local models of irrigation in the highland community of Cabanaconde, I show that different fields of contention—among members of a differentiated community on the one hand and between the state and the community on the other—are intimately bound together. My analysis of these contested domains sheds light on Peruvian cultural politics and "development," Andean communities and production, and the different means by which highland peasants defend their resources and cultural identities.

If there is magic in the world, it is found in water. I have always thought as much, having grown up in the arid southwestern United States. I remember the magic I felt, at eleven years old, watching a "water witch" divine a well on a relative's property. His switch occasionally twitching as he walked here and there, it finally and definitively bent at ground zero, raising shadowy visions of underground lakes and rivers. Other tantalizing images associated with water filtered through my formative years. So when, in 1979, as an undergraduate exchange student in Peru, I first participated in an elaborate ritual celebrating water, it struck a chord deep within me. The "Water Fiesta" (*Fiesta de Agua*), the physical cleaning and spiritual blessing of an irrigation system, is a cultural form found in hundreds of Andean communities. The horse racing, feasting, dancing, singing, and ceremonial divisioning of the community during the fiesta, as well as the ritual offerings to mountains, springs, and ancestor deities, gave me an immediate appreciation of the spiritual, social, and emotional centrality of water in the Andes.

I returned to Peru and carried out six months of fieldwork in the central highland town of San Pedro de Casta, located in the Huarochirí region, while pursuing a master's degree in anthropology at the Pontificia Universidad Católica of Lima from 1982 to 1984.[1] It was during this research that I first encountered the conflict between local and state models of irrigation. In Casta, the state-sponsored Irrigators Commission ordained a new form of water management that challenged the cultural orientations and model of authority found in the Water Fiesta. Similar conflicts in neighboring communities convinced me that the clash between state and local models of irrigation was a widespread and significant process in highland society and that it deserved further study.

I first visited Cabanaconde, the community examined in this book, in 1985. Since that brief first visit, I have returned many times. My longest stay in the community was for my dissertation research, from July 1987 to December 1988. I have since gone back for short stays, in 1991, 1994, 1997, and 1998. My research methods have consisted primarily of "deep hanging out," as Clifford Geertz has put it: that is, participant observation, informal interviews, and immersion in the community's lifeways. I also undertook a land and crop census of several hundred households and conducted archival work in the community and in the city of Arequipa. My different visits to Cabanaconde, previous research in Huarochirí, and studies in Lima, have all contributed to the understanding of highland society and Peruvian cultural politics presented in this book. I could not have written it, however, without the kind support of many people and institutions.

My first debt of gratitude is to the people of Cabanaconde who extended their homes, food, and friendship to me. My deepest appreciation goes to the families of Hilario Herrera and Natividad Amañe, Teodocio Quispe and Julia Salazar, and Susana Valdivia and Adrián Casaperalta. I am also extremely indebted to Cansio Valdivia, Adán Condori, Pancha Valdivia, Mario Flores, Genoveva Chukihuayta, Claudio Benavides, Benildo Feria, Gladys Villavicencio, Teófilo Valdivia, Aurelia Valdivia, Walter Tinta, Isaías Cano, Godofredo Ticona, Nilo Abril, Sara Picha, Ricardo Torres, Braulio Amañe, Prudencia Flores, Juan Ura, Cornelio Ticona, and Hilario Bernedo. Special thanks go to Hilda Quispe and Braulio Ramírez, who have greatly contributed to my understanding of community life.

I also thank the water mayors and their families, as well as the members of the Irrigators Commission, for teaching me about water and allowing me to participate in their work. Communal authorities, especially Melitón Huamani, Pedro Quispe, Braulio Adrián, Guillermo Vera, and parish priest Jorge Silva, welcomed me into the community and provided access to communal archives. As I have traveled throughout the Cabaneño diaspora, several people have facilitated my understanding of this extended community. Here I limit my thanks to Hipólito Miranda, Isidro Miranda, Gladys Herrera de Denham, Gareth Denham, Viviana Vera, Glen Parschalk, Tania Mendoza de Quispe, Hipólito Quispe and his siblings, and to the Cabanaconde City Association of Washington, D.C. Soledad Gálvez shared the discoveries and hardships of fieldwork, and her support was fundamental to its successful completion. To these individuals and institutions, to many other Cabaneños not mentioned here, and to Edgar and René Coa, I offer my sincere appreciation.

Elsewhere in the Colca Valley and in the cities of Arequipa and

Lima, many others assisted my research. Madre Antonia Kaiser and Sister Sara in Yanque always had the latest news from the valley. Ricardo Valderrama and Carmen Escalante provided housing during my occasional trips to Chivay, and helping them make blood sausage was a small price to pay for good conversation and strong coffee. In Arequipa, Guillermo Galdos, Helard Fuentes, Alejandro Málaga Medina, Alejandro Málaga Nuñez, Roberto Ruelas, and Alberto Salinas greatly facilitated my archival research. I would also like to thank René Apaza, Herman Sven, Frieda Both, Andrés Chirinos, Miguel Martínez, Liz Paredes, and Liliana Mendoza. In Lima, I have learned a great deal from my former professors, now colleagues, Juan Ossio, Alejandro Ortiz, Teófilo Altamirano, and Fernando Fuenzalida. Thanks to all.

I would also like to thank the Anthropology Department at the Pontificia Universidad Católica of Lima, the institution with which I have been affiliated during different periods of my research in Peru. The Tinker Foundation, the Fulbright-Hays Commission, the Social Science Research Council, the Interamerican Foundation, the Ciriacy-Wantrup Postdoctoral Fellowship at the University of California at Berkeley, and the Anthropology Department at the University of California at Riverside, supported different stages of my research, for which I am grateful.

Scholars working in the Colca Valley, such as William Denevan, David Guillet, Enrique Delgado, Karsten Paerregaard, María Benavides, Lisa Markowitz, and the late John Treacy, have taught me a great deal. Special thanks go to Blenda Femenias, who has stimulated my thinking about the Colca in many ways. So, too, thanks go to Robert Hunt, William P. Mitchell, Steve Lansing, Jeanette Sherbondy, Rutgerd Boelens, Paul Hoogendam, Gerben Gerbrandy, Teresa Oré, Zulema Gutiérrez, Paul Trawick, and Barbara Lynch, whose work on irrigation, Andean and otherwise, has greatly informed my own.

Many other individuals have influenced my thinking, supported the research, or otherwise helped bring this book into existence. Here I will limit my thanks to Seth Macinko, Melissa Everett, Eric Deeds, Nancy Peluso, Vinay Gidwani, Ann Hawkins, Sara Michaels, Louise Fortmann, Emery Roe, Orin Starn, Gabriela Martínez, Pia Maybury-Lewis, Stanley Tambiah, Nur Yalman, Pauline Peters, Carlos Vélez-Ibañez, Maria Cruz Torres, Konane Martinez, Ramona Pérez, Daniel Rodriguez, Monica Galván, Michelle McKinley, Teresa Lorden, Steve Wenzell, Diana Carr, Jim Huebner, Amy Cale, Roberto Calderón, Juan Palerm, Phil Boise, Ellen McLaughlin, Kit and Bev Boise-Cossart, Stephen Gudeman, Richard Norgaard, Paul Brodwin, Bartholomew Dean, Hugh Gusterson, Bapa Jhala, Jay Levi, Debbie Tooker, Terry O'Nell, and Chris Steiner.

For their close readings and generous comments on different versions of the manuscript, I would like to send special thanks to David Maybury-Lewis, Izumi Shimada, Gene Anderson, Gina Crivello, Michael Kearney, Alena Simunkova, Ben Orlove, and Catherine Allen. The editorial comments and suggestions offered by David Myers at Rutgers University Press and the fine copyediting work by Alison Kerr Miller have shaped the text in important ways and have made this a better book. To all of these people and to my wife, Cristina, for her support during the final stages of this book, I offer my sincere thanks.

I dedicate this book to my mother, father, sister, and brother, and to my friends in the Andes and in Lima.

Note to the Reader

I have italicized glossary words on their first usage in the text. Entire sections that have been italicized indicate the use of ethnographic vignettes (here, glossary words stand out by not being italicized). Quechua words are spelled according to the 1985 standardized alphabet for Peruvian Quechua, except for towns, villages, mountains, personal names, and other words conventionally known by some other Spanish-based spelling (e.g., Cuzco rather than Qusqu). Rather than use the Quechua pluralizer (-*kuna*) for untranslated words, I use the English method (e.g., *mistis* rather than *mistikuna*). The names of particular deities from native Andean religion (e.g., Earth Mother) are capitalized to accord them the same status as the Christian God and saints. Pseudonyms have been used to protect the privacy of the Cabaneños and other individuals.

The original maps and diagrams were drawn by Nancy Lambert-Brown, except for numbers I.1 and 4.2, which were drawn by me; number 2.4, which was taken from Autodema n.d.; number 2.5, which was drawn by Liberato Maki; number 2.8, which was drawn by Braulio Ramírez; number 4.3, which was drawn by Chuck Bouscaren; and number 4.4, the original of which was taken from de la Vera Cruz 1987. All photographs and the translations from Spanish and Quechua are mine, except where noted.

Water and Power
in Highland Peru

INTRODUCTION: CHANNELS OF POWER, FIELDS OF CONTENTION

The central Andean highlands cover the better part of the largest mountain chain in the world and are home to one of the largest indigenous peasantries in the Americas (fig. I.1).[1] They live at over 10,000 feet above sea level, in thousands of hamlets, towns, and cities spread over a rugged and vertical terrain. Found in warm fertile valleys, on steep mountainsides, and on frigid high plains, indigenous peasant communities control vast territories in the highlands of Ecuador, Peru, and Bolivia. The millions of Quechua-, Aymara-, and Spanish-speaking people who live in these communities are firmly tied to, and greatly affected by, national and international political and economic forces. However, members of this cultural majority also have religious beliefs and rituals that are distinctly Andean, providing important meaning and identity for their lives. Ignored or denigrated by dominant sectors in the Andean nations, native Andean religious beliefs and ritual practices have long been a fundamental component of local systems of agricultural and pastoral production, those activities that sustain life.

Irrigation water, one of the most culturally and ritually elaborated resources in Andean society and civilization, is today central to production in thousands of highland agricultural systems. As such, water is a highly contested resource, both in terms of irrigation

1

FIGURE I.1. The Central Andes

development and the different meanings assigned to water. In Peru, as in many other parts of the world, we find social groups fighting not only over the physical control of irrigation systems but also over the right to culturally define and organize these systems. By studying diverse ethnographic and historical materials for Cabanaconde, a large peasant community located in the lower Colca Valley of southwestern Peru, I illustrate how different, competing structures of power and meaning are conceptually mapped onto the community's irrigation system over the course of its annual agricultural cycle.

The 5,000 or so people living in Cabanaconde, which is well known throughout the southern Andes for its excellent maize, derive their irrigation water from mountains that they consider to be sacred. When one flies south from the metropolis of Lima toward Cabanaconde and the city of Arequipa, the arid highland valleys and mountains appear with barren, tiny patches of green barely discernible amid the vertical terrain. The seemingly desolate *sierra* falls abruptly to the even drier desert of the coastal plain. Occasional glacial peaks, many towering at close to 20,000 feet, interrupt the brown highland landscape. Mount Coropuna, considered by many peasants in southern Peru to be the abode of the damned, stands tall to one side as one enters the sierra of Arequipa. In the distance, El Misti holds vigil over the fertile valley and terraced fields surrounding Arequipa, which is called "the white city" and is the second largest in Peru. Directly below is Mount Ampato, joined to nearby Hualca-Hualca and Sabankaya peaks, their white snow necklaces shining brilliantly against the intense blue Andean sky. Sleepy smoke rings rise and disperse like evaporating shadows from the Sabankaya Volcano, active since the mid-1980s.

This mountain chain, the source of Cabanaconde's irrigation water, is revered by the Cabaneños in many diverse rituals throughout the year. Although the Cabaneños and their ancestors have imbued these volcanic peaks with spiritual power for a documented four hundred years, the irrigation and agricultural systems organized around the snowmelt of the mountains date back to at least the middle part of the first millennium of the common era. This longstanding ritual, agricultural, and hydrological formation has to be understood within wider historical, cultural, and political contexts.

During pre-Columbian times, and well through the Spanish colonial period, people and polities throughout the Central Andes traced their origins to sacred features of the landscape, such as mountains, lakes, and springs, which were often sources of irrigation water.[2] This peculiarly Andean definition of ethnicity continues to find expression in contemporary highland communities. As providers of fertility and life as well as of disease, death, and destruction, mountains and other features of the sacred landscape, along with Catholic saints, serve as protector spirits and emblems of local identity. The ritual offerings, libations, and religious celebrations that are directed toward these deities are an integral part of social life and agricultural production. But these local beliefs and rituals are also joined to wider fields of power.

This fact was brought home, so to speak, with the discovery in 1995 of the frozen remains of the "Ice Maiden," a girl sacrificed to Ampato, one of Cabanaconde's sacred peaks, by the Inka state some five hundred years ago. Several months after her discovery, she was presented to the public at the National Geographic Society in Washington, D.C. In attendance were first lady Hillary Clinton, President Alberto Fujimori of Peru, and several Cabaneño migrants. The latter were a small fraction of the several hundred migrants from Cabanaconde now living in Washington, D.C. The event underscored the strong tie that the Cabaneños and their ancestors have always had to larger political processes, be it the Inka's use of mountain worship to legitimate state power in the fifteenth century or the transnational migrant circuits in the late twentieth century.

Transnationalism and mountain ritual would seem to be at opposite ends of the anthropological spectrum. Transnationalism evokes world systems and the postmodern condition, with migrants on the move, plural identities, and hybrid cultural borderlands, whereas mountain ritual conjures the image of an older, modernist anthropology concerned with discrete social entities, fixed identities, and enduring social structures. Such a divide, I believe, reflects more on the discipline than on the cultural reality of the Andean nations or contemporary indigenous peasant communities.

Through an in-depth look at highland irrigation practices, I show that, at the end of the twentieth century, enduring patterns of belief and ritual are compatible with the porous and transnational character of Cabanaconde and many other Andean communities.

My focus is on the clash between local, ritualized models of water distribution and the secular, monetary model put forth by the Peruvian state. Officially, all water in the highlands belongs to the state, which ostensibly has the right to decide not only the uses and allocation of water, but also the organizational models by which it is managed. But highland communities dispute the state's control over "its" water and often refuse to allow the state to determine local irrigation practices. By examining Cabanaconde's peasant "water mayors" (*yaku alcaldes*) and their correlates in the Peruvian state's model ("controllers"), I demonstrate how these authorities embody fundamentally different historical processes, as well as distinct, competing cultural rationales concerning resources, power, efficiency, equity, and ethnic identity.

In addition to analyzing these largely covert and contested cultural domains regarding irrigation, I also explore less subtle forms of domination and resistance. Illuminating a larger cultural politics in Peruvian society, the study of irrigation takes us below the surface of highland history and provides one channel for understanding cultural and agricultural production in Andean communities today.

ANDEAN IRRIGATION DEVELOPMENT OVER TIME

The beliefs and rituals that link local identity and production to wider political contexts must also be examined in terms of Andean irrigation development, past and present. Irrigation, used today in over half of the more than 4,500 officially recognized highland communities in Peru, has a long history in the Andes.[3] Together with terracing, camelid herding, and the vertical control of different production zones, irrigation facilitated the development of the Inka empire and other pre-Columbian states in the rugged environment of the central Andes. Indeed, the surplus production provided by irrigation helped to bring about and increase state power. Covering countless thousands of mountain slopes, the canals and terraces that indigenous states and local polities built are truly monumental structures and represent millions of days of human labor. Unlike the pyramids, palaces, and fortresses that pre-Columbian polities also built, the "congealed labor" evident in terraces and canals reproduced their investment in this form of "humanized nature."[4]

This massive highland infrastructure also affected the development of extractive boom economies in Spanish colonial and postcolonial times. In contrast to those in the neighboring Amazon basin (see, e.g., Bunker 1985, Hecht and Cockburn 1990), extractive industries in the Andes and on the coast, such as those based on silver, guano, oil, and other resources (see, e.g., Thorp and Bertram 1978), have drawn on highland communities that possess well-established territories and relatively stable systems of agricultural and pastoral production. These productive systems have been the material basis for maintaining a cheap labor force and for extracting foodstuffs, tribute, and taxes over the last five hundred years. In the Andes, then, the political economy of extraction has always been bolstered by an extensive and ancient agricultural infrastructure.

However, with the great decline in population that followed the Spanish invasion, close to three-quarters of the pre-Columbian terraces were abandoned (Masson 1987), as were countless thousands of irrigation canals. Although the 4,500 recognized communities in Peru control well over a third of the nation's vast highlands, only a tiny percentage of this land is arable. Over the last century, the rapidly growing highland population has put pressure on communal resources and has engendered attempts to recover some of the lost infrastructure.

But because of Peru's coastally oriented political economy of development and the negative stereotypes of highland peoples and their resources that predominate there, the productive potential of this infrastructure is far from realized. An interpretive and historical examination of the cultural politics of irrigation, community, and development in highland society can contribute to both theory and practice.

IRRIGATION AS A CULTURAL SYSTEM

Over the last several millennia, irrigation has greatly transformed the environment and social formations across the globe. Today, irrigation systems and conflicts over water continue to proliferate around the world. Most approaches to the study of irrigation in anthropology and applied research share a positivist theoretical legacy. These approaches draw on models and metaphors from the natural sciences and, taking an entirely objectivist approach to the relationship between technology and society, theoretically divorce this relationship from particular historical and cultural circumstances.

Now, some will claim that I am beating a long-dead horse. Karl Wittfogel's "hydraulic hypothesis" about so-called Oriental Despotism (Wittfogel 1957), which asserted that irrigation necessarily leads to social stratification and a centralization of power, was refuted long ago. Even in China, where Wittfogel originally made his case, archeological evidence reveals that the rise of political authority needs to be understood not in terms of water control but in terms of art, myth, ritual, and shamanism and the ways that these were controlled by dynastic families (Chang 1983). But despite the many critiques of Wittfogel's basic premise, an emphatically objectivist bias continues to guide scholarly and applied research on irrigation and other forms of common property resource management.

The most forceful call for contextualizing analyses has come from the interpretive anthropology of Clifford Geertz.[5] In Geertz's view, the task of the anthropologist is to interpret the cultural models and expressive action that determine social and political practices, including those associated with irrigation. Like riddles, rituals, palaces, myths, maps, and melodies, irrigation systems are "texts to be read." They are vehicles for both water and meaning, existing through the cultural ideas and social organization invested in them. By studying indigenous models of irrigation, we come to understand the social theories of the people themselves, theories that are "paradigmatic, not merely reflective, of the social order" (Geertz 1980, 13).

Studying the cultural construction of irrigation systems,

however, is of little value if the political forces that underlie them are ignored. Bringing power into the picture is especially important when dealing with nations in which state policies reflect and deploy the political will and cultural hegemony of a dominant ethnic group. As Michael Herzfeld (in a different context) puts it, "Nationalist ideologies usually lay claim to some kind of constructed 'national character.' Their bureaucracies have the task of calibrating personal and local identity to this construct" (1992, 3). In a word, the institutional cultures generated within irrigation bureaucracies are inevitably shaped by the particular kind of "imagined community" (Anderson 1983) to which they belong.

Largely the product of each nation's colonial and postcolonial history, national irrigation institutions and policies are also tied to an international "bureaucratic tradition" (Lynch 1988). The symbolic roots of this tradition are common to the European nations and, through colonialism, to many industrializing countries. As such, bureaucracies are directly tied to "long-established forms of social, cultural, and racial exclusion in everyday life" (Herzfeld 1992,13). They treat particular individuals and groups differentially, depending on whether they are seen as sharing the bureaucrats' social world and cultural orientations; this is often expressed with metaphors of race and blood lines.[6] And, as Barbara Lynch (1993) has shown, this devaluation and exclusion extends to women, as the gender discrimination found in the field and in irrigation offices is part and parcel of this bureaucratic tradition.[7]

International development discourses have many of the same historical roots as the bureaucratic tradition and the nation-state. In Richard Norgaard's words, "Modernity promised control over nature through science, material abundance through superior technology, and effective government through rational social organization. . . . Accelerating progress through planned development has been the recent project of modernity" (1994, 1, 2). One of the key tenets of modernism is that Western science constantly produces more efficient technologies and ways of organizing, and that "cultural differences will fade away as people discover the effectiveness of rational Western culture" (1994, 7).

The power of modernity and Western models of irrigation "development" is clear, for example, in contemporary Balinese irrigation, where Stephen Lansing's work (1989, 1991, 1996) provides keen insight into both bureaucratic myopia and the sophistication of indigenous water management.[8] In the 1970s, Balinese irrigation bureaucracies, based on the policies of the Green Revolution, challenged a model of irrigation that had been in use for centuries. But the water symbolism, priestly authority, temples, and ritual practices of the traditional system were inseparable from cropping schedules, coordination of irrigator groups, and pest control. State and development officials, oblivious to the managerial role of the water temples and their rituals, regarded agriculture as a purely technical process. Farmers were viewed as backward, their cultural orientation an impediment to development. As a result, the temple system lost control of irrigation scheduling, and pests and diseases ran wild. Today, Balinese irrigation officials have reluctantly accepted the power of the temple priests over water control.

What is noteworthy is that Balinese agricultural departments are staffed by individuals who have many of the same basic cultural and religious orientations as the farmers. And yet these state officials were oblivious to the agricultural significance of the water temples and the instrumental power of the priests. I would argue that the examination of local beliefs and practices is necessarily precluded because any legitimation of these local norms calls into question the state's supposed monopoly on rationality and legitimate culture.

THE CULTURAL POLITICS OF ANDEAN IRRIGATION

The divide between local irrigation systems and the state takes on an added dimension in ethnically differentiated and culturally plural societies such as Peru, where the deployment of irrigation bureaucracies, development initiatives, and secular, "rational" forms of social organization reflect and reproduce the legitimacy and hegemony of a dominant culture and ethnic group. In Peru, as in many other culturally plural societies, bureaucratic myopia is often compounded by a deep-seated racism.

State officials in Peru and many other nations throughout the Americas ignore indigenous models of resource management not only because of the alleged superiority of "modern" Western cultural forms and organization, but because the power-holders and dominant cultures of these nations regard indigenous peoples as racially and culturally inferior. Thus, the cultural logics underwriting irrigation use among the Andean majority in the Peruvian highlands are completely joined to ethnic conflict. Irrigation politics, development, and interaction between local and bureaucratic forms of knowledge in Peru must also be understood in terms of the wide geographic and conceptual divide between the coast (*costa*) and the highlands (sierra).[9]

Although there is constant and dynamic interaction, melding, and transference between these two areas (see, e.g., Paerregaard 1997), they are spoken of and conceptualized as iconic of two different cultures, the criollo culture (*cultura criolla*) of the coast and the Andean culture (*cultura andina* or *lo andino*) of the highlands. The inhabitants of these two areas are often referred to as coastal-dwellers (*costeños*) and highlanders (*serranos*), respectively. Although Andean migrants, as well as urban criollos, often restrict their movement to their own particular cultural enclaves in these two regions, their plural identities are conditioned by the radically different cultures associated with each region. Both geographic and cultural spaces are recognized as forming part of the larger imagined community. But it is criollo culture and coastal society that is at the center of Peruvian nation-building. The term *criollo*, which was originally used to designate people of Spanish descent born in the Americas, refers to the "social unit defined in cultural and class terms . . . that has directed state operations since the birth of the republic" (Turino 1991, 260). Today, popular and national cultural discourses present the Spanish-speaking, white, West-facing minority as the model of modernity, the embodiment of legitimate national culture, and the key to Peru's future.

Just as the coastal cities are iconic of criollo culture in popular national discourse, highland communities are iconic of indigenous culture. Many of the negative stereotypes directed toward the people of the Andes, who are referred to as "serranos" or *"indios"* ("Indians")—that they are backward and unproductive—are extended to the mountains and their systems of production. In sum, Peru is a nation in which a dominant cultural minority deploys its worldview throughout the provinces by means of its educational system, civic ceremonies, language, and, as I demonstrate here, through its water policies and irrigation bureaucracies.

Andean communities make up the agropastoral productive units that provide, among other things, the better part of Peru's production of cattle (62 percent), potatoes (99 percent), and corn (79 percent) (Ossio 1992b).[10] If, as I demonstrate in the following chapters, these "productive units" are guided largely by non-Western Andean rationales that are closely tied to communal and ethnic identities, we can ask: How do development organizations and the bureaucracies of the Peruvian state interface with these units? What is the nature of this interface, both politically and culturally?

ANDEAN CULTURE AND THE POLITICS OF REPRESENTATION

The politics of indigenous identity, production, and community necessarily takes us into anthropological debates concerning Andean culture and its representation. The concept of Andean culture, or "lo andino," has recently come under attack from different quarters (see, e.g., Abercrombie 1991; Montoya 1987; Poole 1990; Urbano 1992; Starn 1991). As Thomas Abercrombie puts it, "To suggest the existence of *a* rural/indigenous culture in the Andes, what is often called, in the literature, 'the Andean,' is usually to fall victim to non-Indians' essentializing stereotype of 'the Indian.' In other words, the 'Andean' is only rightly studied as a (usually utopian) image projected by various urban groups" (1991, 97). Questioning "Andeanism" has been salutary for the field, forcing anthropologists to examine the dynamic movement and plural identities of highlanders (see, e.g., Starn 1991). Yet I believe that the critique and subsequent devaluation of all things Andean can also play into the dominant cultural discourses of Peru that effectively deny the validity of highland lifeways. And given the success of ethnicity-based mobilization in Ecuador and Bolivia, dismissal of lo andino seems premature.[11]

The fact is that millions of Quechua-, Aymara-, and Spanish-speaking indigenous peoples living in the highlands of Ecuador, Peru, and Bolivia, while participating in diverse social and cultural worlds, also have similar beliefs and ritual practices that are distinctly Andean and are tied to fundamental notions of community and ethnic identity. These beliefs and practices, forged in a colonial context and today ignored or denigrated by dominant cultural discourses and policy-making in the Andean nations, are fundamental components of local systems of agricultural and pastoral production. But how does one write about mountain and earth rituals, dual organization, traditional staff-holding authorities, and the other aspects of indigenous irrigation without evoking Andean culture as exotic and timeless?

I believe that it is possible to take the historical and cultural specificity of Andean lifeways into account while showing these lifeways as dynamic, adaptable, and compatible with modernity. Andean culture is best viewed as having been created from a hybrid mix of local mores with the political forms and ideological forces of hegemonic states, both indigenous and Iberian. As I demonstrate here, some native institutions are with us today because they were appropriated and used as a means of extracting goods and labor by Spanish colonial authorities and those of the Peruvian state after independence; others were used to resist colonial and postcolonial regimes. These institutions, reproduced and transformed through the everyday practices of millions of people, vary from one locality to the next. Andean cultural production is dynamic and adaptable, providing orientation and identity for villagers as well as for migrants who transit different national and international frontiers.

COMMUNITY LIFE AND FIELDWORK IN CABANACONDE

Arriving in a Transnational Community

In a coffee-table book about the Colca Valley, in which Cabanaconde is located, Mario Vargas Llosa writes, "Those of us who live immersed in the ugliness of Lima sometimes forget the beautiful things of Peru. One of them is this southern valley, to the northwest of Arequipa . . . which until a few years ago was incommunicado with the rest of the territory. . . . Modern man has not had time to depredate the valley . . . although horrible corrugated zinc has replaced the ancestral straw roofs on some of the dwellings" (Vargas Llosa 1987, 23). Such a view of the Andes contrasts with that of José María Arguedas, who says, "But on the coast there are no mountain passes. They do not know how their towns look from afar . . . from the joy of a heart that is familiar with distances" (Arguedas 1985, 2).

Cabanaconde, a large and growing community of some 5,000 bilingual Quechua and Spanish speakers, is flanked by mountains on one side and the precipitously deep Colca Canyon on the other. While the community sits at 10,500 feet, Mount Hualca-Hualca stands almost twice that high at 19,500 feet. The water from its snowmelt courses down the Hualca-Hualca River to the community and is the lifeblood—or as the Cabaneños put it, the "mother's milk"—of the agricultural fields and the townspeople. All agriculture in Cabanaconde is irrigated, and because it produces a valuable commodity for subsistence and trade—"cabanita maize" (*maíz cabanita*), famous throughout the southern Andes for its taste and quality—irrigated land is the primary source of wealth in the community.

From a distance, Cabanaconde appears relatively small, and this perception persists as one enters the town itself. The eight-hour, rocky bus ride from Arequipa, the town's rutted dirt streets, and the elaborately embroidered dress of the Cabaneñas reinforce the sense that one has entered a "traditional" community that is "incomunicado with the rest of the territory," as stated by Peruvian writer, politician, and monolingual Spanish-speaker Vargas Llosa. But nothing could be further from the truth.

Rather, as the bilingual Arguedas, who was fluent in both Spanish and Quechua, suggested, people in the Andes are "familiar with distances." Whereas government officials, tourists, and other outsiders such as Vargas Llosa tend to consider the town a remote outpost and a timeless community only recently contaminated by the first signs of modernity, the residents of the region regard Cabanaconde as a large urban center and a major thoroughfare.

Cabanaconde, the largest of the twelve major communities in the Colca Valley, is in fact a transnational community with colonies of migrants in Arequipa, Lima, and Washington, D.C. The residents of the town itself often refer to other communities in the Colca Valley as "in the Provinces." Municipal documents from the early part of this century often begin with the words, "In this City of Cabanaconde," showing that this urban and cosmopolitan self-perception has been around for some time.

On my first visit to Cabanaconde, I was made aware of just how connected the town was to larger worlds.[12] Neither I nor my partner at the time, Soledad Gálvez, who is from the metropolis of Lima, had been to the Colca Valley or the sierra of Arequipa before. Our rickety bus chugged through Arequipa, which is the second largest city in Peru and is located at 7,500 feet. Passing its outlying shanty towns, we began a slow, steep ascent parallel to the towering El Misti, a cone-shaped volcano that is the emblem and pride of the "white city." After we had arrived at 14,000 feet, it took another few hours to cross the expansive, brown, steppelike pampa. On the way we passed several herd steads, dozens of alpacas and llamas penned at their sides. Although the Colca Valley was beginning to be known as a tourist attraction because of its beautiful colonial churches, deep canyon, condors, thermal waters, and terraced fields, we were the only *turistas* (tourists) on this bus.

As we made our descent into the valley six hours later, the sear moonscape of the barren high steppe gave way to towns and terraced fields glimmering below in the late-morning sun. The landscape took yet another dramatic turn as we descended into the canyon. Beautiful terraces now lined both sides of the ever-deepening canyon, while snow-capped peaks loomed overhead. We passed through several other towns, stopping in the central plazas to let passengers on and off. The local dress of the women, truly dazzling, became more ubiquitous with each stop. Most sported short-brimmed, ivory-white hats made of fine straw and white lace with a huge silver or colored ribbon on the side. The women also wore flowing long skirts, sleeveless vests, and long-sleeved shirts embroidered in different colors. Some of the passengers wore a different kind of hat, made of cloth and embroidered with colorful animal and floral designs and a five-point star on the crown. They, I was told, were the "Cabaneños," the people of Cabanaconde.

We struck up a conversation with a nattily dressed couple, Alcides and Elena. Elena had on the embroidered five-point star hat, but also a down jacket and blue jeans. When I told them I was from the United States, Elena replied, "We, too, live in the U.S."

It turned out that not only they, but more than 150 other Cabaneños, were living in the Washington, D.C., area at that time.[13]
Although they were returning to Cabanaconde after a four-year absence, Elena and Alcides offered to put us up. Thus began my for-
tuitous relationship with the Montoya and Mamani families.

A few months later, Alcides and Elena visited us in Boston.
Gone was the five-point-star hat, and Elena had gotten a speeding
ticket on her way up from Washington. We took in some of the
local sights and drove along the Charles River. Later, over Korean
food and Mexican beer, they told us more about Cabanaconde, as
well as whom to contact and whom to avoid. Two years later we
again found ourselves in Cabanaconde, this time for a year and a
half.

We arrived in July 1987, rushing straight to Cabanaconde for
the *fiesta* of the Patron Saint, the Virgin of Carmen, and the very
active ritual period that accompanies it. Together with Catholic processions and veneration of the saints, the Mamanis and other families were performing rituals from native Andean religion, including
q'apas or *irantas*, which are offerings burned for the mountain deities known as *cabildos* (called *awkis*, *wamanis*, and *apus* in other
Andean regions) and for *pachamama*, Earth Mother. Mount Hualca-
Hualca, the jagged, gray, snow-shrouded summit of which stood
tall in the distance, was invoked in each offering.

Just weeks before our arrival, a Polish mountaineer had per-
ished while attempting to scale Hualca-Hualca. People lamented the
climber's death ("pobre gringito") but considered his attempt fool-
ish, his failure proof of the mountain's power. I had no idea at the
time that an adjacent glacier peak, Ampato, held the bodies of several youths who had been sacrificed by the Inka to this same chain
of mountains. Reverence for the power of mountains joins the ritual
logic of these imperial sacrifices to that of contemporary mountain rituals in the Andes, including the q'apas and *tinkay* libations
being carried out by the Mamanis.[14]

Elena's extended family was marking their calves, and these
particular q'apas and tinkays were given in thanks for the fertility
afforded their cattle; after the offerings, we had a ritual meal of
toasted corn flour. Q'apa and tinkay are used for many purposes:
to heal illnesses caused by the earth (see Appendix A), to bless

houses, for protection of one's family, to increase one's cattle and crops, and even to do harm to one's enemies. As I later came to understand, q'apa and tinkay do not represent some "sacred" domain discrete from the "secular" practice of day-to-day life, but rather are part of a worldview that guides everyday practice. The sweet and pungent air of a burning q'apa, the mountains' preferred food, became a familiar smell.

My first notes, written during the euphoria of the fiesta, referred to "great communal solidarity." But I soon learned that the community was riven by factionalism. One of the Mamanis confirmed this, confiding that although the town had been known to unite on some issues, there were deep divisions in the community. "The Spaniards left their bad blood in the town," he went on to say. "There's a tremendous amount of envy . . . and no one cares about the good of the community. Look at the authorities, they can't agree on anything."

A communal assembly of the Peasant Community—this being the officially recognized and most representative political institution in town—was held in the town plaza on July 26. I was nervous—the president of the community had already granted our stay in the community, but the communal assembly is, by law, "the maximum authority" in town and could decide differently. The church bell had been ringing all morning, calling the townspeople to the assembly, and finally, a few hours later, it began. About sixty men, standing, formed a wide circle, and to the side a handful of women sat and watched as the meeting was called to order.

A director of debates was named and the minutes of the previous session were read—in Spanish, as is all official business—by the secretary. The president, mayor, and governor were enjoined by several people to stop fighting, to cooperate for the good of the town. The points of discussion were then read out: conflicts over communal lands, education and transportation, and the recovery of abandoned fields and canals, among others. The hostility and lack of coordination between the authorities soon became apparent. The governor, Osvaldo Milla, had had an unauthorized meeting with provincial authorities to help Acpi, a small village annexed to Cabanaconde, to relocate to a sector of communal territory known as Castropampa. This relocation was necessary, he argued, because Acpi was perched dangerously on the side of a precipice.

Milla declared, "We have to help our brothers in Acpi—if we don't and an earthquake wipes them out, it'll be on our conscience."

One man, stepping forward from the ring of men as he was given the floor, vigorously challenged Milla's motives, citing purported bribes and Acpi's ambitions to gain more land. Especially incensed that plans had already been drawn up without community approval, several *comuneros* (community members) spoke about the pitched physical battle between Acpi and a group of Cabaneños that had taken place five years earlier. Slings had been used, and although the Cabaneños had retained their lands, a few people had been injured. Another man stepped forward to decry the actions of Milla. "Since they couldn't do it by force back then, they think they'll buy off authorities and engineers. There's going to be civil war. I'll die first!" People shouted approval, and other speeches against Milla and the Acpeños followed. Milla left shaking his head, saying, "It's good as done." The assembly, ignoring his assessment, agreed to reject the motion by Acpi and to develop the fields and canals of Castropampa for the Cabaneños. There was applause once consensus was reached and they moved on to the next point.

There were heated discussions on other motions, rhetoric flowed, and jokes and emotional outbursts occasionally punctuated the generally formal proceedings. Some people were especially good orators, and these individuals repeatedly voiced the general sentiment of a particular faction. It was soon apparent that the communal assembly was an important arena for negotiating political power as well as social theater at its best. When I took out my notebook, however, I found myself at center stage.

"Señores comuneros, one moment please," one of the younger authorities stiffly declared. "We have in our presence a stranger who has been observing our assembly. I suggest we ask him who he is and why he's taking notes. If, for some reason, he doesn't want to tell us, I suggest we retire him, always respecting his person, from this meeting." All eyes were on me, and, although I had prepared for the moment, the pressure was great. Stepping from the edge of the circle into the center, I explained the purpose of my research and its relevance to the recovery of abandoned agricultural lands. Promising to leave the results of my research with the community, I also offered to teach in the high school.

The director of debates stepped forward. "Well, if this man, a student, is here to study and help the community, and won't interfere with the proceedings, we should offer him our recognition." I felt a surge of relief as the men applauded me. They quickly moved on to the next agenda item—I had been an interesting interruption, but they had important things to do. A minor point in their assembly, a major rite of passage for me.

People's perception of us was of course conditioned by their contact with other outsiders. We were categorized as *mistis* (nonindigenous outsiders) and *gringos*; the latter term is also applied to Peruvians who do not follow the cultural mores of highland society. However, over time these categories gave way to other imagined identities as the Cabaneños' perception of us changed.[15] Despite the lingering doubts of some as to our purpose, many Cabaneños began to trust us. As we settled into community life, developed friendships and godparenthood ties (*compadrazgo*), and took up the symbols of the community, we gained more and more acceptance. As word spread that I would freely help in agricultural chores (*por voluntad*) without expecting a return service (*ayni*), people sought me out.

Our acceptance in the community was also greatly enhanced by the family with whom we lived, that of Elena's uncle, Toribio Aguilar, and his wife, Exaltación Acuña. Toribio had been an enterprising muleteer before the road was built in 1965. Through hard work he had slowly acquired cattle and plots of land. The front room of the house served as a small store, which Exalta, a large woman who spoke little Spanish, managed with the help of five of their children. Two older children lived in the United States near Alcides and Elena. Just as Toribio, a well-respected figure in the community, became a father figure to us, Exalta became our "mother." She had a great sense of humor, was unabashedly frank, and, with her many skirts, wide figure, and roly-poly gait, she was a presence.

We slowly adapted to community life. The days would start with the honking of buses leaving at 4:30 A.M., often the only traffic during the day. As night fell, a gasoline-run generator installed in 1986 would light up the central street, the plaza, and a couple of small video theaters for a few hours after dark. The eighteenth-century church bells would chime across town, the strident rings or somber, slow tolling signaling everything from baptisms, deaths, and church services to political assemblies and emergencies. Town criers, with two or three musicians, would also loudly announce upcoming events from the major street corners. Occasionally a squeaky and barely intelligible microphone would less effectively broadcast these events from the town plaza.

The radio brought different messages, from Radio Havana, the BBC, Radio Moscow, and the Voice of America, to local stations from Arequipa featuring *huayno* and *chicha* music, the preferred genres in town. On these local stations, messages would be sent out to the people in Cabanaconde and other nearby towns telling of the coming of a relative or offering birthday wishes from a family member who had migrated.

Envy, Conflict, and Violence

Envy and conflict are part of life in Cabanaconde, and the town is considered by the inhabitants of the region to be especially aggressive and conflicted. The Cabaneños themselves often attribute this to the fact that many more Spaniards settled in Cabanaconde than in other towns in the Colca Valley. Many other factors—such as rising demographic pressure on resources, interfamily feuds, and economic differentiation in the community, as well as neglect by the Peruvian state—also account for the conflictual nature of community life. And, in the larger Peruvian society to which Cabanaconde is well connected, there has been great political upheaval and a steady decline in the standard of living since the late 1970s; the years 1985–1988 saw even greater economic deterioration.[16]

Envy is one idiom used to discuss and express conflict and social power, and its assumed presence appears like a cloud over many activities. Irrigation, weaving, healing, and other activities all have prescriptions for avoiding or countering envy. Black magic curses, spells, hexes, and counterhexes are performed by both the layperson and witches (*layqas*). Witchcraft also figures in struggles over land and water, where interfamily fights sometimes last for generations. Ambitious individuals make use of political parties and offices to advance their family's interests.

People keep their doors locked tight in Cabanaconde and often use guard dogs; they are also vigilant against the theft of the animals and crops they keep outside of town. During my stay, there were several incidents of maize theft at harvest time, and cattle rustling occurred throughout the year. People often know who is stealing but do not denounce the thieves for fear of reprisals. "The rustlers only eat at night," Toribio tells me. "But we know who they are because you can smell the meat cooking. How are they, being poor, eating meat when those of us who have cattle aren't tasting any? Everybody knows each other here." One cattle-rustling family in town was known to be especially violent. They had successfully intimidated the entire town and even some of the resident police. Several months into my stay, an elderly woman was raped and murdered by one of the sons of this family of criminals. He hid out for several weeks in a cave in the Colca Canyon, robbing local travelers who used the isolated trails that lead to nearby villages. He was finally caught and imprisoned.

I learned more about the nature of interfamily conflict as I became further involved in the town's political life. The proceedings of the Peasant Community's Qualifying Commission, whose charge it was to oversee the recovery and distribution of agricultural lands in Castropampa and other areas, were conflict-ridden, as certain powerful families had old land titles to some of these fields. These families were still trying to block the community from distributing this land, and at one point they had the local police incarcerate the president of the Peasant Community.

When word of this spread, several people quickly swung into action, climbing the church tower and ringing the bell. A crowd of several hundred soon gathered in the square, and we marched on the police station. Two guards clung nervously to their machine guns as the crowd shouted insults, demanding the president's release; communal officials entered to speak with the chief of police. Finally, the president was released—land recovery went on as scheduled.

Studying the diverse archives of the community, I found that communal conflict over land and water had a long history. Powerful families, many of which descended from the Spaniards who once ruled the community, had introduced new forms of irrigation and had maneuvered to increase their land base for decades. My attempts to track down old documents were often frustrated for this reason. The worst case involved a man who had inherited not only the land of his powerful father-in-law, but also two trunkloads of communal documents. After pursuing these documents for several months, I finally found out that he had been using them as kindling over the years; illiterate, and in conflict with some of his relatives, he was afraid the papers would be used to take away his land.

There was conflict of a far different nature in much of the Peruvian countryside during the 1980s. More than 27,000 people, mostly Andean peasants, died in the war between Peru's brutal military and Shining Path, a revolutionary movement that took up armed struggle in 1980. Hundreds of thousands of people were displaced from their homelands, both sides abused human rights and massacred entire villages, and the military carried out thousands of extrajudicial executions. Cabanaconde, however, felt only distant reverberations from the war, not the devastating impact that it had on nearby regions.[17]

Sacred Geography and the Water Mayors

Although I was concerned with these larger conflicts, my day-to-day goal in the community was to better understand the local politics and cosmological foundations of irrigation. This required that I immerse myself in water distribution and ritual, as well as expand my knowledge of Cabanaconde's sacred geography, especially Mount Hualca-Hualca, source of the town's water. One of the high points of my fieldwork came when Toribio agreed to take me to Huataq, a faraway pasture that even most community members had never seen.

We left at 3:30 A.M., sometimes walking, sometimes riding mules up the Hualca-Hualca River basin. By sunrise, the town was far behind us, and looming up ahead was Mount Hualca-Hualca. Finally, there we were, directly below the "mother mountain" of Cabanaconde. In the middle of its gray slope, surrounded by the brilliantly white snowpack, a small track of water descended. The incipient Hualca-Hualca River was dirt brown as it passed us. We were now at 16,000 feet, but Hualca-Hualca still towered above. I thought of the Polish climber, his body suspended in an icy crevasse somewhere on the mountain.

We continued over the ridge, and as we crossed the unworldly moonscape of the high plateau we came upon an eerie sight. The ancient tracks of a large canal, apparently a failed Inka effort, crossed and disappeared into the barren, desolate, boulder-strewn plain. Other snow-capped peaks grew closer as we approached the Huataq valley. One of these was Sabankaya, the recently active volcano.[18] To my right was Mount Ampato, the largest in the area at over 20,500 feet. A few years later, Sabankaya would erupt, its ashes covering the area we now rode on and melting the snow on both Hualca-Hualca and Mount Ampato. But for now, only small puffs of smoke rose lazily from Sabankaya's pyramidal crest and the as-yet-undetected bodies of the Ice Maiden and other human sacrifices remained entombed on Ampato's frozen slopes.

We made our descent into the fertile valley of Huataq. Two abandoned canals, departing from a spring at the head of the valley, cut across and then disappeared into the valley side. On a distant hillside in front of smoking Sabankaya, a dozen wild horses watched our approach and then galloped away. Below were Toribio's cattle, a herd of alpacas, and a few thatched huts. The raw natural power manifest in the towering peaks, smoking volcano, rapidly rushing Huataq spring, and wide green valley made it clear to me why the earth was considered much more savage and undomesticated here. I was warned not to fall asleep anywhere but in the hut, the earth of which had been tamed through q'apas.

Although I later returned to the high pastures and made trips to the orchards deep in the Colca Canyon at the other extreme of the communal territory, that first trip to Huataq gave me a new, more encompassing view of Cabanaconde's sacred geography. Morever, I had felt the immediate presence and power of Hualca-Hualca, mother to the Cabaneños, whose life-giving fluid is domesticated by alternating water mayors.

The water mayors, colorful local authorities who carry snake-headed staffs and often have flowers adorning their hats, are in charge of water distribution during the longest and most crucial period of the yearly irrigation cycle, from June through December. During this period there are four complete rounds of water to the fields. Each round, which lasts about six weeks, is managed by two water mayors who alternate, each spending four consecutive days and nights in the fields "together with the water." One oversees water distribution for the fields classified as belonging to "upper half," *anansaya*, and the other irrigates the fields classified as *urinsaya*, those of "lower half." The water mayors alternate not only in managing water but also in carrying out important rituals.

This once-in-a-lifetime *cargo*, or civil office, which rotates among the irrigators, became my key entry point into the micro-politics and ritual correlates of irrigation. The office of water mayor is tiresome for the water mayor and his family, and I tried to en-dear myself to these overworked men by helping them. By taking food to them from their wives, sometimes several times a day and sometimes at night, and by carrying ponchos, irrigator lamps, matches, coca leaf, corn beer (*chicha*), liquor (*trago*), and cigarettes to and from the fields, I became quite close with many water may-ors and their families. One of these men took me to his herd stead in the high pastures; another took me to his orchard deep in the Colca Canyon. Still another asked me to be a godfather to his two grandchildren. The water mayors grew to not only tolerate my presence, but to expect it, and several of the future office-holders solicited my aid. By the end of our stay in the community, my close affiliation with these men and their families led many to consider me an irrigation authority—and, quite possibly, bewitched by water.

I also participated in the local Irrigators Commission and stud-ied its archive. My research also led me to develop a relationship with the extension agent, a representative of the Ministry of Agri-culture who resided in town and who enacted the state's agenda. During the local Irrigators Assemblies and meetings of the Irriga-tors Commission, I would normally just observe, but occasionally I would be called upon for an opinion or to record the minutes. Initially I feared that my interest in such an important resource could cause concern among the townspeople. Ironically, it soon justified my presence.

People perceived my participation in water management as impartial, and, several months after our arrival, many began to thank me for being a "good example" to the townspeople. Word had spread that I was helping the water mayors, and people looked favorably on my aiding these overworked men and their families.

I explained that my actions were not selfless—I was studying irrigation for a book that was going to benefit me.

People insisted that I was having a positive effect on water management and that, unlike the extension agent and the Ministry of Agriculture, I respected the customs and beliefs of the community and did not attempt to challenge the authority of the water mayors. Rather, without knowing it, I was apparently reinforcing it. At one point, several months into my research, it came as a strange revelation to find out that word had spread that I was *in charge* of distribution and that was why it was proceeding in an orderly fashion. After trying to gain acceptance and legitimize my presence in the community through different means, it was through the culturally and politically charged resource of water that I achieved this.[19]

Departing Thoughts

After a year and a half of living and doing research in Cabanaconde and Arequipa, I returned to the United States. A short while later, I visited Elena and Alcides in Washington, D.C., and gave a presentation of my findings to several dozen Cabaneños in a meeting of the Cabanaconde City Association. It was disorienting, yet reassuring, to be drinking Coors beer and dancing to traditional *wititi* music in our nation's capital. I also felt a real sense of displacement when served some microwaved maíz cabanita as we watched videos of fiestas from "back home." But during return visits and follow-up research in Cabanaconde (1991, 1994, 1997, 1998) and in its Washington-based colony, I have gotten used to such cultural hybridity, and it no longer surprises me when I run into Cabaneños at airports and hotels along the way.

By 1998, the colony of Cabaneños in the United States had grown to over six hundred. Elena's parents, most of her siblings, and several of the Aguilar children had arrived in the United States by the early 1990s. And amazingly, in 1995, Exalta and Toribio, whom I had always imagined as being too tied to community life to leave Cabanaconde, also arrived to live in Washington, D.C.

Soon thereafter, a special migrant from the area also landed in Washington. In 1991, Sabankaya Volcano had erupted, the ash wiping out the pastures of Huataq that Toribio and I had visited together. It also melted the snow on nearby Hualca-Hualca and Ampato Mountains, and in 1995 the "Ice Maiden" was discovered on the summit of Ampato, bringing international attention to Cabanaconde. In May 1996, her frozen corpse was presented to the public at the National Geographic Society in Washington, D.C.; among the Cabaneños who attended this event were Exalta, Toribio, Elena, and the president of the Cabanaconde City Association. It seemed strange to me, the recently arrived Toribio and Exalta viewing their sacred mountains on National Geographic's big screen. But, to again invoke Arguedas, such transitions do not appear to be difficult for those who are used to seeing their town from afar and who are "familiar with distances."[20]

In June 1996, Elena and the president of the Cabanaconde City Association were invited speakers at a conference on transnationalism at the University of California at Riverside. Elena brought her teenaged niece and nephew, and after the conference they demanded that we go to Universal Studios. Soon, in the virtual reality ride known as Back to the Future, I was careening with my Cabaneño friends through deep canyons, mountain caves, and smoking volcanoes, our voices raised in a single scream. Such an image provides some idea of the outer limits of the Cabaneño diaspora, the transformations and plural identities of many Cabaneños, and the ease with which they move back and forth between extremely different cultural realities.

We have seen, then, that the Andean peasant community—of which the Washington Cabaneños still consider themselves members—is complex and dynamic. In the pages that follow, I show that irrigation is an excellent medium for exploring this complexity and for examining key political and cultural processes within Andean society and history. Indeed, a detailed look at the diverse histories, cultural models, political forces, and power struggles found in highland irrigation provides a window into both the enduring patterns of belief and the rapid social change that characterize Cabanaconde and many other Andean communities.

1

HISTORY, COMMUNITY,
AND ETHNICITY
IN CABANACONDE

W ater, ethnicity, and power in Cabanaconde must be understood
against the backdrop of the region's colonial history and contemporary Peruvian systems of stratification. Before, during, and after
Spanish rule, the Andes have been characterized by a great diversity of indigenous polities and ethnic groups. The Cavana polity,
which had its political seat where Cabanaconde is currently located,
was one of two major nations that occupied the Colca Valley at
the time of the Spanish conquest (fig. 1.1). Throughout the colonial period and still today, Cabanaconde has remained ethnically
distinct from other communities of the valley.[1] This chapter provides a selective history and contemporary overview of community,
ethnicity, production, and different kinds of power relations in
Cabanaconde.

HISTORY

Indigenous States, Mountains, and Andean Ethnicity

The productive potential of the Hualca-Hualca River basin and
Cabanaconde's warm valley led at least two pan-Andean empires,
Wari and Inka, to colonize this hydrological system and the people
dependent on it. A long defensive wall outside of town, a Wari con-

[[[[[[[[[[**Territory of the Cavana polity**   ≡≡≡   **Territory of the Collagua polity**

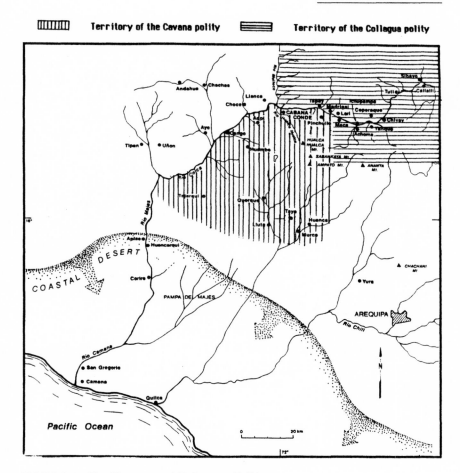

FIGURE 1.1. The Cavana and Collaguas Polities

struction probably built around 700 A.D. (de la Vera Cruz 1987; Schreiber 1992), suggests that this part of the Colca Valley was already politically and economically important by that time.

During Inka rule, Cabanaconde's warm valley was the seat of the Cavana nation and was "more important politically and in productive terms than other zones of the Colca Valley" (de la Vera Cruz 1987, 10).[2] The *kurakas,* or ethnic lords, of Cavana controlled distant villages and resources (see fig. 1.2); they continued to do so well into the eighteenth century (Cook 1982).[3]

There was considerable intensification of agriculture in Cabanaconde during Inka rule, and the rich volcanic soils and temperate climate that favored the production of maize allowed for greater population density (de la Vera Cruz 1987, 10). Here and in hundreds of other areas, the Inka state invested in its periphery, expanding pre-Inka canals and terraces. The Inka also imposed different social and administrative divisions in Cabanaconde, such as the anansaya/urinsaya moiety divisions explored in later chapters. So, too, Quechua, the general language of the Inka, was used to administrate and consolidate the largest indigenous political system ever to develop in the Americas. Yet the Inka also perpetuated local ethnic differences of the conquered groups and established a system of indirect rule through local kurakas, such as those of the Cavana and Collagua polities.

The ways in which these two polities distinguished themselves in the early colonial period provide great insight into a "primordial" type of communal and ethnic identity found throughout the Central Andes, one related to religious beliefs and practices concerning mountains and irrigation water. As mentioned in the Introduction, indigenous peoples in the Andes, like those in the past, often trace their origins to sacred mountains, lakes, springs, and rivers. Irrigation water is usually perceived as an extension of subterranean waters, the latter uniting highland lakes, rivers, and mountains with the "mother lake" (*mama qucha*), that is, the ocean (Sherbondy 1982b). Together these form a hydraulic network through which the gods and ancestors travel, and from which the human world originated.

The importance of mountains within this symbology of power also needs to be stressed. In the words of Johan Reinhard, "Whatever the ultimate source of water, the mountain deities at the local level were usually the controllers of it. They thus were the ones who directly affected the fertility of crop plants, animals, and—in the end—people" (1985, 418). In sum, this Andean cultural logic and definition of ethnic identity, intimately tied to water and mountains, posits a strong bond between a "place deity" (Salomon 1991), the territory it controls, and a dependent social group.

In the case of the Cavana polity, such meanings make their way through the historical record loud and clear. In his 1586 description of the "province of the Collaguas and Cavanaconde," a Spanish Crown official wrote that "according to their ancient beliefs, those of the province of the Cavanas came to the place where the town of Cavana is today from a mountain which is in front of it, snow-capped and crowned, which is called Gualca-Gualca. . . . They take advantage of the water from its snow-melt for their irrigated fields" (Ulloa Mogollón 1965 [1586]). This was in contrast to the neighboring Collaguas polity, which emerged from "a snow-capped mountain in the form of a volcano . . . called Collaguata; they say that near this mountain or from inside of it many people emerged and came down to this province and valley."

Mountain worship and ethnic identity were literally inscribed on peoples' bodies as each group employed cranial deformation to imitate the shape of the mountains from which their people had emerged: "By the shape of the head, one can easily tell those who are native to Cavana and those who are from Collaguas" (ibid.). According to Juan de Ulloa Mogollón, both groups actively worshiped their mountains of origin with many rituals and the sacrificing of guinea pigs, llamas, and other goods.

In his report, the Crown official also says that "when the Inka wanted to make an important sacrifice and placate one of the holy mountains . . . he would have people sacrificed." The recent discovery of the Ice Maiden and other human sacrifices on Cabanaconde's Mount Ampato and other high peaks of the region shows the truth of this sixteenth-century testimony.[4]

Colonial Categories and Andean Ethnicity

Andean ethnicity was irreversibly changed with the Spanish invasion in 1532, when the Spaniards introduced the category of "indio" ("Indian"), gathering under one term a great number of ethnically distinct peoples. The term was used to define the conquered, those to pay tribute and service. The colonial categories of *indio, español* or *blanco* (Spaniard or white, respectively), and *mestizo* ("mixed race") have been fundamental to Spanish and Republican political economies, and they still exert strong power in Cabanaconde.

The importance and wealth of the Cavana polity in the early colonial period is apparent in the documentation. Cavana was the second *encomienda*—a grant of "Indian" labor and tribute given to powerful Spaniards by the crown in the early colonial period—

awarded in the Arequipa region (in 1535 and by Francisco Pizarro himself). During the early colonial period, two encomiendas were carved out of the Cavana polity, Cabanaconde anansaya and Cabanaconde urinsaya, and several powerful Spaniards maneuvered to control them (Barriga 1955; Manrique 1985; Cook 1982).[5] Many Spaniards were intent on returning to Spain and wished to get as much out of their encomiendas as they could in as little time as possible. Spanish officials tried unsuccessfully to curb the outright sacking of communities as well as the custom of making the natives "bleed without just cause," as it is stated in a sixteenth-century official communication (Barriga 1955, 4–6).[6]

In 1549, for example, a Spaniard who was recommended for one of the Cavana encomiendas is implored by a Crown official to conform "to the Royal Ordinances": "Leave the caciques their women, children, and servants . . . demand moderate tributes so they can pay . . . the wars and troubles of these Kingdoms have reduced the natives in number, and they are tired and lacking in food . . . let them cultivate their lands and [leave] them seed; [otherwise] it is clear the future damage that will be done to both Spaniards and natives" (Barriga 1955, 174).

That same year, in addition to provisioning the local Spanish priest, the anansaya Cavanas were required to pay a tribute of three hundred pieces of cloth, six hundred bushels of maize, thirty loads of potatoes, six bushels of quinua, 130 sacks of cotton and wool, fifty sheep, twenty-five goats, forty llamas, 150 birds, ninety quail, twenty loads of salt, and four loads of fodder (Manrique 1985, 62, 63, 88). That such a large tribute could be obtained a scarce fifteen years after the conquest further demonstrates that Cavana was a productive and wealthy polity.

This was not to last. Diseases, civil wars, and exploitation in the nearby mines of Caylloma led to a demographic loss, which reached an extreme in the late seventeenth century. From the 1570s—when the dispersed villages of the immediate area were brought together to form the nucleated settlement or *reducción* of Cabanaconde—to the 1680s, the number of "Indian" tribute payers decreased from 1345 to 256 (Cook 1982, 17, 25). With the population loss, the Cavanas were unable to maintain their pre-Columbian

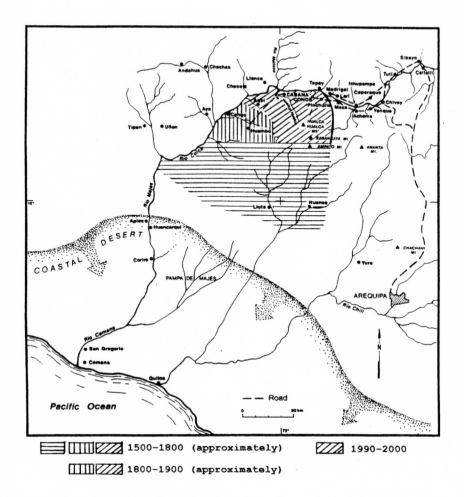

FIGURE 1.2. Contraction of the Cavana Polity

infrastructure, and dozens of canals and thousands of hectares of terraced fields were abandoned.

After the Spanish conquest, the Cavana polity lost land on another front—the outlying lands of the Cabana polity began to be usurped as early as 1562.[7] This trend continued until the end of the nineteenth century, by which time Cabanaconde's territory had become restricted to the lands belonging to the communities of Huambo, Cabanaconde, and Pinchullo (fig. 1.2). Cabanaconde was established as a municipal district in 1857; Huambo later established itself as a separate district.

With the population decline and reorganization of highland society, indigenous worldviews were reconfigured. Unlike the Inka, the Spaniards attempted to destroy the native belief system of the people they conquered. In the Arequipa regions there was both accommodation and resistance (see, e.g., Salomon 1987; Marzal 1981; Millones 1978). Pre-Columbian concepts of ethnic identity linking local deities, territories, and peoples were reconfigured through fusion with Iberian beliefs, practices, and institutions. Catholic saints were joined to preexisting beliefs at the time when the reducciónes were formed (see, e.g., Fuenzalida 1970). In Cabanaconde, the Virgin of Carmen became the most revered saint. Ethnic identity, then, often became reformulated as a community-based identity, and this was tied to both the sacred geography and the patron saints of each town. Today, this Andean form of differentiation of social groups is submerged beneath the racial categories and ethnic identities established during the Spanish colonial period.

While the native population of the Cavanas decreased, there was a large influx of Spanish and criollo (again, people of Spanish descent born in the Americas) residents. Cabanaconde had a greater concentration of Spaniards than any other community in the region with the exception of the Caylloma mining center. A census for Cabanaconde anansaya in 1790, for example, lists 489 Indians, twenty-three Mestizos, and 122 Spaniards (AAA).[8] The nature of exploitation changed little after Peruvian independence in 1821. Well into the twentieth century, marriage, baptismal, and death records continued to be recorded in Cabanaconde as indio, mestizo, and blanco, the term *indio* being synonymous with *tribute payer*.

England and the United States, which became increasingly involved in the exportation of wool and minerals from Peru, came largely to replace Spain in the regional economy of Arequipa in the nineteenth century (Flores Galindo 1977, 45, 55). This process surely had less of an impact on the maize-producing community of Cabanaconde than on mining and herding communities. Extensive trade networks and muleteers supplied Cabanaconde with products from the coastal area of Majes, the highland regions of Yauri and Puno, and the city of Arequipa until the road opened in 1965.

Cabanaconde in the Twentieth Century

This brief sketch of Cabanaconde's history shows that the town has always been joined to larger political and economic forces and that its present identity and communal institutions were forged in a colonial context. Equally apparent, I hope, are the historical roots of Cabaneño communal identity, that special highland sense of kinship and belonging *in terms of the place itself.* Today, Cabaneño communal and ethnic identity resides in the spiritual connection that bonds the town to Mount Hualca-Hualca, other deities residing in the surrounding landscape and the Virgin of Carmen and other saints. Providers of both life and death, these different protector spirits and emblems of communal identity must be regularly honored with ritual offerings, libations, and religious celebrations.[9]

The population of Cabanaconde has more than doubled over the last century. As of 1987, there were at least six hundred households and some 4,000 people in the community.[10] This demographic expansion and the rampant partitioning of landholdings have been factors in permanent out-migration. A road linking Cabanaconde to the city of Arequipa was built in 1965, which also increased migration and participation in the market economy. Improved transportation changed community life dramatically. Today buses arrive and leave daily, and there is a continual flow of people, goods, and ideas between the community and its colonies in Arequipa, Lima, and Washington, which in 1987 had Cabaneño populations of approximately 1,000, 3,000, and 150, respectively.

Cabanaconde already had its own migrant associations operating in both Lima and Arequipa by the 1940s. These became the model for the Cabanaconde City Association in Washington, D.C., established in the early 1980s. The associations formed by migrants in these cities are part of community life, channeling resources back to the community and intervening decisively in conflicts between the community and outside interests.

Today, Cabanaconde is a bilingual and relatively literate population. A primary school was established in the late 1920s, the high school in 1965. Today, most Cabaneños under age fifty know how to read and write in Spanish.[11] The Cabaneños express themselves a good deal of the time in Quechua, their mother tongue. Quechua is a "fenced in" and "oppressed" language (see, e.g., Mannheim

1985, 1991; Albó 1973), one that is widely spoken but which rarely finds its way into print. Although Quechua receives no institutional support, it colors much of life in the community. People move easily from Quechua to Spanish in the same conversation and even in the same sentence.

COMMUNITY

Political and Economic Organization

Cabanaconde is an economically differentiated community, and people there have conflicting interests. Different types of assets (e.g., land and cattle holdings, social networks, godparenthood ties [compadrazgo], migrant remittances, and access to market opportunities) vary greatly from family to family. Competition, factionalism, and envy, therefore, are part of community life and play an important role in the political processes of the community.

The official political structure of Cabanaconde, like that of many highland communities in Peru, consists of the municipal council (*concejo municipal*), the governor (*gobernador*), the Peasant Community (*comunidad campesina*), and an Irrigators Commission (*comisión de regantes*). Before the 1970s, as I detail in a later chapter, the central political forces were the municipal council and governor, nonrepresentative offices that were easily controlled by a few powerful families. Although the power of these local elites was increasingly challenged from the 1940s onward, it was Cabanaconde's official recognition as a Peasant Community in 1979 that ended their domination. Today, although the different political institutions of the community (i.e., the municipal council, the Peasant Community) often cooperate on projects of mutual interest, they also compete over local resources, personal loyalties, and funds from government and nongovernmental organizations.[12]

Individuals known for their competence and probity are often compelled to take office by community consensus and pressure. Other families and interest groups accede to communal offices to secure power and influence over community decision-making. Conscientious authorities are often hindered in their attempts to challenge powerful families encroaching on communal resources. As a former authority put it, "One wants to serve the town and help it progress, but people say you're just out for yourself. One has to be strict, but not too strict or they'll bewitch you. They'll screw up your animals or your crops; your burros will disappear."

The most respected and democratic institution in communal life is the Peasant Community, which can legally act as a corporate body to defend communal interests from internal or external threats. Individuals are inscribed as comuneros into the Peasant Community. In return for attending communal assemblies and carrying out cargos and communal work service (*faena*), the comunero gains access to the common property resources of the community, such as irrigation water, grazing lands, medicinal herbs, and firewood. Other benefits, such as fiesta celebrations and sometimes even access to new agricultural land gained through community-sponsored land rehabilitation, are also enjoyed by the comunero.

There were 463 comuneros inscribed in the Members List of 1988; these comuneros are generally "heads of household" representing nuclear families, often the same as domestic units. Of these, 82 percent (379) were men and 18 percent (eighty-four) were women.[13] Unlike many other officially recognized peasant communities, Cabanaconde has many residents, wealthy and poor, who are not inscribed as comuneros (i.e., they do not belong to the formally constituted Peasant Community) but who de facto have many of the rights and obligations of comuneros. Another sign that the boundaries of comunero status are fairly permeable is that several comuneros do not reside in town, but in Arequipa, Lima, and Washington, D.C. Yet these same individuals participate in the reproduction of local notions of communal and ethnic identity.

Cabanaconde is the primary urban settlement of the lower Colca Valley (fig. 1.3). Yet there is little occupational specialization and the great majority (94 percent) of the comuneros make their living from agricultural and pastoral activities.[14] As is detailed in the next chapter, Cabanaconde has production zones ranging from 6,500 to 14,500 feet and reaching from tropical orchards deep in the Colca Canyon to high pastures, where alpaca, llama, sheep, and cattle herds are kept. The bulk of agricultural production takes place in the fields surrounding town, where the cabanita maize is grown.

Although cattle are bought and sold regularly and some individuals sell part of their potato and maize harvests, production is

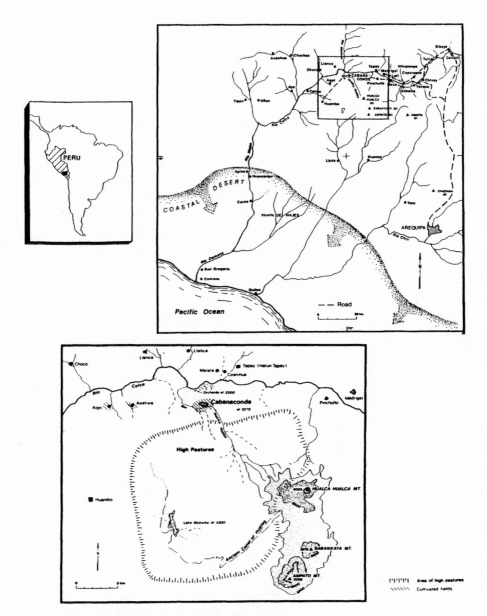

FIGURE 1.3. Cabanaconde and Surrounding Area

overwhelmingly for consumption and for barter. Most households produce their own weavings, tools, rope, and other such goods. But other specialized activities do play an important role in community life. According to the Members List, there are thirteen merchants or entrepreneurs, nine herders, two carpenters, one brick mason, two state "employees," and an artisan, each of whom considers these activities to be his or her primary means of livelihood. "Secondary activities" include store owners, *cochinilla* traders, and artisans.

Embroidering the elaborate ethnic dress of the Cabaneñas is a widely practiced and lucrative skill in the community, performed mostly by men using foot-pedal sewing machines; women weave mostly for family use (see Femenias 1991, 1997). Cochinilla, small insects that grow on prickly pear cactus and which contain a red colorant that is used in the manufacturing of lipstick and other cosmetics, have altered the local economy in the last years. Individuals have made fortunes harvesting and selling this product, and there is a good deal of theft, even physical assault, over the unharvested and harvested product.

There are more than thirty-five small, family-run stores in town, and there are also those who fulfill key services, taking roles such as electrician, photographer, and brick mason; there is also a state employee who runs the generator that provides the town's electricity.[15] Electricity has allowed for the emergence of a couple small "movie halls," Betamax/T.V. setups that project varied "B movies" to small groups, usually teenagers. There are a few small hotels and restaurants that cater to local travelers and backpacking tourists, as well as the priest, schoolteachers, a doctor, police, and Ministry of Agriculture officials.[16]

The presence of most of these outsiders is determined by the education, health, and political agendas of the Peruvian government, and their presence in the community changes unpredictably. While the outsiders provide needed skills, they often consider themselves above the comuneros and see it as their duty to civilize them. For example, a doctor's report (Cuba 1988) and a Ministry of Agriculture report (ORDEA 1980) both refer to the Cabaneños' "main problem" as being "their low cultural level."

Family and Gender Relations

To understand the micropolitics of community and water, we must examine local conceptions of kinship and the family, that is, how relations of descent and affinity are given meaning, how families oppose and unite with other families, and how families conceptualize their relationship to spiritual forces. While Cabanaconde kinship is patrilineal in that children take their father's name, they also retain their mother's family name as their second name. Women keep their family name after marriage. Inheritance of land is bilateral in that male and female children receive equal amounts of this valued resource. Other goods, such as cattle, are divided equally, although preference is sometimes shown to certain children.

Ascertaining correct paternity and naming in general are important in Cabanaconde. In the last decade, names such as Saturnino, Marcelino, Epifania, and Fortunata have been joined by names such as Willy, Hagler, Jackson, Franklin, Susy, and Katy. Even stranger are political names, such as Mao-Tse-Tung, Hitler, Marx Piero, and Nixon Richer.

In Cabanaconde, as elsewhere in the Andes, horizontal relationships of affinity and alliance are stressed over vertical ones of lineage and descent, and this emphasis is highlighted in the proliferation of terms for affinal relationships.[17] The importance of alliance is exemplified by marriage ritual. The marriage process begins with a type of bride service, in which the son-in-law must irrigate his in-laws' fields and help with other agricultural and pastoral activities. In return, the son-in-law becomes like a true son to the new family, enjoying many of the same rights. Formal marriage by the Church is usually undertaken after a couple has had children and has some economic means. The marriage festivities last three days, during which the bride and groom each receive gifts (aphrus) from their entero munaqkuna, their friends and loved ones. There is competition to see who can assemble the most munaqkuna and gifts, which are publicly displayed.[18] On the third and last day the aphrus are counted to see who won, and then they are brought together in the aphrutinkay, the wedding rite. The joining of the gifts symbolizes the merging of the two families, and competition dissolves into a series of alliances that people can enact as they see fit.

The marriage ritual also embodies essential notions about men and women and provides insight into the cultural construction of gender at the local level. Although highland women have a great deal of power physically and socially, they still suffer the double burden of racism and sexism in not only the larger Peruvian society but in peasant society as well. Gender relations and sexual dualism, as metaphors for unequal power relations, are deployed metaphorically into other social and political domains. For example, as detailed later, dualism and local fertility beliefs and rituals have been manipulated by indigenous states. As such, dualism is used both as a cultural medium for the domestication of nature and as a means of subordinating social groups through an idiom of opposed complementarity.

At the same time, women gain a certain amount of autonomy, power, and control through this highly gendered worldview, which places emphasis on the generative power of female forces. Because the earth and Mount Hualca-Hualca are considered to be female, it is women who transport the harvested corn from the corrals where it is stored to the dispensary in a ritual known as the *sarastallaman*. Only women are allowed into the dispensary. Women have "hot hands" (*q'uñi maki*) which hold onto maize and money, whereas men have "wind hands" (*wayra maki*), which make the dispensary empty quickly.

Local gender constructs are also reflected in *solay*, the sowing ritual carried out by all households in Cabanaconde. After the men turn the soil, the family places the seed on top of a wrap shawl spread out on the ground, and the women sit next to the seed. Standing in a semicircle, the men face Mount Hualca-Hualca. Men occupy the higher position, both physically and conceptually. Both women and men labor: men provide the brute labor for the sowing, and women prepare and haul food and corn beer to the fields. It is the men, however, who are served, symbolically exalting their labor and status. Reinforcing local notions of fertility and the socialization of gender hierarchy, it is the youngest married woman who individually serves each man. As the corn beer makes several rounds through the semicircle of men, each man sprinkles a few drops to Earth Mother before drinking.

Although women in Cabanaconde are simultaneously

celebrated and subordinated by this gender ideology,[19] they have almost no control over the formal political sphere, from which they are largely excluded. And as has been well documented for other Andean regions (e.g., Bourque and Warren 1981; Gose 1994; Weismantel 1988), in Cabanaconde there is a relatively low value placed on female labor. But while women are undervalued in economic and political spheres traditionally assigned to men, they exert great power over home and hearth. They are also at the center of many forms of alliance, such as accruing and maintaining munaqkuna, which is crucial to the power of men in almost all cargos.

The importance of alliance to both men and women is also illustrated by the ubiquity of godparenthood ties in community life. The most important compadrazgo relationships are those of baptism and marriage, but *padrinos* (godfathers) and *madrinas* (godmothers) are solicited for many events, including a school graduation, a first haircut, and a house-thatching. In forming these relationships, many considerations—status in the community, reliability, generosity, and potential benefits—are taken into account by both sides. Having many godchildren, or a powerful godfather, permits an amount of political maneuvering unavailable to most of the townspeople.

ETHNICITY

Status and the Racialization of Ethnicity and Class

We have seen that there are different material and social means for acquiring power, status, and wealth within Cabanaconde. The terms *qhapaq* (powerful) and *ricachón* (rich one) are given to those Cabaneños who have material wealth and/or extensive social ties, these usually, but not always, being found together. Poorer individuals within the community are referred to as orphans (*wakcha*), poor (*pobre*), or plucked clean (*q'ala*). Land is publicly measured for communal work and cargo obligations, and individuals are categorized as major land owners (*mayoristas*), medium land owners (*medianos*), and minor land owners (*minoristas*). These distinctions are also applied to cattle holdings.

As mentioned above, land is inherited by both men and

women, and it can be bought, sold, leased, and mortgaged. Whereas almost every Cabaneño has some landholdings, many individuals are land-poor and must sharecrop, rent land, or sell their labor to make ends meet. In recent years, as I discuss in the next chapter, many land-poor Cabaneños have obtained more land through the communally sponsored recovery and distribution of abandoned terraced fields. But no matter how much land or cattle one has, one also needs a strong network of friends and family to effectively use one's productive holdings; those who have limited social ties are also vulnerable to the abuses of more powerful families.

The extent of one's social status and wealth is exhibited on various public and private occasions. In the passing of cargos, at marriages, birthdays, and sowing parties, one's family, godchildren, and other munaqkuna gather in a show of support and solidarity. It is in death that a person's status is perhaps most clearly revealed, with wealthy, powerful, or especially respected individuals within the community receiving the most elaborate and well-attended funerals.[20]

Although differences in wealth, social status, and power are recognized by all, there is an ideology of parity within the community. As one man expressed to me, "Yes, some here have more than others. But really we're all the same. Even the wealthiest don't have that much." Most individuals have had some experience outside the community in the urban centers of Arequipa or Lima and realize that, by comparison with urban mistis, even the wealthiest community members are relatively poor.

Because of the greater Spanish presence and miscegenation in Cabanaconde, the relationship between ethnicity, class, and the racialized colonial categories of indio and misti is different from that of the other Colca Valley communities.[21] Derived from the Spanish word *mestizo, misti* is the term used by indigenous people in the southern highlands to refer to nonindigenous people. As with other terms such as *indio* or *cholo* (derogatory term akin to "half-breed" or "uppity Indian"), *misti* is part of a racial idiom used to express class and ethnic differences.

Many people in Cabanaconde insist that the term *misti* has to do only with phenotypic features (e.g., fair skin, light eyes) and not class; "It's just color, not economy," as one man put it. Others say that the term refers to non-Quechua speakers who wear shoes instead of tire sandals (*usutas*). While the term is used to designate white-skinned insiders and outsiders, it is also applied to transculturated Cabaneños. Those who leave the community and return with city ways and clothes are often seen as putting on airs, as acting like *misticitos*, "little mistis." These newly minted mistis become the object of both respect and envy.

The polar opposite of misti is the racial stereotype of *indio*, a term which has a negative connotation and which can be used as an insult. Although the Cabaneños do not use *indio* for self-reference, they are aware that the people they define as mistis, criollos, or gringos place them in the denigrating category of *indio*. The status system of the community is not a closed one, then, and the Cabaneños understand that a peasant background is a handicap in mainstream Peruvian society.

Nevertheless, because of the culturally and economically valued maize they produce, the Cabaneños have a good deal of power and enjoy a relatively high status within the region. What is more, the Cabaneños use the denigrating term *indio* and concepts of race (*raza*) as idioms of power to differentiate themselves from the herders that arrive every year for the harvest.

Caballeritos and Maíz Cabanita

Highlanders descend from herding communities in the upper Colca Valley (see fig.1.1), as well as from neighboring regions such as Yauri and Puno at harvest time. In addition to bartering their wool, potatoes, and llama meat, many herders trade their labor for Cabanaconde's most renowned and valued commodity, cabanita maize. They arrive either on foot, accompanied by large caravans of llamas and alpacas, or in trucks and buses. The herders are treated as migrant farmworkers by the Cabaneños, with the pastoralists being paid anywhere between forty and one hundred cobs of corn per day plus room and board.

Among themselves, many Cabaneños refer to those who help them bring in the harvest as *caballeritos*. The first time I heard them use this word I was surprised. The word *caballero* is a term of respect, meaning gentleman. The -*ito* is a diminutive, making *caballerito* an ironic commentary on a person's status, something akin to a superior addressing an inferior as "little fellow." I had only heard the term used once before, in an Irrigators' Assembly by a Ministry of Agriculture official who fit the stereotype of criollo and misti: tall, white, and condescending. By the way he spoke to the group it was clear that he considered the peasants to be culturally and racially beneath him. When one of his assertions was challenged, he affected a mocking tone, saying, "Listen here, *caballerito.*"

Why would Cabañeños use *caballerito*—as well as *indio*—to describe the herders who come from the high pastures? A good many Cabañeños consider the herders to be economically, culturally, and even racially, inferior.[22] The reasons for the Cabañeños' attitude of superiority are many. Not only is agriculture generally perceived as an activity of higher status than herding, but maize is particularly valued in highland society.[23]

Another reason that Cabañeños refer to the herders as caballeritos (emphasis on the *ito)* is that the herders are often small in height and relatively dark. These characteristics contrast with the relatively taller statures and fairer complexions of the Cabañeños, which are, again, the results of a greater miscegenation because of the large number of Spaniards who settled in Cabanaconde. Cabañeños as a group are known throughout the region as being tall, white, and, in some cases, as having green or blue eyes. But again, these are stereotypes, and, as with other levels in the Peruvian system of stratification (see, e.g., Bourricaud 1975; Fuenzalida 1971), there is often only a minimal, if any, phenotypical difference between those deploying the stereotype and those being thus characterized. Rather, ethnic, cultural, and class differences become racialized.[24]

The herders view the relatively wealthy and powerful valley people of Cabanaconde as more criollo, that is, being more oriented to the coast and having more of the cultural orientations of Hispanic Peruvian society. The Cabañeños are bilingual, whereas many of the herders are monolingual Quechua speakers. And, in addition to being at a lower altitude and warmer climate, Cabanaconde is a large, nucleated settlement firmly tied to national society through its high school. Herders sometimes leave their children in town to work as servants so that they can obtain an education. The Cabañeños who receive these children are obliged to feed and clothe them, as well as pay for their education; many become foster parents.

The Cabaneños consider the herders to be inferior but also view the pastoralists as being closer to the untamed power of the mountain deities. Thus, pastoralists are thought to be the most accomplished spiritualists.[25] The maize farmers of Cabanaconde and the herders share this cultural orientation, one that finds expression in mountain and earth rituals and which is tied to identity. This orientation joins both groups in a common cultural framework and differentiates them from members of the dominant ethnic group in Peru.

COMMUNITY AND ETHNICITY OVER TIME

In this chapter I have shown how community, ethnic categorization, and production must be understood in terms of the larger political economy of the colonial period and the cultural politics of the contemporary Peruvian state. Clearly, the large concentration of Spaniards in Cabanaconde has greatly influenced its ethnic dynamics. The direct descendants of a small group of Spanish families who settled in Cabanaconde retained power, in part, through a separate cultural identity from those whom they defined as indios, and whom they continued to exploit as such. Today, the terms *indio* and *misti* are part of a racial idiom used to express differences of class and ethnicity among individuals, and the tie of whiteness and power is strong in Cabanaconde.

However, I have also demonstrated that the politics of identity and ethnicity in Cabanaconde—as in the Andes as a whole—involves much more than the differentially positioned usages of *indio, cholo, mestizo,* and *criollo.* On the one hand, because of the ways that native Andean religion and ritual practice atomizes power among thousands of mountains, each of which has a subject population dependent on it (and a patron saint) for fertility and prosperity, there is an almost endless differentiation of ethnic identity among social groups in the Andes. On the other hand, it is the shared conviction that mountains and the earth possess spiritual properties which, among other things (e.g., language, dress, diet), differentiates indigenous peoples from mistis and mainstream criollo society, a society that denies the validity of these Andean cultural orientations.

Ethnic stratification and the politics of cultural pluralism are, of course, intimately linked. The way in which colonial categories have been assimilated by Andean peasants is joined to the process whereby their cultural frameworks are marginalized by the Peruvian nation. The colonial categories and racist attitudes that were instituted in Peru during the colonial period, and which were intimately linked to tribute exactions, have survived with incredible virulence.

The everyday speech of *Limeños* and highlanders alike is laced with references to race, and the negative stereotypes associated with the term *indio* have been internalized by Andean peoples. In this sense, the Cabaneños' references to the pastoralists as indios and caballeritos mirror their own subordination within the larger system of stratification. This is also expressed in some Cabaneños' choice to use their maternal name if it is less "Indian" than their paternal name. As Abercrombie (1991, 96) says, "Given their advantage in force, it is not surprising that aspects of the colonizer's value systems have become hegemonic, so that the stigma attached long ago by Europeans to 'Indianness' has worked its way into 'Indian' self consciousness as well." Because indigenous people are denied opportunities within Peru, many individuals choose to sacrifice their cultural orientations and their ethnic identity to achieve greater prosperity and status.

In fact, the goal of many Cabaneños is to educate their children so that they can escape peasant status and become "professionals"—people with steady salaries in "respectable" jobs (e.g., schoolteachers, police officers, secretaries), a move that usually requires that the individual deny or downplay his or her highland cultural roots. While the change to misti status may bring about economic and social progress for the individual, it helps reproduce the structures that marginalize and stigmatize Andean culture and identity. These same hegemonic structures have an impact on state, regional, and communal irrigation politics, where issues of cultural identity and agricultural production intersect.

2

THE POLITICAL ECOLOGY AND CULTURAL POLITICS OF IRRIGATION AND LAND RECOVERY

It was March 1983. Every night, after the town was well asleep, the "eleven heroes"—as the people of Cabanaconde would later call them—would meet in the parched, water-starved fields outside of town and, picks and drills in hand, ascend the almost dry riverbed of the Hualca-Hualca River basin. As they arrived to Tomanta, the moonlit cement casing of the Majes Canal stood out against the clear Andean night like a wide, white sidewalk—or a white scar, a permanent reminder of the abuses and broken promises of the Peruvian state and the billion-dollar Majes Project. Financed in part by the World Bank and constructed by companies from England, Sweden, South Africa, Spain, and Canada, the project was supposed to expand agriculture and promote regional development in southwestern Peru by channeling water from the upper Colca Valley to the dry coast for large-scale irrigation development and cash cropping.

Promised an offtake valve and a generous amount of the "Majes water" to intensify and expand its agricultural land, Cabanaconde had allowed the project to gouge through its communal territory. The project, however, had then proceeded to usurp resources and wreak havoc on the social and ecological fabric of the community for the next five years. Once the canal was built, the administrative unit of the Majes Project denied Cabanaconde the water it had been pledged. Now, in 1983, as the worst drought in thirty years devastated the community, Majes remained stead-

fast in its refusal. While the remaining plants withered under the intense Andean sun, a virtual river was streaming by the community, sequestered in a thick cement canal and destined for cash crops on the coast. Enough was enough.

Two stood guard while the others, laughing and cursing, went at it again. They'd already been working on it for several nights and were making little progress cracking open the canal. It would have to be dynamite, they decided. Dynamite it was, and the rest is history. Maybe not "official" history, but history at least for the people of the Colca Valley.

Cases of successful resistance to large-scale irrigation projects such as Majes are rare in the Andes. But highland peasants do regularly deploy subtle forms of cultural resistance to defend their control over irrigation water. This chapter, drawing on the portrait of ethnicity, politics, and community developed in the preceding pages, examines the Majes conflict and other fields of contention that exist in the development of Cabanaconde's hydrological resources and irrigation system.

Irrigation water in Cabanaconde and throughout the Andes is a form of common property. Common property, understood as a type of property relationship in which a particular resource is controlled by an identifiable community of interdependent users, usually excludes outsiders while regulating use by members of the local community (see, e.g., McCay and Acheson 1990). In this sense, irrigation water and its regulation has much in common with range lands, shellfish beds, fisheries, forests, and other resources managed by communities.

Since at least the turn of the century, the Cabaneños have attempted to expand their irrigation commons and rehabilitate some of their lost agricultural land. In Cabanaconde, where there was a population loss of over 80 percent from the 1570s to the 1680s, several pre-Columbian canals and over a thousand hectares of cultivated terraced fields were abandoned.[1] Over the last century, as in much of the Andes, the growing population of Cabanaconde has put pressure on communal resources. The Cabaneños' successes and failures in expanding their water supply and recovering abandoned terraces necessarily take us to the political ecology of irrigation

development, that is, the way that political forces at the local, regional, national, and international levels condition Cabanaconde's
relationship with its resources.[2]

ECOLOGY, PRODUCTION, AND THE COMMONS

Lying on the arid west slope of the Andes, the territory of Cabanaconde is environmentally diverse and supports an extraordinary
amount of wildlife.[3] Yet, there is little hunting or fishing. Instead,
Cabaneños depend on domesticated plants and animals, employ-
ing a wide range of "production zones" (see, e.g., Mayer 1985), all
within a few hours' walk of the community (fig. 2.1). Most agricultural production takes place in the warm valley (quechua) fields
surrounding the town, which are at between approximately 9,500
and 10,800 feet and are where the famous maíz cabanita is grown.

All agriculture in Cabanaconde is irrigated, and approximately
three-quarters of the 1,250 hectares of irrigated land in the main
fields is dedicated to this crop (see fig. 2.2).[4] Irrigated landholdings
become more fragmented with each generation. In a survey of 322
households, I found that 44 percent had six to ten plots of land,
22 percent had eleven to fifteen plots, and 6 percent had sixteen
to twenty different fields to cultivate! This abundance of plots does
not mean an abundance of land, as these plots are generally small
in size. Of these 322 households, 56 percent had one hectare or
less, 31 percent had one to two hectares, 10 percent had two to
three hectares, and 3 percent had more than three hectares of land.[5]

Deep in the Colca Canyon at 6,500 feet in the yunga area are
the orchards and the associated small outlying hamlets of Ayon,
Awaliwa, Saqerqa, San Galle, Saqasñirwa (below Acpi), Suysuywa,
and Cenillo (see fig. 2.3). Here the Cabaneños cultivate varied fruit,
as well as alfalfa and cochinilla.[6] These hot and dry orchards are
generally associated with fertility and romance, as well as malaria,
which used to claim many lives. Most Cabaneños own or have access to land in at least one of these orchards, though many do not
keep up their plots, usually "for lack of time." The steep cliffs of
the Colca Canyon that lead down to the orchards is a commons,
that is, a common area that provides comuneros with resources

PRODUCTION ZONES

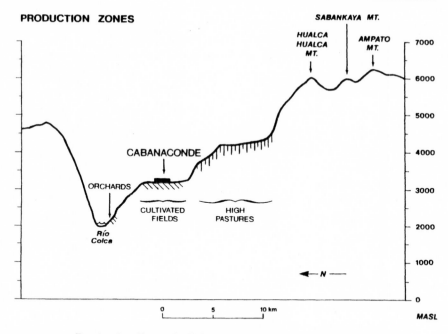

FIGURE 2.1. Production Zones in Cabanaconde (altitude given in meters)

such as medicinal plants and the prickly pear cactus, which yields fruit and cochinilla. These resources lie outside the regime of private property, which is made up of the relatively small irrigated lands in the orchards themselves.

At the other extreme of the communal territory is another commons, the high pastures located at between 12,000 and 14,500 feet, where alpaca, llama, sheep, and cattle herds are kept (see figs. 2.1 and 2.3). After agriculture, herding is the most important economic activity of the community.[7] Life at over 13,000 feet is hard and solitary, and this *puna* region is perceived by the Cabaneños as uncivilized and possessing an almost unlimited amount of untamed natural energy. Large grassy plains and sparsely forested ravines contrast with steep mountains higher than 19,000 feet. Small forlorn hamlets of one or two families are interspersed amidst the rugged landscape, usually separated by several miles. There are some ten of these herd steads (*estancias*) in the high pastures; the permanent herders who live there make only occasional trips to the community. The high pastures, in addition to being a grazing common, also yield medicinal herbs and firewood. Access to this commons is one of the most fundamental rights that a Cabaneño enjoys.[8]

Herding and agriculture are intimately related. During the sowing, cattle are needed to plow the earth, and they are fed cornstalks, which are highly valued as quality fodder. Immediately following the harvest, the date of which is decided by the municipal council, the agricultural fields become a common area. Communal stone fences surrounding the cultivated fields are opened to allow transport of the harvest and to let the cattle feed on the stubble, abandoned cornstalks, and grasses that have grown on these fields. People must gather their harvest quickly or risk having it turned to fodder. For the next few weeks, privately held, irrigated land becomes common property for cattle grazing.

THE IRRIGATION COMMONS AND WATER MANAGEMENT

Cabanaconde's irrigation water originates in Mount Hualca-Hualca's snow-shrouded summit and in the small springs that furrow down the slopes. The Hualca-Hualca River picks up more water from other springs and the Majes Canal as it winds its way down from the snowmelt of the looming mountain. Annual rainfall is extremely variable in Cabanaconde, and periodic drought occurs in this region.[9] The Hualca-Hualca River supplies Cabanaconde's agriculture with an estimated seventy-five to 150 liters of water per second during the dry season, the months of May to December (Abril Benavides 1979; ORDEA 1980). Before the water of the Majes Canal became available in 1983, each round of irrigation water, that is, the time between waterings, lasted seventy-five to one hundred days. Today each round lasts forty-five to fifty days; there is still, however, only one harvest a year.

Well above the community itself, the water from the Hualca-Hualca River is diverted by rustic stone dams into the main canals. The latter snake through the agricultural fields and connect to secondary intakes and smaller feeder canals by means of small earthen dams. By adjusting large rocks, which are sealed tight with *champa*, grassy clods of earth, water is channeled to each individual field; these intakes have to be prepared for each new round of water. The principal canals, when taken together, are more than thirty miles in length. With the exception of approximately one mile that is cement-lined, these are earthen canals. These canals average a yard in width and half a yard in depth.

The large dams and smaller intakes are all made with stone and champa. Whereas the large intakes from the river usually wash out in the rainy season and are rebuilt every year, the smaller ditches and intakes are continually refurbished by the users. Small bridges (*chimpanas*) and paths that provide access to these canals are an important part of the hydraulic infrastructure, and they are also maintained by the users. So too, offtakes, called *tinkunas* in Cabanaconde and *wikchas* in upper valley communities (Treacy 1989, 1994a, 1994b), are an important feature of this canal system; these are generally used to channel excess water back to the Hualca-Hualca River.

The Cabaneños practice continuous nocturnal irrigation. River water passes directly to the fields twenty-four hours a day (fig. 2.2), and reservoirs for storing water at night are not a feature of the system in Cabanaconde.[10] Nocturnal irrigation, which requires stomping through drenched fields during the chilly Andean nights, can be deadly: several people have died from hypothermia or from falling off a terrace.

Irrigation is an important arena of social interaction. Although the heads of households and the water authorities are predominantly men, both women and men are skilled and active in irrigation from a young age. Many women are consummate irrigators and carry out the most burdensome tasks, such as nocturnal irrigation and water theft; the latter is accomplished by rechanneling a portion of the irrigation water, usually under the cover of nightfall, to one's field from its designated place in the irrigation round. Family and interfamily disputes over land are often expressed in water use—one waters land that one intends to cultivate. Water can also be used as a weapon: a slight turn of a rock can send water streaming into the already irrigated plot of an enemy, destroying the small plants.

As a common property resource, individual access to irrigation water is managed and controlled by a village-wide association of water users, the Irrigators Commission. The commission, usually made up of literate men, has an elected governing board of president, vice president, secretary, treasurer, two aldermen (*vocales*), and two controllers. The commission appoints the water mayors, as well as additional controllers, each year. The state is represented at the regional level by a water engineer (*ingeniero de aguas*), who resides in the provincial capital, Chivay, and, at the local level, by an extension agent (*sectorista*), who resides part-time in Cabanaconde. These state officials, generally monolingual Spanish-speakers from the coast or from the city of Arequipa, are viewed as powerful misti outsiders by the Cabaneños.

The water engineer and the extension agent are ever-loyal to state irrigation policies and development and are in charge of seeing that the national water laws are implemented correctly. While it is made up of locally elected peasant irrigators from Cabanaconde itself, the Irrigation Commission should, in theory, report to the state's irrigation bureaucracies and should enact the state's policies. But the Cabaneños who serve on the Irrigators Commission are expected by the townspeople to put the interests of the community first, and they usually do. As explored later, members of the commission take advantage of their position to favor friends and family with water, and the relationship between local and state officials is characterized by both cooperation and conflict.

The meetings of the commission are held in a small, dusty room with a desk, five chairs, some weathered wheelbarrows, a few bags of cement, and books that date from the 1940s. These books record the minutes of the Irrigator Assemblies, the organization of canal cleanings, the water allotted different sectors, the naming of water mayors and controllers, the assessment of fines to water thieves and absentee faena workers, and legal battles over communal waters.

There were some 865 irrigators (usually heads of households) in Cabanaconde in 1980, according to the Ministry of Agriculture. In Cabanaconde, the irrigation cycle determines the planting schedule and other agricultural activities, such as the preparation of the soil, weeding, and buttressing of the plants. The activities of the individual, then, are constrained by the irrigation calendar established by communal authorities, which follows the same basic schedule from year to year.[11]

The principle of the commons is also manifest in relation to

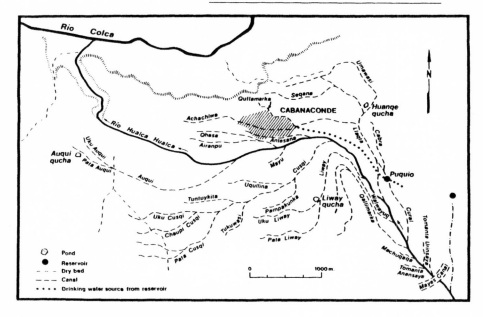

FIGURE 2.2. Cabanaconde's Irrigation System

canal cleanings and other important obligations—such as assuming the office of water mayor once in one's life—that irrigators must fulfill to gain access to irrigation water. Each large canal that feeds off of the Hualca-Hualca River (see fig. 2.2) has its own group of users. The Irrigators Commission organizes the irrigators by posting notices and using town criers. Almost every Cabaneño possesses land along several canals, and therefore he or she ostensibly has canal-cleaning obligations. Although the owners of larger plots of land should, in theory, bring an extra worker to the canal cleanings, they rarely do.

There is less communal regulation of water in the orchards and the high pastures. In the orchards there is a relative abundance of water but a lack of land. People irrigate when they feel the need, and there is no nocturnal irrigation.[12] Planting is not determined by rounds of irrigation water as it is in the main fields, but rather each farmer is free to decide when to plant; the decisions are usually based on the full moon or the appearance of certain stars. In the high pastures, water is used in accordance with pastoral needs, and irrigated pastures (*bofedales*) provide an especially luxuriant grass.

In the main fields, the organization of the irrigation commons is anything but a cooperative affair. It was mentioned in chapter 1 that a few powerful families that descended from resident Spaniards controlled the political structure of the community until the 1970s. As will be elaborated on in chapter 5, from the 1920s through the 1950s, these families used their political offices to sell—mostly among themselves—untitled *eriazo* lands, that is, lands not authorized for any kind of cultivation, whether they are irrigated (*de riego*) or dry-farmed (*de secano*). However, when it came to irrigating the unauthorized lands—which would have meant prolonging the round of water for the main fields—the community refused. Nevertheless, as discussed later in this chapter, this conflict continues to militate against the total recovery of abandoned terraces.

SCRATCHES AND GOUGES, COMMUNITY AND STATE

Conflict and cooperation within the irrigation commons and land-recovery initiatives must be understood in relation to the availability of water. Power and different attempts to capture water are inscribed in the scratches and gouges that cross Cabanaconde's broken territory. In some places the inscriptions are fresh; others are well routed from years of heavy use. Still others have been almost entirely erased. The community has tried to expand its water supply and land base since at least 1916. Some of these efforts have been successful; many have not.

The principal means of expanding the annual availability of water has been the cleaning of the high springs that feed the Hualca-Hualca River through the maintenance and rehabilitation of canals built in pre-Columbian times and through the seeking out of new sources of water. The latter includes attempts to gain water from the contested area of Huataq and the opening of the Majes Canal in 1983.

The ancient canal of Huataq represents a massive undertaking, surely the work of the organizing force of the Inka state. The Majes Canal involved not only the modern Peruvian state but an international consortium. At the other end of the scale, small scratches next to the large gouges of Huataq and Majes, are the tiny springs and channels of water at the high end of the Hualca-Hualca River basin that, until recently, were dug out every year to increase the flow of water (fig. 2.3). In between these two extremes are the heavily used canals, intakes, and secondary canals of the fields themselves. Although these canals receive constant minor and occasional larger modifications, they have been in continuous use for at least five hundred years. Here, too, power is inscribed in the different culturally determined forms of distribution that guide their use today.

CABAÑEÑO ETHNOHYDROLOGY AND THE SOJOURN TO HUALCA-HUALCA MOUNTAIN

It is impossible to overstate the symbolic importance of irrigation for the Cabaneños—it pervades their lives and is cause for great joy and great suffering. Irrigation structures the private and collective calendars of the Cabaneños during much of the year. It gives life to their terraced fields and to many of their conversations, and—as evidenced in the centuries-old religious observations to Hualca-Hualca Mountain—water is a basic part of their ethnic and communal identities. The Cabaneños are also proficient hydrologists with a vast store of knowledge concerning water flow, subterranean filtration, canal and terrace construction, and the changing chemical composition of river water at different times of the year.

This technical knowledge, combined with religious ideas concerning the correct formulas of rituals for assuring fertility, abundance of water, and personal safety, constitute the Cabaneño variant of Andean ethnohydrology (Sherbondy 1982b), the particular "hydro-logics" (Lansing 1991) that guide local water management in town. Mountains are gendered, and for Cabaneños it is generally the female mountains that provide water. Unlike other highland regions where people conceptualize irrigation water as semen or blood, water is likened to mother's milk, another essential, life-giving fluid. And unlike the single eight-day communal catharsis associated with canal cleanings in the Water Fiesta described for many other parts of the highlands and even in other Colca communities, Cabaneño irrigation rituals are carried out by the water mayors and the irrigators throughout the distribution cycle.[13]

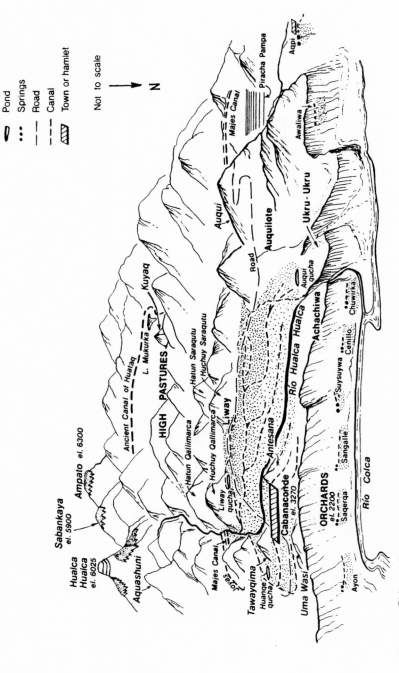

FIGURE 2.3. Oblique View of Production Zones (altitudes given in meters)

Legend:
- Cultivated fields
- Pond
- Springs
- Road
- Canal
- Town or hamlet

N

Not to scale

Hualca Hualca el. 6025
Sabankaya el. 5900
Ampato el. 6300
Aquashuni

Ancient Canal of Huatoq
L. Mukurka
Kuyaq

HIGH PASTURES

Hatun Qallimarca
Huchuy Qallimarca
Hatun Saraqutu
Huchuy Saraqutu

Liway qucha
Liway

Antesana

Majes Canal

Tawayqima
Huange qucha
Uma Wasi

Cabanaconde el. 3270

ORCHARDS el. 2200
Saqerqa
Sangalle
Ayon

Suysuywa
Cenillo
Chuwirka

Río Hualca Hualca

Achachiwa

Río Colca

Auqui
Majes Canal
Auquilote
Road
Auqui qucha
Ukru-Ukru
Awaliwa
Piracha Pampa
Aqpi

Until 1983, however, there was a ritualized communal work project, the annual sojourn to Hualca-Hualca Mountain (*la salida a Hualca-Hualca*). The purpose of this event, which involved the entire community, was to increase water availability for irrigation. The people of the community accomplished this goal by physically cleaning the small tributaries that flow into the Hualca-Hualca River. Availability was also enhanced by the ritual appeasement of the mountain through individual offerings. Because of its ritualistic nature, the salida resembled pilgrimages made to sacred mountains by other communities in the southern Andes (see, e.g., Allen 1988; Sallnow 1987). In Cabanaconde, the purpose of these rituals was to honor the mother mountain, secure the personal safety of the irrigators, and create an abundance of water.

Communal authorities decided the date of the expedition, which would happen between the months of September and November. During years of drought they would go twice. "It used to look like an army," one man told me. The townspeople, organized into their respective quarters (*cuarteles*), marched their mules and burros over ten miles and up 6,500 vertical feet (see fig. 2.3) to clean the small rivulets and channels (*zanqas*) that emerge from the high slopes and furrow down through the boggy pastures to the Hualca-Hualca River. Although the first expedition of which I found record was in 1922 (BMC), this annual pilgrimage is most likely an ancient feature of the complex of rituals and irrigation associated with Hualca-Hualca Mountain.

A good part of the community used to make this march, remaining at the foot of Hualca-Hualca for three days. Not only would the participants dig out the small furrows on the lower slopes but they would also climb to the snow of the mountain itself at around 17,000 feet. Here they had to cut a central channel through the snow to redirect the snow melt to the main channel, thereby increasing the overall volume of water. The work was strenuous. "You'd hit the snow three times with your pick, and you'd be out of breath," one person explained. Many people were known to faint, become ill, and even die. Indeed, in November 1934, a state representative who arrived to "organize the irrigators of the district" was told by the communal authorities that "the small flow of water to irrigate the fields each year is due to the efforts of this Town's inhabitants, who, making great sacrifices on snow-covered Hualca-Hualca, toil in the snow for eight days and at times even longer. It is well known that all who go there become snow-blind and gravely ill, many heads of family having passed away in the sacrifice to increase the water" (BMC).

The journey to Hualca-Hualca has not been made since 1983, when the water from the Majes Canal was secured by the community. Many people with whom I spoke lamented the water lost by not going to Hualca-Hualca, also noting that these cleanings used to build solidarity among the townspeople, solidarity that spilled over into other communal initiatives. Ironically, the courageous effort to open the Majes Canal, which required great communal unity, brought to an end the yearly sojourn—part work party, part pilgrimage—to Hualca-Hualca, and with it an end to the annually renewed solidarity that it provided.

THE OLD HUATAQ CANAL

In addition to these communal efforts, conflicts between the community and regional forces have a great impact on the availability of water. Competition between communities over highland sources of water is often intense. An example is the case of Huataq, a spring in the high pastures of the community that provides more than six hundred liters of water per second. Since at least 1916, the community has attempted to rebuild through communal work projects the twenty miles of canal that, during Inka times, apparently brought water to what were then cultivated lands (fig. 2.3).[14]

The community of Lluta has fought legal and even physical battles with Cabanaconde over the Huataq waters since at least 1933. In that year there was a trial over Huataq, and in 1937 the entire town of Cabanaconde went "to take possession" (BMC). Attempts by the Cabaneños to repair the ancient canal throughout the 1930s, 1940s, and 1950s met with continued opposition from Lluta. The struggle became especially intense in 1968. Each community had national decrees to demonstrate their lawful possession of the Huataq waters, and each accused the other of trying to steal the water (BIC). The mayors of Lluta and Cabanaconde each presented the subprefect of the province with documents asserting their rights. The waters of Huataq were then legally divided into three parts, two for Cabanaconde and one for Lluta.

The conflict, however, did not die there. In September 1969 Cabanaconde denounced the people of Lluta "for the abuses committed to the water of Huataq" (BMC). In 1971 a new resolution appeared, stating that the waters of Huataq belonged to Lluta. In December 1979 the legal battle had shifted again, this time to Cabanaconde: "The transfer of the Huataq waters . . . was favorable" (BMC). Other resolutions have since appeared, however, and in 1988 Lluta was still threatening violence if the Cabaneños were to renew their efforts to divert this water.

The numerous and contradictory national decrees over Huataq demonstrate the capricious nature of state intervention in highland water politics. And in this case, some of the most powerful representatives of the state in the Ministry of Agriculture were in fact beholden to regional elites with a personal stake in the Huataq waters. These obstacles did not, however, diminish the Cabaneños' resolve. As late as 1985, the community was continuing to send engineers and communal work parties to rehabilitate the Huataq Canal. Because of political influence, the conflict with Lluta, and the fact that this difficult project clearly demanded the logistical support of the Peruvian state, the Cabaneños never completed it. The community did prevail in a different case, however, and, when it did, the Huataq waters became an important bargaining chip.

THE MAJES CANAL

As illustrated in the opening vignette, an important source of water, as well as of contention, is the large canal built in the late 1970s by the Peruvian state and the international construction companies that made up the Majes Consortium. The purpose of the canal, which was financed by the Peruvian state, the World Bank, the Banco Interamericano de Desarollo, and other international banks, was to channel highland water to the coast and bring over 50,000 hectares of barren desert land into production (see, e.g., Obando 1992, 60).

Although there had been serious discussion since before the

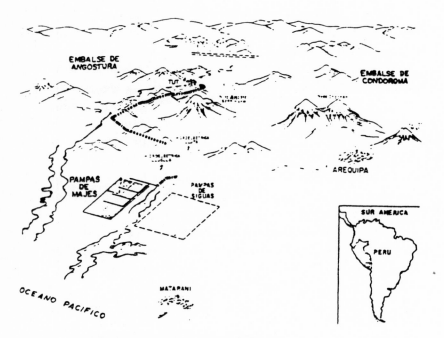

FIGURE 2.4. Majes Project's Map of the Region

1940s to develop the pampas of Majes, it was only in 1971 that
Peruvian President Juan Velasco introduced legislation to move the
Majes plan forward and to, in his own words, "make Arequipa's
dream a reality" (Obando 1992, 43). Thirty years later, however,
the project has fallen well short of its goals and has to a large degree lost its connection to regional development and the needs of
the people of Arequipa.

But the project had other costs as well. As figure 2.4 shows,
the map proposed by this billion-dollar development project neglected to show that in the path of the proposed canal lay more
than a dozen communities and tens of thousands of peasants. This
is symptomatic of the low regard that Majes and the Peruvian state
had for the inhabitants of Cabanaconde and the Colca Valley.

The role of the state is clear. As early as May 6, 1967, the Ministry of Development and Public Works by way of the Arequipa
Board of Rehabilitation and Development stated that Cabanaconde
"is being considered for three thousand hectares" to favor the irrigators there (BIC). Various other government agencies convened

later that year. An entry in the books of the Irrigators Commission states that the community is "soliciting some three thousand liters [per second] of water from the Main Canal of Majes to be used in the irrigation of the fields now being cultivated and in the expansion of new lands." This same entry, dated November 10, 1966, reports that the Ministry of Development and Public Works, the Board of Rehabilitation of Arequipa, the National Fund for Economic Development, and the national office of the Agrarian Reform were going to study the springs of the entire area so that if the Majes Canal affected the town's resources, Cabanaconde could claim damages (BIC).

Promises were made but not kept. Until 1983 there were no benefits from the project, except an improved road and some jobs, but these jobs were temporary, dangerous, and poorly paying. The project brought widespread social and environmental problems for the communities of this region (see, e.g., Hurley 1978; Benavides 1983; Sven 1986). Workers from the project, who came from other highland regions and the coast and who were housed in a large encampment near the community, abused the local townsfolk. Many workers would not buy products from women accompanied by their husbands, and there were incidents of prostitution and rape. Although the improved road provided the means for greater mobility up and down the valley and to and from Arequipa, the community was also subjected to economic, cultural, and political forces it had never experienced before. More money began to flow into the community, and stores were opened to meet the needs of a boom economy. Most Cabaneños with whom I discussed the Majes Project lamented the changes and abuses the project brought. "Everything became money, money, money," one man complained.

Harder to express are the profound social and cultural changes the community experienced, including the way local society defined itself. "Criollo" views, disparaging toward the "simple" and "backward" ways of the highland dwellers, became widely felt. As the president of the community ruefully expressed to me, "The workers would come rolling into town. They were from all over—Cuzco, Puno, the coast—all over. They'd come in, saying in Spanish, 'Son of a bitch, it's hot! Hey, give me a case of beer,' and pretty soon all the boys in town were walking around saying, 'Hey, son of a bitch.'" Less respect for elders, an increase in vandalism, and the breaking down of social mores were other consequences of the Majes Project. The local culture was denigrated, and several rituals, such as the cattle rite (*torotinkay*) during the sowing, disappeared. The workers even instituted a new saint in the community.[15]

The social impact was paralleled by an ecological one. Economic dependence on income generated by the project increased as the community's resources suffered. During a series of drought years, when the volume of river water was already extremely low, the project used large amounts of water from the Hualca-Hualca River for its operations, without the community's permission (BIC). Canals and terraces were damaged by project roads. The underground tunnels built by the project also affected subterranean sources of water.[16] Because of the drought and the Majes workers' insensitive use of the little river water that remained, the cultivated area decreased dramatically. A petition sent by the Irrigators Commission to the Ministry of Agriculture on March 18, 1980, states that the devastation caused by "the last droughts" and the water supplied to Majes had "horrific results . . . our agricultural fields have diminished by 80 percent."[17]

Abuses were tolerated, in part, because of the irrigation water and the extended land base that the community expected to receive from the project. The project also promised to use its engineers and heavy machinery to improve the drainage of the Hualca-Hualca River basin and to recover the Huataq Canal (BIC). Through 1979 and 1980 the Majes Project continued to promise support for these projects as well as enough water, 1,000 liters per second, to recover several thousand hectares for the community.[18] But it soon became clear to the community that Majes, intent on channeling all of the water to the coast, had no intention of carrying through with their promises.

The first hint of resistance soon became manifest. In March 1980, a commission made up of the president of the Peasant Community, the president of the Irrigators Commission, and the mayor of Cabanaconde again requested water from the Majes Canal in the form of an offtake valve and assistance in improving the waters of the Hualca-Hualca River. They stated that "the District of Caba-naconde has been forgotten" and that "everyone will unite as one man" if their demands went unanswered. Later that month, a memorandum was sent out to the Ministry of Agriculture and to the president of the republic "clamoring for one thing alone, which is water" (BMC). A letter to the Majes Consortium from August 1981 states that if the community was not recompensed for its water, "the agriculturists will stop the services they provide. . . . The higher authorities are fooling us." More ominously, the letter continues, "The townspeople will take action to the last consequences if an immediate solution is not arrived at." Yet no water was allotted to the community. An entry in the books of the Irrigators Commission from September 1981 refers to the drought of that year as "a frightful crisis."

In January 1983, another letter was sent by the mayor of Cabanaconde to the president of Peru, Fernando Belaúnde Terry, stating,

> Cabanaconde is the most populated district in the Province of Caylloma . . . all community members are small holders, a situation that generates the massive exodus of the population. [Our] current water capacity is just 80 liters per second, insufficient for 1200 hectares. We irrigate every 100 days . . . this generates poverty, undernourishment, infant and adult mortality, alcoholism, and illiteracy. Cabanaconde has been forgotten by the Majes Macon Project, whose canal crosses our jurisdiction, destroying natural resources such as land and water, making even graver the already precarious economic situation of this community. (BIC)

They asked President Belaúnde to authorize an offtake valve from the Majes Canal; money, machines, and technical assistance to reconstruct the Huataq Canal; the construction of a cement reservoir in Joyas; and the settlement of families in the Pampas de Majes (the target area of the project). The letter was signed by the communal authorities and several hundred people. A few days later, a memo was sent to the Ministry of Agriculture asking for "an offtake valve in the Tomanta Sector," which is where the Majes

Canal crosses the Hualca-Hualca River. Their numerous cries for help—the many delegations and various pleas the community had sent to the consortium and to the regional authorities, letters written, articles printed in Arequipa newspapers—fell on deaf ears. Usually kept below the surface, the cultural politics and racism embedded in Peruvian national development were clearly revealed in the negligent and unethical position of the Majes Project. With the remaining plants withering in the most serious drought in thirty years, the possibility of famine in Cabanaconde became real.

In March 1983, the Cabaneños opened the Majes Canal in a classic show of peasant resistance. As described in the opening vignette, the now-renowned "eleven heroes" of the community, some of whom were authorities of the Irrigators Commission and Peasant Community, went nightly to drill a hole in the thick cement casing of the canal where it crossed Hualca-Hualca River (see fig. 2.3). Finally, they used dynamite. People in town soon began to comment that the volume of the Hualca-Hualca River had increased, and an assembly was hurriedly called. The entire community swung into action.

A permanent guard kept watch in the church tower, ready to sound the bell should the police arrive. A trumpeter was stationed at the entrance of the town, and barricades were built on the road. The eleven heroes left the community or slept in the orchards deep in the Colca Valley. A committee made up of local authorities traveled to Arequipa to report what had been done, and they were immediately arrested. But the Cabaneños had skillfully published several news clips in Arequipa newspapers in the weeks before they opened the canal, decrying the drought and the way that Majes had lied to the community, as well as the lack of government support. This was done not only to assert the Cabaneños' rights to the water but to ensure that their actions would not be confused with those of terrorists.

A police contingent was sent to the community, but when they arrived the entire community confronted them. The community claimed collective responsibility for the opening of the canal and demanded that the water not be withdrawn. Several large machines belonging to the consortium were taken hostage. A few days later, the subprefect of the region, the mayor of Cabanaconde, and other important authorities were present in the plaza of the community to talk about "the problem of the offtake opened by the townspeople in the Tomanta Sector" (BIC). The mayor exclaimed, "The Ministry of Agriculture is guilty because it has never taken any steps to help the agriculture of Cabanaconde." The subprefect agreed to provide a legal transfer of the waters within the briefest time possible, promising that there would be "no repression against the townspeople." But when he asked that the machines be returned to the Majes consortium, the community denied his request. Further, the mayor demanded that three hundred liters per second be given to the community. After he agreed to the conditions set by the community, the subprefect received an ovation. People still talk excitedly and proudly about how the entire community took responsibility, and how they were ready to fight to the end for the water.

The communal authorities, with help from the migrant associations of the community in Arequipa and Lima, continued to negotiate with the regional authorities, explaining that they were not terrorists but were dying of hunger. Out of fear of further conflicts, Autodema (Autoridad Autónoma de Majes)—the administrative unit of the Majes Canal since 1982—finally agreed to cede 150 liters per second to Cabanaconde. The Cabaneños also demanded that the state's water tariff, instituted a couple of years earlier, be rescinded.

In August 1983, the hole was patched and a valve was installed at Tomanta. The next day the entire community went to Tomanta in a procession, with a brass band leading the way. The books of the Irrigators Commission note, "After the blessing by the priest the two valves were opened in the presence of the president of the Irrigators Commission and the townspeople" (BIC). With this victory, the Cabaneños became heroes in the region. The other communities of the left bank of the Colca Valley threatened to take similar action against the Majes Project "or call in the boys from Cabanaconde," as several Cabaneños proudly told me. These other communities were soon given access to the "Majes water."

Today the eleven heroes meet in secret to celebrate that day in March 1983 when they opened the canal. Although everyone in the community knows who they are, they still keep their identities from government officials for fear of reprisals. When the abandoned fields were later recovered with the Majes water, the heroes were given choice plots.

THE LAND RECOVERY PROJECT

After the flow of 150 liters per second from the Majes Canal was secured in 1983, there was a betterment of agriculture in the main fields, and attempts to increase the area of cultivation soon began. Canals in the lower part of the agricultural lands were extended through communal labor, and abandoned terraced fields in the area of Auquilote were distributed through lottery (see fig. 2.3). To decide which families could participate in the lottery for the thirty-six hectares (ninety acres) being recovered, the Peasant Community held a communal assembly. As the name of each comunero was read, the public decided who met the established criteria: full-time and responsible farmer, head of household with dependent children, permanent resident in the community, and small landholder. More than two hundred people qualified. The thirty-six lottery winners quickly organized into an association, elected a president, and began to rehabilitate their lands through cooperative labor. Many of the newly recovered fields were soon yielding good harvests.[19]

Auquilote was the first step in recovering more than 1,000 hectares of agricultural land in Cabanaconde; this plan was predicated on an increase of water from the Majes Canal. The Majes Project Administration promised an additional 350 liters per second if the community could provide a suitable plan for the use of the water. The peasant community commissioned an engineer to study and delimit 340 hectares of agricultural lands in three areas: Ukru-Ukru, Pirachapampa, and Liway (fig. 2.3). This study, which took several months, cost the community more than 2,000 U.S. dollars.[20] A "qualifying commission" was named to evaluate eligibility for the 340 one-hectare lots, and another lottery was then held. This time, all who qualified obtained lots.

However, this land-recovery project met with problems resulting from the communal and regional conflicts discussed previously.

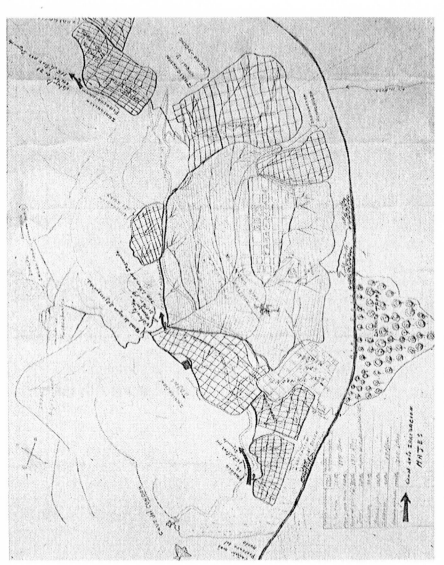

FIGURE 2.5. Local Representation of Land Recovery

First, the grown children and grandchildren of the elite families who illicitly purchased and appropriated land earlier in the century entered into an intense legal battle with the peasant community over the lands of Ukru-Ukru and Liway. This legal battle brought the land-recovery process in these areas to a standstill. The elite families even used their influence to have the police detain the president of the Peasant Community. Although he was released, such threats from the powerful families kept the community divided and impeded the recovery of some lands.

This community infighting further endangered land recovery, as the Majes Project Administration would not release the promised water until the issue of the contested fields was resolved. Release of the water was also contingent on the community signing away their rights to the water of the Huataq. The reason for Majes Administration's generosity comes to light: by releasing 350 liters per second to Cabanaconde, they retain the six hundred liters per second of Huataq water for the Majes Canal and for the powerful Arequipeños who currently use it.[21]

When the Majes water was secured, other groups within the community besides that of the powerful families opposed the allotment of new lands by the Peasant Community. One group argued that the new water should be used to better the existing fields. Community members who had been disqualified from the lotteries because their children were adults or otherwise had no dependents also complained. Their discontent resulted in a promise that they would receive land in the next allotment. This has come to pass.

Since 1990, Cabanaconde's efforts to recover its lost infrastructure and agricultural lands have been extremely successful (see fig. 2.5). As of 1998, the community had recovered over eight hundred hectares; another three hundred will be brought into production in the next few years. By the year 2000, the community will have essentially doubled its agricultural lands. And although this land recovery has been anything but a trouble-free process, it has succeeded where previous attempts failed.[22] After a century of efforts, the Cabaneños' courageous actions and astute maneuvering have provided them with a relatively large and growing land base.

FIGURE 2.6. Different Models of Water Management

June to December Irrigation	January to Mid-April First heavy rains	Dry spells
Local Model water mayors saya system	Informal System el que pueda anarchic	State Model controllers de canto

FROM POLITICAL ECOLOGY TO CULTURAL POLITICS: STATE VERSUS LOCAL MODELS OF DISTRIBUTION

The materials from Cabanaconde demonstrate that land recovery and the expansion of water availability are primarily political, rather than technical, issues. At the communal level, political and economic divisions militated against complete rehabilitation of terraces. In the case of the Huataq and Majes Canals, regional and national interests greatly influenced water availability and the possibilities for land recovery. And as the Majes conflict clearly illustrates, local Andean systems of production must be understood within the political economy of the Peruvian state, where the coastally based national economy's need for highland water has wide-ranging effects at the local level.

But the Majes Canal and national development policies in Peru are part of a larger cultural politics in which power-holders and dominant cultural discourses consider the human and natural resources of the highlands as inferior to those of the criollo coast. Besides overt instances of domination such as Majes and other large-scale, coast-oriented development, the Peruvian state marginalizes Andean communities and cultural frameworks in many subtle ways. This marginalization is evident in the cultural underpinnings of local and state models of water distribution and management, models that provide varying degrees of efficiency, equity, and local control.

In Cabanaconde, these models are applied to the same fields during different moments in the annual irrigation cycle (see fig. 2.6). Initially, local, informal, and state models of water distribution—anansaya/urinsaya, *el que pueda*, and *de canto*, respectively— appear to be merely different options for apportioning water (see

State Model of Irrigation Distribution: De Canto

de canto sequence   **fields are watered without distinction of the dual divisions**

1	2	3
4	5	6
7	8	9

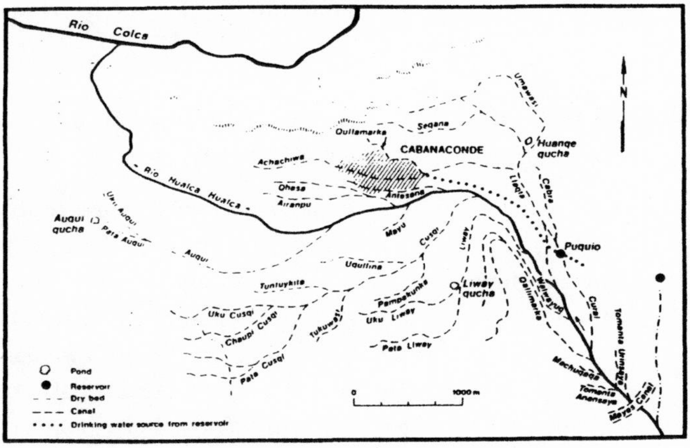

↑
these are
the same fields

↓

Anan/Urin Sequence   **fields are watered according to the dual divisions**

Local Model of Irrigation Distribution: Dual Organization

A	U	U
A	A	A
A	U	A

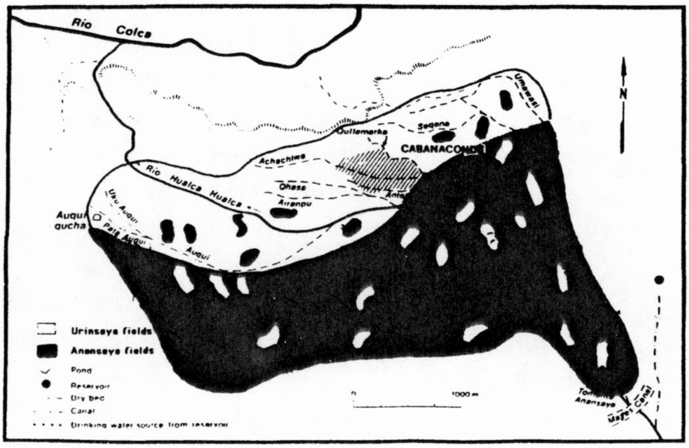

A=fields watered by
Water Mayor of
Anansaya

U=fields watered by
Water Mayor of
Urinsaya

FIGURE 2.7. State versus Local Models of Water Distribution

fig. 2.7). But, in fact, they embody different historical processes and widely diverging cultural rationales.

From June through December, the water mayors, carrying the snake-headed staffs of authority, alternate in distributing irrigation water. They follow the conceptual dual *saya* grid that overlays the agricultural fields of Cabanaconde (figs. 2.8 and 2.9), one watering the land classified as anansaya, or upper moiety, the other watering urinsaya, lower moiety.[23] As mentioned in the Introduction, the water mayors alternate not only in managing water, but in carrying out rituals. The attainment of fertility and the symbolic control over water through mountain and earth rituals are crucial aspects of the local model.

When the first strong rains of late December or early January fall, an informal system of distribution, of el que pueda—whoever gets to the water first or has the most social or physical muscle—is set in motion. As soon as the rains let up even temporarily, the absence of any water official provokes many conflicts and even physical violence. This is when the state model of irrigation is put into action.

During the state model's annual hold on water management, there is a different type of "repartitioner," the person in charge of distribution. These individuals, community members like the water mayors, are called controllers (*controladores*). They distribute water to the fields de canto, that is, sequentially from "one end to the other," ignoring the dual classification of the plots (anansaya and urinsaya) operative in the local model. The state takes a secular and bureaucratic view of water management, whereas the local model is highly ritualized and perceives water as part of a larger social and symbolic universe.

At the heart of this conflict are issues of local autonomy, state control, and different cultural understandings concerning availability, efficiency, and the means by which to obtain an abundance of irrigation water. For the last fifty years, local elites and state officials have attempted to completely supplant the local saya model of distribution with the state's de canto one, a struggle that continues today. Although the state model has gained ground over the years, many aspects of the local model remain firmly entrenched.

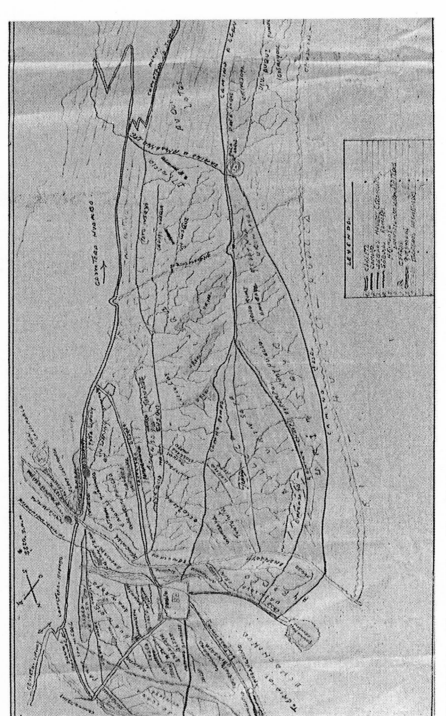

FIGURE 2.8. Local Representation of Saya Divisions

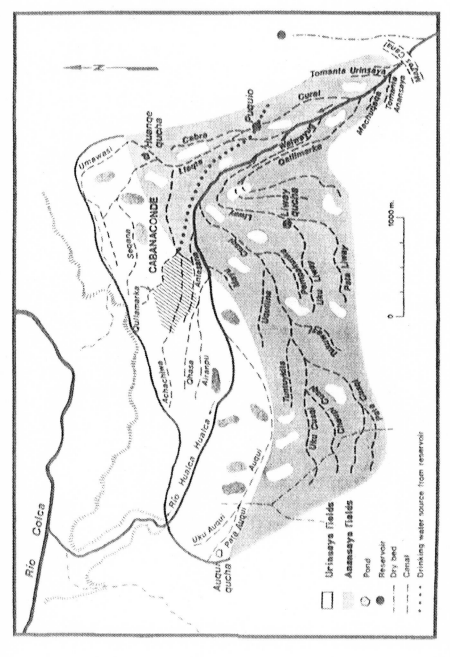

FIGURE 2.9. Generic Representation of Saya Divisions

To understand this persistence, in the following chapters I contrast the histories, rituals, and management practices of the water mayors with their counterparts in the state model. By tracing the transformations of different religious concepts and cultural logics through pre-Columbian, colonial, and contemporary times, I show how these concepts and logics are used by, and against, states trying to extend their cultural hegemony and political power. We begin with the cosmological referents and ritual practices of the office of water mayor.

3

EARTH MOTHER, CABILDOS, AND WATER RITUAL

There's no mountain, none anywhere in the world, like mine.
[Como mi cerro no hay, no hay en todo el mundo.]

"Chirihuayrita," song by Sávia Andina

[W]hen the Inka wanted to make an important sacrifice and placate one of the holy mountains . . . he would have men sacrificed.

Statement given by the kurakas of Cabanaconde to Spanish Crown official Juan de Ulloa Mogollón in 1586

It has been a long morning.[1] Mariano, the water mayor of anansaya, lower moiety, has been busy this first day of the new irrigation round. With his wife, Genoveva, other family members, and a hired ritual specialist (paqu), he has already made numerous offerings to Mount Hualca-Hualca, Earth Mother, and Water Mother (yaku mama). Mariano has also been plugging up the leaky earthen canals and helping irrigators prepare their ditches. For the next four days and nights—before the other side, upper moiety, takes over—he will be at the water's side, never leaving the fields. Hurrying over terraces, cajoling and controlling the irrigators, and patrolling the canals for leaks and water theft, he will just take catnaps, never really resting well as the sear, dry days give way to frigid Andean nights. His wife will be busy too, cooking and shuttling food, ponchos, and lanterns between town and field.

Preparations for the initiation of the round began the night before. I had arrived at dusk, and the two snake-headed staffs, symbols of the water mayor's authority, were already adorned with flowers and leaning against the wall. Mariano, his wife, his three grown daughters and their husbands (his "sons"), and a handful of grandchildren were carefully observing Donato the paqu as he prepared and arranged the ritual paraphernalia: llama fat, coca seeds, coca leaf, trago, kunuka herb, and special cornflower. He carefully handled the fetus of a vicuña, an *undomesticated camelid from the high reaches, which had cost Mariano three hundred intis in the central market of Arequipa.*

Donato, who has worked for both anansaya and urinsaya in past irrigation rounds, is known around town as an excellent paqu who, as one man put it, "really makes the water fly." We drink a few rounds of trago, chew coca, and smoke cigarettes, pouring a few drops of trago over the snake-headed staffs with each round. After making these and other libations, Donato passes each of us a small piece of the llama fat. Invoking our godfather and godmother mountains, we breath heavily on the fat, praying, "ay padrino, madrina." Saying our names, the paqu places each piece of fat onto the q'apa offering—this will protect each of us from the dangers associated with the upcoming irrigation rounds. "If you don't, you'll just fall by the wayside," he tells me.

Donato then rubs llama fat on the bent, snake-shaped crowns of Handsome Lion and Saint Peter, the so-named staffs of authority. He then passes around a stone, embers burning on its flat surface. As each of us receives it, the paqu places a pinch of incense on top, whereupon each of us passes it over and below the head of the staffs, then in the direction of Mount Hualca-Hualca, all the time whispering prayers to her: that there be no accidents and that the water arrive swiftly and safely to Auqui, the last fields of the round. As he carefully wraps the q'apa offerings and vicuña fetus in old newspaper, Donato gives detailed instructions to Cornelio, one of Mariano's "sons," who is an aspiring paqu in his own right and who will fulfill the role of ritual specialist during the water rite (yakutinkay) the next morning. As I am leaving, Mariano calls after me: "Remember, Pablo, three-thirty. If you're not here, we'll leave without you."

When I arrive at the appointed hour, they are already sipping coffee, bundled up in their ponchos and rubber boots. Shovels in hand, with their wrap shawls and my daypack bulging with ritual goods, the four of us—Mariano, sons-in-law Cornelio and Juan, and myself—set out from town toward the Puquio intake. Mariano and Cornelio are carrying the staffs. The full moon has yet to dip over the horizon, and, with the help of a tiny irrigator's lamp, it lights our way. We stop along the trail to drink some trago, smoke a cigarette, and chew leaf. The water swishes by in a nearby canal, a constant drone coming from the river further below.

We hike for an hour, passing Puquio and the highest intakes. Now

*we are well above all the canals and cultivated fields, walking along the
undomesticated Hualca-Hualca River. Really a large mountain stream,
the Hualca-Hualca noisily sloshes and slithers beside us as it winds its
way down from the snow-shrouded, moonlit peak of the same name towering in the distance. As we arrive at the ritual site, the ridge above us
blocks the moonlight and the early morning sky grows darker. We begin
the ceremony.*

*Cornelio places the staffs in the ground with the snake heads fac-
ing downriver, and while the others gather kindling he begins to prepare
the ritual holding case (caja). Dislodging a large stone and several smaller
ones from the wet mud next to the rushing river, he then digs out a small
rectangular hole and places the vicuña fetus inside, together with five
flasks of wine, trago, and different kinds of corn beer. The first hint of
light is just showing, and there is the slightest shift from dark grayness
to deep blue in the predawn obscurity; as before in the moonlight, the
shapes of our surroundings are once again distinguishable.*

*Mariano decorates a large boulder in the river with confetti tape,
and we make libations, showering the river and confetti-clad boulder with
special corn beer from ritual wooden cups and dripping some onto the
snake-headed staffs. Cornelio closes the earthen offering case with a stone
and covers it with a large rock followed by smaller ones. "It stays there
for the river, Pablo," Cornelio tells me. We pass around coca, trago, and
cigarettes, and then make more libations and burn incense to the snake-
headed staffs, the earthen offering case, Earth Mother, Water Mother,
and especially to Mount Hualca-Hualca and the other cabildos, or mountain deities. "Just like with us humans who have a judge and a governor, like here in Cabanaconde, so too each mountain is an authority
which has been named and appointed. That's the way it is," Cornelio
explains. Then, supplicating Hualca-Hualca and other cabildos with a
reverent tone, he burns the q'apa offering. The kunuka herb, coca leaf,
and llama fat send off a sweet smell, one especially appreciated by the
cabildos. Several more rounds of drinking, incense-burning, and special
libations follow.*

*We then pack up quickly and start back toward town. We stop and
plug some smaller leaks on our way to Ullpaq, where lower moiety has
its "chimney," or ceremonial hearth for burning q'apas. At Ullpaq one
must always burn q'apas, Cornelio tells me, "because that's the way the
ancients, the Inkas, taught it." Soon Genoveva, Mariano's daughters, their*

comadre, and a friend arrive there with bulging wrap shawls and skirts. Out of these materialize pots full of food, as well as pans, cups, and bottles. A small fire is built in a well-worn cooking hearth. Donato arrives and we are now a gathering of some twelve people.

The women serve hot punch followed by trago and wine, after which we pass the coca bags and chew a lot of leaf. Before the ritual meal, we burn several more q'apas in the chimneys, make libations, and burn incense. Then comes the food—and lots of it! After we eat, Cornelio and I walk up the canal some fifty yards to take care of a large leak; using breaker bars and shovels, we cut out thick chunks of champa to plug the holes. Upon our return to Ullpaq, friends and family adorn Mariano's, Cornelio's, and my own hat with rings of roses, placing confetti wreaths around our necks. There is more coca, trago, and hanpi *(trago mixed with medicinal herbs).*

This is just the start—there will be several more rituals and a huge feast and celebration later on today. But even now, with the sun just up, the day seems well advanced. Mariano sets off two large skyrockets that explode loudly overhead, echoing off the steep walls of the surrounding mountains. Shaken out of its slumber, the town is alerted that the water rite has been performed. Lower moiety has begun its round—the water is in route to the fields.

FERTILITY RITUALS, MOUNTAINS, AND MUMMIES

The yakutinkay and other irrigation rituals performed by the water mayors occupy an important place in Cabanaconde's annual cycle of rituals, and they constitute a powerful medium for transmitting and reproducing beliefs about fertility, disease, power, authority, and ethnic identity. In Andean society, wherein the "communication of deeply held values and of ideas about the order of things is accomplished by preference in ritual acts, that is in symbolic action and not verbally" (Rasnake 1988, 220), ritual holds special importance. Irrigation ritual in Cabanaconde, then, "actively produces practices and policies that constitute social reality" (Tambiah 1990, 2).

The yakutinkay ritual that each moiety uses to initiate the irrigation sequence is followed by countless formal rituals and small performative acts throughout the irrigation cycle. Through redundancy, powerful symbolism, the use of multimedia, and a sense of heightened and intensified communication, the yakutinkay and countless daily rituals enact and incarnate "archetypal cosmic truths" of Cabaneño native belief that are tied to ethnic identity and production. As we saw earlier, the people of the pre-Columbian Cavana polity claimed Mount Hualca-Hualca as their origin place, and, through cranial deformation, they inscribed Hualca-Hualca's holy crown on the bodies of her human charges; until the mid-1980s, the community made an annual pilgrimage to revere her and to procure additional water from her. Hualca-Hualca's water, likened to mother's milk by many Cabaneños today, remains the most essential, highly valued, and ritually elaborated natural resource of the community.

These same rituals and beliefs are those most easily exoticized and romanticized in representations of the Andes. But, conversely, critiques of such representations often relegate native Andean religion to the margins, thus trivializing a key component of highland cultural identity. Forged within indigenous and Iberian colonial contexts, native Andean religious belief and practice is dynamic and varies greatly from place to place, interacting with other cultural spheres and ideologies. The latter include Catholicism, a market economy, right and left political discourses, and the images and ideologies brought by teachers, merchants, anthropologists, transnational migrants, evangelicals, and the radio. And, with the introduction of Beta Max miniature movie theaters in 1987 and television in 1993, the Cabaneños are constantly exposed to new cultural products from afar.[2]

However, even the seemingly autochthonous, local worldview associated with Mount Hualca-Hualca is not entirely indigenous to Cabanaconde but was forged in a colonial context, albeit that of an indigenous empire. In the late fifteenth century, atop the icy ledge of neighboring Mount Ampato's 21,000–foot-high, frog-shaped summit, a twelve- or thirteen-year-old girl, attended by priests and Inka state officials, received a sharp blow to the back of the head. She was the victim of an indigenous empire that took the longstanding pan-Andean tradition of mountain worship and sacrifice to, literally, new heights and violent extremes. The Inka was the only state to construct religious shrines on dozens of peaks at over 17,000 feet, reaching heights of over 20,000 feet that were not reached again until the second half of the twentieth century. It is possible that the Ice Maiden came from the imperial center of the Inka empire, Cuzco, or perhaps she belonged to the Cavana polity.

Five hundred years later, archeologist Johan Reinhard and mountaineer Miguel Zarate found the Ice Maiden, as well as other sacrificial victims that were further down the flanks of Mount Ampato. Reinhard's important studies have contextualized these kinds of sacrifice and revealed their logic within Inka statecraft and Andean society in general (see, e.g., Reinhard 1985, 1986, 1998). Nevertheless, the media, both in Peru and the United States, concentrated on the most exotic aspects of the mummy. A National Geographic television special, for example, focused on the "mysteries of the mummies," a cross-cultural look at embalming and funerary practices.

The reports could have examined the ways in which the Ice Maiden was part of a pan-Andean and ongoing religious tradition of worship that gives power, authority, and agency to mountains, the earth, and other elements of sacred geography. This religious tradition existed long before the Inka empire and remains important in the lives of millions of people in Peru, Bolivia, and Ecuador. But the relevance of contemporary belief in the Andes—and the fact that the mountain chain where the Ice Maiden was found continues to be a strong locus of religious belief and ethnic identity—received no airtime.[3]

Using long wooden poles, the Inkas also reached the craggy summit of Mount Hualca-Hualca and probably carried out human sacrifice there, as well (Johan Reinhard, personal communication, 1997). Clearly, then, the Cavanas' cult to this mountain—source of their irrigation water, primordial origins, and identity as a people—was consecrated and symbolically appropriated by the Inka. By establishing high-altitude ritual shrines and religious sanctuaries on Ampato, Hualca-Hualca, and dozens of other high peaks throughout the central Andes, the Inka state established its legitimacy, extended its hegemony, and used the most local and primordial of religious beliefs for its own purposes. The Cavanas' cranial deformations and the Inka state's human sacrifices, then, embody political processes, both literally and figuratively. Clearly, then, the local mountain rituals practiced today by the Cabaneños have been linked to the cultural construction of power and identity that has been in place in this region for many centuries.

DAILY RITUAL AND RITUAL SPECIALISTS

The cosmology that guides the ritual practices surrounding irrigation today is part of a worldview interpreted variously by the individuals who practice it. While some individuals are curious about this model and actively participate in its reproduction and transformation, others perform rituals by rote and are ignorant of its finer points. But everyone accepts that the mountains and the earth are sacred, and that the prosperity of each family is to a large degree dependent on frequent ritual offerings. Adult individuals must have a good general grasp of these ritual practices, as they are seen as an integral part of irrigation and other productive activities.

Each family enacts formal ritual offerings (q'apa and tinkay) at least three times a year for their personal cattle; one major ritual for each plot of land during the sowing; one general ritual after the harvest; and one ritual a year to bless the house and the earth from which it is made. This is the bare minimum; during a normal year most families make many other offerings for their alpacas, llamas, and orchards, and to cure illness. Each family burns q'apas and ceremonially drips, splashes, and sprinkles tinkay libations in the name of Hualca-Hualca, Earth Mother, and other local place deities who have control over their production. In these offerings, no ritual specialist is required; every adult is well versed in the correct proceedings.

In addition to these formalized rituals, which involve the nuclear or extended family, there are lesser rituals that each individual enacts personally and that form part of daily life. For example, it is necessary to take a coca bag when one goes to the fields to protect oneself from illnesses from the earth. Coca leaf, a central part of highland social life and cultural identity (Allen 1988), is carried in coca bags—small, colorful pouches that are beautifully woven and embroidered with the designs and colors of the community and have small tassels at the base.[4] They are thought to have curative and protective powers like the coca itself. One must honor the earth or a mountain by raising one's opened bag with both hands, making respectful invocations. When drinking corn beer during agricultural work or visiting friends, one must again make a small tinkay, proffering a few drops to Earth Mother or Hualca-Hualca. These daily rituals are practiced on a fairly regular basis by almost all Cabaneños.

Certain rituals and a whole realm of esoteric knowledge, however, are the domain of ritual specialists, most of whom are men. Among these specialists are spiritists (paqus), witches (layqas), and healers (*hanpiq, curanderos*).[5] Paqus communicate with mountain and earth deities and carry out agricultural, pastoral, and healing rituals on behalf of individuals, families, and entire communities. Some paqus are general practitioners, whereas others have a reputation for a particular activity, be it curing, water-related ritual, and so on. The most revered and renowned type of paqu is the *karpayuq*, called *altamisayuq* in other regions (see, e.g., Allen 1988).[6]

PACHAMAMA, THE EARTH MOTHER

The Earth Mother (pachamama) is a fundamental feature of a worldview "in which land is experienced as animate, powerful, and imbued with consciousness—a parallel society of Earth Persons with whom one is in constant interaction" (Allen 1988, 24). The earth is alive, and although she is often benevolent and gives sustenance to those who dutifully worship her, she is also capricious and can harm, even kill, those whom she perceives as offending her.

The earth's personality varies from one place to another. In the high pastures, where the earth has not been properly domesticated by offerings, she is more savage and more "virgin" than in the agricultural fields.[7] In the latter, the Earth Mother becomes individualized and parallels human activity and property; each agricultural sector and each plot of land has its own "mama." When people sow and make offerings to their plots of land, they invoke the Earth Mother of each particular area (e.g., "ay Liwaymama"). As is the case with the concept of cabildo, which is reviewed later, the social world is extended to and personified in the landscape. Plots of land talk to each other, comparing the offerings their owners have proffered:

"What did yours give you?"

"Mine gave me guinea pig, excellent chicha, wine, and coca. How 'bout you?"

"Nothing, just some stale old toasted corn!"

The earth resents these stingy offerings and gives little produce, or worse, makes the landowner sick. This sickness is known as *allp'a* or *tierra* ("earth" in Quechua and Spanish, respectively), and it is the most common illness in the town (see also Appendix A). Tierra can also occur when one gets angry at another person or at one's animals and the earth misreads it—taking it personally, she strikes back.

During the ritual to bless the earth of their houses on the first of August, each family invokes Hualca-Hualca, Earth Mother, and other cabildos. The q'apa is made in the names of the members of the household and other family members one wishes to protect. There are many other occasions for the formalized worship of the earth, such as in solay, the sowing, which is a ritualized, family-based work party. This formalized earth-worship—as opposed to the small earth rituals of everyday life—is again manifest when the harvest is in and each family thanks the earth and Hualca-Hualca with another q'apa.

CABILDOS, THE MOUNTAIN DEITIES

The term *cabildo* designates the mountain deities who regulate the health of humans, cattle, and plants under their jurisdiction. Some cabildos provide water for the agricultural fields as well and are worthy of special attention. The use of the word *cabildo* is interesting in itself. Although most Cabaneños suppose the word to be of Quechua origin, it is in fact a Spanish term imported during the early colonial period, which has the general connotation of council of authority, such as that of a town council. The cabildos, then, are the mountains that have authority over the town of Cabanaconde; they are the power figures to whom the Cabaneños owe allegiance and respect and to whom they must make sacrifices and pay tribute. In return, the cabildos watch over and protect the Cabaneños; the truly devoted are rewarded by an increase in their animals and crops.

In visits to the high pastures and during sowing and harvest rituals, one makes offerings to both the cabildos and to the earth. The mountain deities, however, differ in that they have greater control over the cattle and animals that live within their domain. Condors and foxes belong to the mountain and are sent out to kill animals whose owners have not paid the proper respects—that is, those who neglect q'apa payments (*pagos*) or those who "don't have faith." Such is the respect for these mountain deities that when one comes upon a condor chasing and trying to trip up a calf, one should not interfere; it is better to let the mountain have its due than to risk offending it.

Hualca-Hualca, the principal cabildo of the Cabaneños, gives life to the fields with her water and accepts her children's many offerings, responding vengefully when the latter are insufficient or made in bad faith. Invoked in almost all ritual offerings, Hualca-Hualca is a striking mountain, with its snow-covered base peaking in a jagged rocky crest. People are proud of this feature, and it appears in many stories, myths, children's drawings, and everyday conversation. While the Cabaneños see Hualca-Hualca as theirs, they also see it as one of many important mountains in the region, each of which is the protector and ethnic emblem for other communities. Arequipa, like other Andean regions such as Cuzco (e.g., Sallnow 1987; Allen 1988), has its own unique regional configuration of worship.

The people of the neighboring community of Tapay make their offerings to Sepregina and Bonboya Mountains, and the people of Chukibamba and Cotahuasi make offerings to Coropuna Mountain. This is the way of the world, and the Cabaneños do not feel isolated in their belief system. In other words, the Cabaneños situate their allegiance to Hualca-Hualca within a larger religious context, in which these other mountains are seen as powerful, and even sometimes deserving of mention in their offerings.

Like the political councils for which they are named, the sacred cabildos have their own hierarchy, constituted by gender and rank. Mother Hualca-Hualca is the chief cabildo, whom one must always be sure to mention in libations and prayers. She is often invoked together with Sabankaya, the smoking volcano next to her, as well as with other tall peaks, such as Ampato, Kuyaq, and

Aguashuni. A few of the cabildos found in the immediate environs of the town, such as Qallimarca, Sarajoto, and Antesana, will also be invoked. After Hualca-Hualca, Aguashuni is the most important mountain and is considered a principal cabildo. Whereas Hualca-Hualca is associated with agriculture, Aguashuni, which is considered to be male, is important for cattle. Some people speak of Aguashuni and Hualca-Hualca having sexual relations, symbolizing the interdependence of agricultural and pastoral fertility.

Although there appears to be a consensus about the importance of Hualca-Hualca and Aguashuni, people differ in the way they view the other powerful mountains of the community (see fig. 2.3). People often speak of the "twelve cabildos," but they provide different lists when asked to name these. They also have differing ideas as to the genders of these lesser mountains. The conceptualization of the cabildos, then, varies. However, the general idea that they are powerful and can control the well-being of one's family and animals is not open to interpretation. In short, the average Cabaneño cares little about the exact details of the mountain hierarchy but makes sure that all the cabildos (*entero cabildokuna*) are invoked in rituals and prayers.

That peasants list different cabildos reflects, in part, each person's orientation to the sacred geography and productive systems of the community. This is determined largely by the location of their personal cattle holdings—which mountains their cattle graze on and which water holes their cattle drink from.[8] During the fiesta of Candelaria in February or March, families walk to different parts of the high pastures to mark their calves and to make libations to those mountains that protect their cattle. Special trips are made at other times to make offerings at the herd steads, where families keep their alpacas and llamas. Still other herding rituals are performed by each family when a calf is born and when cattle are bought or sold.[9]

FERTILITY AND ILLNESS: KUYA AND QAYQA

As we have seen, the life-regulating powers of mountains, the earth, and water are at the center of much religious thought and practice, and this cultural logic is an integral component of production.

The concepts of *kuya* and *qayqa* are an important part of this cultural logic. *Kuya* has the connotation of miracle or fortune and is firmly tied to the cattle/mountain ritual complex. This concept is clearly expressed in the libations and offerings to the water holes, known as *pozotinkay*, which occur in the week following the patron saint's fiesta. "Captains" or *devotos*—cattle owners who volunteer each year to sponsor the ritualized labor of the water hole with music, food, and drink—lead the offerings to the water hole, and in return the pond gives them kuya: their cattle multiply.

This ritual efficacy is also manifest in the offerings made to the high lakes during Candelaria. As one of my compadres related it, one offers q'apa to the water hole or cabildo, imploring, "Please give me a sweet little cow, a dear little bull, a little donkey, any little thing." By this act, "out of nowhere one's cattle will be suckling their newborn . . . a little calf can give way to a whole herd." "It's like a god," another man told me, referring to the water hole. Another person explained, "It's like this. I have special faith in Huataq, so I ask Huataq to please give me kuya, and out of nowhere a little calf appears among the herd."

The mountains, Earth Mother, and the water holes have not only the potential to make one's cattle and crops increase but also the power to cause illness and death. A concept important to understanding the relationship between illness and cosmology is that of qayqa. Qayqa is related to a series of concepts and overlapping semantic domains concerning bewitchment, illness, and envy.[10] One appears to be especially vulnerable to qayqa during the pozotinkay. When the water hole is offended by lack of reverence or faith, it makes one's entire body ache "as if it was totally destroyed." The fox's gaze, the vapors of the deceased, and envious people can also cause qayqa, and there are prescribed ways of avoiding or countering these ill effects.

Assuring fertility, health, and prosperity, as well as avoiding disease, accidents, and envy are fairly universal concerns. The practices and beliefs found in the agricultural, pastoral, and irrigation rituals of Cabanaconde address these concerns, and they provide a cultural framework for obtaining fertility and enhancing production.

THE CULTURAL LOGICS OF WATER RITUAL

Irrigation ritual, then, is part of a larger constellation of belief linked to other productive domains. At the same time, by looking at the relationships among gendered mountains and irrigation water, the water mayors' symbols of authority, and other conceptions of water communicated through ritual, meanings fairly specific to irrigation water become apparent.

For the ritual specialist and the average Cabaneño alike, almost all of the mountains designated female are those that are the sources of water. Such is the case for Mount Hualca-Hualca, "a virgin who spews water." The "virgin" here refers not to sexual matters, but to Hualca-Hualca's quality as a goddess. That is, when the Cabaneños speak of Hualca-Hualca as a virgin, they are referencing the miraculous, life-giving qualities associated with the Virgin Mary, other female saints, and the sacred landscape. Many of the other "mother mountains" provide water: Qoranqima to Lake Mukurka, and Santa Cuqasqa to Leqlehani Lagoon. This is also true in the case of Mount Seprigina, which provides water to the neighboring town of Tapay, and Mount Coropuna, which provides water to the many communities of that area. In the case of Cabanaconde, the female qualities of Hualca-Hualca Mountain are transferred to water, referred to as Water Mother.

As in other Andean societies (see, e.g., Sherbondy 1982b; Bastien 1985), some Cabaneños explicitly connect irrigation water, subterranean water, and the ocean (*mama qucha*)—Hualca-Hualca is often referred to as a "water volcano." One woman told me that the earth is like a giant root suspended in water, the water welling up through certain mountains and springs. Another person likened the earth to a piece of paper floating on the ocean. He explained that the salt gets filtered out as it rises through the minerals inside the earth before emerging "pure and crystalline" from Hualca-Hualca and other mountains. Others expressed that Hualca-Hualca's water comes from the mother lake (mama qucha) by way of veins. Yet, in contrast to the constant invocations of the cabildos and the Earth Mother, the beliefs concerning how water is filtered up from the ocean are rarely discussed.[11]

However, the reverse process, *filtración*, wherein water filters down from the high mountains and lakes through subterranean layers to emerge as springs at lower altitudes, is a widely recognized process. Local images of filtration allow us to understand how the ecological and technical knowledge of this process is fused with mountain cults and how each orchard, field, mountain, and community is linked to particular fields of power. The irrigation practices of the main fields, then, must be contextualized not only in terms of mountain cults and irrigation in the region as a whole, but also in terms of the micro-hydrology of different ecological floors within the communal territory.

In the orchards, one performs rituals to the mountains and lakes, which are seen as providing water, through filtration, to the small springs that emerge from the steep cliff sides of the Colca Canyon. For example, in the case of Ayun, Mount Hualca-Hualca is worshiped, whereas in Awaliwa and Aqpi (see fig. 2.3), toward the western end of Cabanaconde's territory, Mukurka Lake and Ampato Mountain are revered.

For the water mayors of the main fields, Hualca-Hualca assumes a special importance as she directly provides the water for which they are responsible.[12] She can favor them with plenty of water when they make proper and repeated offerings, or she can kill them if she perceives them to be insolent (see Appendix B). The snake-headed staffs that the water mayors use as symbols of their authority are also important ritual objects that conceptually link the water mayors to both Hualca-Hualca and Earth Mother.

Staffs of authority are "dominant symbols" related to a wide range of semantic and political domains in the Andes (Rasnake 1988). The "symbolic complexity of the [staff of authority] links it to fundamental cosmological and supernatural forces . . . in which there is an identification of the person in the authority role with the [staff], and both of these with Pacha Mama and the gods of the mountain peaks" (Rasnake 1988, 268). Moreover, snakes are often conceptually linked to Earth Mother in the Andes (Zuidema 1967, 50).[13] In Cabanaconde, then, the water mayors' snake-headed staffs of authority vividly evoke a native Andean cosmology.

The snake-headed staffs are the object of libations and are treated with great reverence. During the days that they are not used, they are often placed next to small family altars and the crucifix in the water mayors' homes and receive occasional blessings. They are thought to be powerful spiritual instruments, and many of them are baptized and have names. When supervising nocturnal irrigation, the staffs are used to frighten off evil spirits and wandering souls: one clangs the staff against a rock and they disappear. Moreover, the staffs can be efficacious in increasing the flow of water: one rubs the snake head with vicuña fat or wool and then dips the staff in the water and the water races along. Whenever the water mayor stops to rest, take a meal, or make libations, it is important that the snake head be fixed in the ground alongside the canal and pointed downstream. This positioning helps maintain and even increase the flow of water, especially when the libations include a few drops for the snake head.

Another element of the irrigation rituals that differentiates them from other rituals is that the q'apas are accompanied by a camelid fetus, preferably a vicuña, which is offered to Mount Hualca-Hualca and her water.[14] Clearly, the fetus is a fertility symbol par excellence. As powerful as the blood of cattle offered to the cabildos, the fetus vividly evokes the concept of life force and is an extremely efficacious payment.

The water mayors are also unique in that, unlike offerings made during family rituals in the field and pasture, their offerings are a public concern. They are major ritual actors and must carry out a well-established series of formalized rituals over the six to seven weeks of their tenure. These rituals are fairly fixed in form and content. The paqus who transmit much of the esoteric knowledge surrounding these rituals are in part responsible for their uniformity. At the same time, most individuals passing this cargo have accompanied other water mayors, and the general features of the sequence are common knowledge.

The following is a description of the ritual sequence that is followed by eight water mayors annually (again, two alternating water mayors in each of the four cycles).

The Day before the Cycle Begins

1. Preparation of offering by the paqu, water mayor, and his family in the house of the water mayor. (This is preceded by the

solicitation of the paqu, the mobilization of kinfolk, and commit-
ments of support for the various tasks associated with this cargo.)

The Day the Cycle Begins

2. The initial tinkay, also called *tomatinkay*, takes place above
the intakes (*tomas*). Only the water mayor and the individuals who
help him in the physical distribution attend this ritual, sometimes
accompanied by the paqu. Here an alpaca, llama, or vicuña fetus
is offered in addition to q'apas and libations.

3. The water mayor's wife, immediate family, and other relatives or helpers await in ritual sites of Qachkarumi (anansaya) or
Ullpaq (urinsaya). A ritual meal creates the correct respect, ritual
attitude, and family solidarity for the upcoming irrigation cycle.
More q'apas and tinkays are made, and a skyrocket signals that the
cycle has begun.

(Stages one through three correspond to the yakutinkay vignette given at the beginning of this chapter.)

4. A *tinkachu* is held. This is a large social event held in another ritual site, which the water mayor and his family sponsors
and which expresses communal solidarity for the water mayor and
his family. One's entire group of loved ones (entero munaqkuna)
attends.

Throughout the Cycle (Six to Seven Weeks)

5. There are prayers and incense every four days or at the beginning of each new major canal. This is a minimum. Every day
small libations with chicha and trago are made to the snake-headed
staffs, to Hualca-Hualca, Earth Mother, and Water Mother. Some
water mayors make q'apas every four days, whereas others will prepare a major q'apa with an alpaca, llama, or vicuña fetus halfway
through the cycle.

On or after the Last Day of the Cycle

6. There is a farewell tinkay (*despedida*) with the paqu and the
water mayor's immediate family members. One must bid farewell
to Hualca-Hualca by offering her another q'apa payment, and usually a camelid fetus as well. Some make an offering on the day the
cycle ends and at a later date make another offering, even hiking

over twelve miles up a steep mountain path to the foot of Hualca-Hualca.

A Few Weeks after the Cycle Has Ended

7. The water mayor and his family sponsor another fiesta in their house for those who attended the tinkachu of the first day.

The cycle must end as it began, with an elaborate ritual bidding farewell to Hualca-Hualca, thanking her for her protection and for providing water. As one water mayor explained, "She expects this and is waiting. If one neglects to make this offering she could punish us and make us sick." In fact, one water mayor attributed his wife's death, which occurred soon after he completed his cargo, to her failure to participate in the farewell q'apa (see Appendix B).

In the event that follows, which is the social correlate of the farewell q'apa, thanks are given to all who attended the tinkachu and who supported the water mayors. Both divine and social forces are required for the successful completion of this office, and each water mayor's personal relationship with these forces is publicly displayed.

WATER RITUAL AND PRODUCTION

We have seen, then, that the system of belief and rituals surrounding irrigation is part and parcel of a larger cosmology concerning mountain, water, and earth deities, which extends to herding and agricultural activities, as well as to health care. Concerns about illness and fertility are central to this system. Moreover, the formalized and prescribed rituals for these different activities are accompanied by a constant set of smaller and "spontaneous" invocations and libations performed on a daily basis. All of these are a fundamental aspect of living in the world and an inseparable part of production.

At the same time, the practices and beliefs that condition irrigation management can be distinguished within this larger constellation. The water mayors use special ritual offerings and the snake-headed staffs to maintain and increase the volume of irrigation water. The crucial importance of irrigation is evidenced by the elaboration and redundancy found in the rituals over the irrigation cycle. As Stanley Tambiah states, "The longer a rite is staged and the grander the scale of the ritual's outlay and adornment, the more important, the more efficacious the ceremony is deemed to be" (1985, 153). No other ritual arena is as elaborated as that presided over by the water mayors.

This ritualized irrigation system, at least five hundred years old and probably much older, has always been intimately joined to local ethnic identity as well as supralocal political forces. In the early Spanish colonial period, the Cavana people claimed that their primordial ancestors had emerged from Mount Hualca-Hualca. A century earlier, the Inka state had symbolically incorporated this same mountain cult and hundreds of others like it into an imperial mountain cult through human sacrifices on the highest peaks. In short, a pre-Inka cultural framework gained further impetus through Inka domination, and it was used as an ideological tool to naturalize state power and extraction—that is, the state's control over local resources and labor.

Yet, mountain ritual was completely antithetical to the Spanish conquerors' belief system, and rather than harness it for extractive purposes as had the Inkas, the Spanish colonial system tried to root out these "idolatries." The historical material from Arequipa (see, e.g., Salomon 1987) and from many other parts of the Andes shows that these cults were not eradicated but instead flourished during, and were even used as a form of resistance to, the Spanish colonial and early republican states.[15] I believe this persistence is partly explained by the strong connection between these cults and production. Today, Mount Hualca-Hualca's life-giving water remains an integral part of production, and the rituals devoted to this mountain still go on behind the back of the local priest.

1. The warm valley of Cabanaconde and the terraced fields surrounding town. Cabanaconde's main fields have a cultivated area of over 3,000 acres (approximately 1,250 hectares).

2. Irrigation water periodically flows through Cabanaconde to reach fields on the other side of town. Many people take advantage of the passing water to dispose of their trash.

3. Irrigation water flowing from one terrace to another. Water is a basic element of production in this arid part of the Andes, and all of Cabanaconde's agriculture is irrigated. Peasants thoroughly soak their fields with each watering.

4. The Majes Canal, which traverses Cabanaconde's territory as it takes highland water to the coast, wreaked havoc on the social and ecological fabric of the community. When administrators of the billion-dollar Majes Project broke their promise to provide water to the community, the Cabanenos blew open the canal in a classic showing of peasant resistance.

5. A water mayor, holding a snake-headed staff and with flowers in his hat, overseeing water distribution. One irrigator waits her turn while another channels water to his field.

6. Women and children with chicha jugs. Women play an important role in the organization of tinkachus and other aspects of the local model of irrigation.

7. Son-in-law of a water mayor with ritual paraphernalia, including incense, a q'apa offering, and a vicuña fetus to be offered to Earth Mother, Mount Hualca-Hualca, and other sacred mountains of Cabanaconde.

8. Hualca-Hualca, the mother mountain of Cabanaconde, rises to nearly 20,000 feet. (This photo was taken at around 16,000 feet.) The irrigation water that originates in her snowpack is likened to a mother's milk by many Cabaneños.

9. Most families in Cabanaconde make a q'apa offering after the harvest to thank Mount Hualca-Hualca and Earth Mother for providing fertility and life.

10. The water mayor of anansaya transferring responsibility for the irrigation water to the water mayor of urinsaya after four days and four nights on the job.

4

DUAL ORGANIZATION
Equilibrium, Extraction, and the
Cargo of Water Mayor

Dualism is the cultural mechanism by which the
random power of the wild is channeled into the
domain of human society.

Michael Sallnow, *Pilgrims
of the Andes*

To facilitate collection, the provinces were
grouped two by two.

Hernando de Santillán, Relación del
origen, descendencia política y gobierno de
los incas, 1563–1564 [cf. Murra 1980]

The local model of irrigation contains another kind of ritual logic
that has to do with the anansaya/urinsaya division of the fields and
which is enacted through the alternation of the water mayors. Dual
spatial divisions and alternation, like local mountain and water rituals, have to be understood within a wider historical and cultural
context. The division of society into opposed halves or moieties,
often referred to as "dual organization" (see, e.g., Maybury-Lewis
1960, 1989), has figured importantly in the social, political, and
spatial organization of Andean polities and communities since pre-
Columbian times.[1]

Under the Inka, for example, the anansaya/urinsaya classification was central to the social and spatial organization of the empire.[2] The imperial capital, Cuzco, was divided by ranked moieties,
anansaya and urinsaya, each of which had its own resources (Sherbondy 1982a, 1994; Urton 1984, 1990; Zuidema 1964, 1989, 1990a,
1990b). This saya system was also used as a model for organizing
subject groups and their resources.

Today, a variety of activities in countless hundreds of Que-
chua-, Aymara-, and Spanish-speaking villages and towns throughout the highlands of Ecuador, Bolivia, and Peru are organized along
dual lines.[3] Michael Sallnow (1987, 145) best summarizes the con-

temporary significance of Andean moieties when he states that "dualism is the cultural medium through which the fertility of nature is conveyed into the human realm." This cultural logic, for example, is found in the well-documented ritual battles known as *tinku* in Quechua.[4] These duels are often thought of as a "game" between moieties (Hopkins 1982) in which sexual play and human fertility are conceptually linked to the fertility of the land and livestock. The men of each moiety take turns letting fly with their slings, and this alternation is viewed as necessary for achieving fertility.[5]

We find a similar cultural logic, as well as the Inka's administrative saya division, at work in Cabanaconde's irrigation practices. In Cabanaconde, well into the nineteenth century, the populace was divided into endogamous halves, the moieties of anansaya and urinsaya. The town was in many respects two separate communities meeting at a dividing line, the central street of the town, and the natural resources of the surrounding area were also apportioned in accordance with this dual saya division. Today it is *only resources, not people*, that are so divided.

All of Cabanaconde's environmentally diverse production zones—the orchards at 6,500 feet, the main fields at 10,500 feet, and the high pastures at 14,500 feet—are currently classified according to the anansaya/urinsaya division (fig. 4.1). But while it structures the spatial and ritual organization of many productive activities, the saya division is most explicitly expressed in the local model of irrigation overseen by the water mayors.

As shown in this chapter, it is no accident that the old Inka saya division is today best expressed in the primary productive activity of the community, irrigated agriculture. Pre-Inkaic forms of cultural and social dualism, like local mountain cults, were appropriated and expanded upon by the Inka state as a means to legitimate its power and to extract surplus production.

After the conquest, dual organization was continued under Spanish colonial rule. Unlike mountain ritual, dual organization was not recognized by the Spanish state as a religious belief and ritual practice. Rather, because of its key role in the organization of production and because it even had some affinity with Spanish models of social and political organization, the Spanish state appropriated the saya divisions, which continued to be used as a

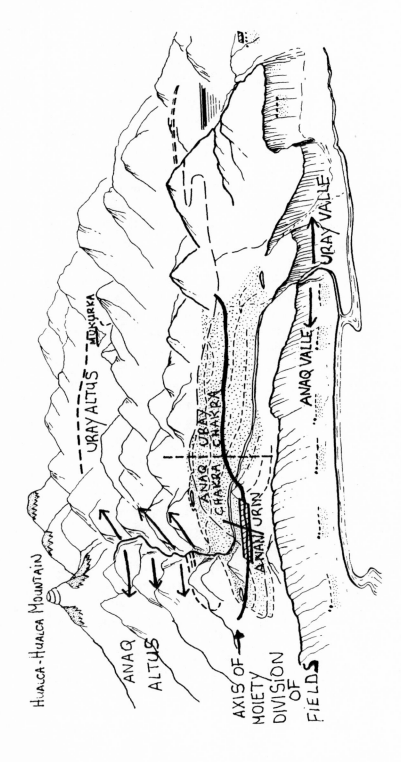

FIGURE 4.1. Dual Division of Cabanaconde's Production Zones

means of extracting surplus from Andean communities.[6] In this chapter, I explore the historical roots of the saya system, the cargo of water mayor, and the complex relationship between imperial and communal uses of dualism.

DUAL ORGANIZATION, RITUAL, AND PRODUCTION

The Cargo of Water Mayor

The office of water mayor, which lasts for an entire round of water distribution (presently forty-five to fifty days), contrasts with the religious cargos of the Catholic religious calendar. While the latter are voluntary and sometimes have long waiting lists, the cargo of water mayor is studiously avoided. It is a once-in-a-lifetime service, a fundamental obligation that irrigators must fulfill to have access to the common property of irrigation water. The dangers of nocturnal irrigation, the diversion of almost two months of labor from personal agricultural and pastoral activities, and the responsibility of managing a politically and spiritually charged resource are some of the reasons why people try to avoid being named to this office. It is considered the most onerous of all cargos.

Although largely independent of the state in day-to-day practice, the water mayors are nevertheless under the aegis of the local Irrigators Commission, which represents the state bureaucracy and is made up of community members who are also irrigators. The water engineer in Chivay is supposed to name the water mayors each year based on their landholdings according to the Irrigators List made in 1980. Today, although those individuals who have larger amounts of land are forced to comply with this office, many escape the obligation. The practice of appointing water mayors is in fact quite capricious (see Appendix C).

Tinkachu, a Social Blessing

The ritual offerings of the yakutinkay on the first morning of the irrigation round are followed later that day by another, different yakutinkay, which I will call "tinkachu" to distinguish it from the former. Unlike the family gathering of the morning, the tinkachu is a large public event that the water mayor and his family must sponsor. It really constitutes a social investiture to office, one that lies outside the institutional domain of the Irrigators Commission.[7]

Family members, neighbors, and irrigators gather in the afternoon event to drink, eat, and pledge support to the water mayor and the family members who help him—generally his wife, sons, sons-in-law, and daughters. The tinkachu begins with a few irrigators, waiting with shovels in hand. Women start to arrive with large jugs of corn beer and pots stuffed with food. The tinkachu soon swells to over sixty people, not including the family of the water mayor, who are busy attending to the guests.

A key purpose of this tinkay is to "receive visits" from munaqkuna, one's loved ones. The munaq embrace the water mayor and his wife, as well as the main support person in the coming ordeal (usually the son or son-in-law). They flower their hats, and put serpentine confetti and wreaths (*qalqinchas*) around their necks. The fertility symbolism of the qalqincha—a wreathlike string of apples, oranges, peppers, maize, cabbages, potatoes, onions, bread, and flowers—is vivid.[8] Before long the water mayor and his wife are completely covered from shoulder to waist, literally weighed down by as many as fifteen or twenty of these wreaths.

It is the women's participation that matters most at the tinkachus, and it is they who supply the qalqinchas and hanpi.[9] Approximately half of those who attend will be family members; others come to assure themselves of the water mayor's favor in the fields. After they present their gifts, the visitors are then enjoined to have some soup, a dish of food, coca, and hanpi. The men stand with the water mayor close to the water at the spot where the snake-headed staffs face down the canal, and they make tinkay libations to the water and staffs with trago, chicha, and wine. The women visit and drink with the water mayor's wife and distribute hanpi. The tinkachu, one of the few occasions in life when all of one's supporters and loved ones (entero munaqkuna) gather together, is an emotionally charged time for the water mayor and his wife.

The cargo of water mayor thus demands a tremendous amount of time, energy, and expense not only in the process of the irrigation activities themselves, but also in the feting of the irrigators at the tinkachu. People informally judge the tinkachu and the performance of the water mayor's family, who run here and there with plates of food, jugs of chicha, and bottles of trago. However, the successful completion of the tinkachu—good attendance, the water mayor and others getting stumbling drunk, a large number of qalqinchas—assures a smooth distribution cycle and raises one's prestige in the community. After one particularly successful tinkachu, the wife and daughters of the water mayor were ecstatic, and they stayed late into the night talking excitedly of their success.

The tinkachu, then, is a collective and social blessing of the work that lies ahead for the water mayor and his family, one oriented to ritually assuring not only their safety but the steady and abundant flow of water for which they are temporarily responsible. It also mobilizes a large group of friends and family who will be supportive in the arduous job ahead. The tinkachu is also one of those few events during the yearly cycle at which a family has the opportunity and the need to manifest publicly the breadth of their social relations. At the same time, the instrumental nature of this gathering, which complements the ritual events of the morning, is known to all. It sets the tone for the successful completion of this hazardous cargo. As one Cabaneño told me, "They do the tinkachu so the water advances."

Dual Organization and Distribution

After the ritual and social events of the first day, the water mayors of the two sayas trade shifts supervising the flow of water, following an established order for the distribution of water: by canal, by sectors, and by the plots of land within each sector.[10] The water mayor mediates conflicts, ensures that water follows the prescribed route and that intakes are opened and closed correctly, and guards against water theft.

In many parts of the Andes today (see, e.g., Mitchell 1981), including the upper Colca Valley (see, e.g., Valderrama and Escalante 1988; Treacy 1994a), the anansaya/urinsaya division creates distinct spatial units and social groups. In these situations, people often live in anansaya, have their fields there, and receive water from the anansaya irrigation system. The same is true for the people of urinsaya, who constitute a distinct social group within the community. In Cabanaconde, however, almost every individual possesses both anansaya and urinsaya lands.

It is important to note that today the water mayors are the only individuals in town who are designated as belonging to anansaya or urinsaya, and then only during their tenure. And in Cabanaconde, although the water mayors distribute water according to whether land is classified as anansaya or urinsaya, these divisions are not geographically exclusive. There are large areas where anansaya fields are geographically contiguous, but a few urinsaya fields are found among them. The opposite is also true: the areas that are predominately urinsaya contain pockets of anansaya fields. Therefore, along any one canal some of the fields are anansaya, others urinsaya (see figs. 2.8 and 2.9).

Cabanaconde's position on a small plateau that overlooks most of the agricultural fields favors the informal networks that guide distribution. The irrigators, by watching the course of the water during the day or by word of mouth, anticipate what time of day or night the water will reach their particular fields. Those in line for water arrive a few hours beforehand and prepare their plots of land and feeder canals; they then await the commands of the water mayor. Small dikes are built up and knocked down at every canal, large and small, and smaller channeling operations are necessary for virtually every field.

"One really gets to know the people," I was told by one water mayor. "Who's responsible, who has fields where, who's stingy and who's generous, and who just doesn't give a damn." On the whole, there is a great deal of respect for the staffholders. People approach with respectful greetings and proffer coca, alcohol, and occasionally food and small amounts of money. Sometimes the water mayor will be the one to offer a drink or some food if the irrigator is a friend or family member. Together they often make small invocations to Hualca-Hualca while passing the coca bag. The chicha and trago will silently be dripped onto the snake-headed staffs, a few drops are spilled on the ground for Earth Mother, and a libation is made to the canal water rushing by.

The water mayors must constantly negotiate the demands and maneuverings of the irrigators, and they must also guard against water theft, which is a socially accepted, if officially condemned, practice.[11] There are "correct" and "incorrect" ways to steal water; the latter are wasteful, cause the water mayor to suffer, and are detectable. People generally rob water at night in the upper reaches of the fields. For this reason the water mayor is usually accompanied by his son or son-in-law at night. One of them oversees distribution while the other patrols the canals.

Nocturnal irrigation is an odyssey for the water mayors, and they carry small irrigator's lamps, rubber boots, thick jackets, and ponchos. They have to remain alert and guard against water theft, evil spirits (*malignos*), accidental falls from terraces, and other hazards. In addition to the snake-headed staffs, the water mayors always carry well-supplied coca bags, cigarettes, and incense, which help protect them. Several men have been seriously injured and some have even died during their tenure as water mayors. With all of the hazards encountered by the water mayor and his family, it is obvious why safety is such a central part of the invocations and ritual offerings made to Hualca-Hualca.

Ritual Competition: Dual Organization and the Playing Fields

The dualism manifest in the alternating activities of the water mayors constitutes another ritual level, one of ludic nature. The two water mayors are said to be working in *suyu*, a notion that refers to a spatial apportionment of tasks (Zuidema 1982; Urton 1984); like two bulls plowing a field, each water mayor has his part marked off for him. The classification and even division of the agricultural fields into anansaya and urinsaya creates a well-defined route for each of the water mayors, providing the basis for their alternation and competition. The complementary opposition and fertility embodied in the saya system is also expressed in metaphors of sexual dualism. The minutes of the Irrigation Council in 1949, for example, make mention of "the Water Mayors of the agricultural fields who are repartitioners of Both Sexes, or in other words, of both Moieties (*Parcialidades*)" (BIC 1949).

Complementary opposition finds its most overt expression in ritualized competition. The two water mayors actively compete with each other in the performance of their office. Each water mayor brings together food, drink, and as many family members and friends as possible for their tinkachus, and townspeople comment on and compare these social events. Water mayors, trading four-day shifts, also compete to be the first to complete the water round.

Ritual offerings during the rounds are made not just to secure safety for the water mayor and his family but to create a greater volume of water in order to proceed more rapidly. Competition between the opposed and alternating water mayors is viewed as the motor of the system, that which "makes the water advance."

To make it a fair race, the fields are carefully measured out so that each water mayor has the same amount of land to irrigate. Like a checkerboard visible only to the Cabaneños—parts of which are seen more clearly than others, depending on the sectors each person knows—the saya division overlays and divides the 1,250 hectares of agricultural fields into equal proportions (fig. 2.9). This culturally prescribed ordering defines the playing field for the water mayors, setting the course for a race that the entire community observes. Although irrigation is serious business, politically charged through and through, there is also this competitive and playful element between the two water mayors in which their alternation constitutes a "game" that provides individual and collective rewards.

As they do in other ritual duels (Hopkins 1982), the notions of battle and play come together in the water mayors' often fierce competition. The townspeople follow the progress of the different water mayors and comment on who is ahead at any given moment. Some water mayors compete vigorously, using different techniques and carrying out small performative actions (trucos) to hurry their water along and slow down that of their competitor. Water mayors, for example, use vicuña fat or wool to grease the snake heads of their staffs, which they dunk in the river water to increase the flow. Some use black magic. One man, for example, told me how, after finishing his four-day period, he had hidden a bottle of river water at a major intake in order to "tie down" his rival's water. Other water mayors even divert their rival's irrigation water back into the river to make them lose time, especially toward the end of the forty-five- to fifty-day round.

One of the rewards for winning is that one's superior command of social and spiritual forces is displayed for all to see. Tinkachu attendance, the conduct of the water mayor and his family in distribution, and the support he has from friends and family are all publicly manifest. A water mayor's success is attributed to his vigilance, fairness, and sense of responsibility, to his knowledge of the fields and their owners, and to his ability to physically manage water. The latter includes overseeing the building and adjusting the rustic dams and smaller intakes, as well as effectively channeling water and plugging leaks (*tapar seco*). Perhaps most important, a water mayor's spiritual control over water and his having the proper attitude toward Mount Hualca-Hualca are viewed as greatly influencing his success. People firmly believe that good paqus and water mayors who are more knowledgeable about the mountain and earth deities make water move more quickly.

The dual system of distribution has changed over the last thirty years and continues to do so, in part because of the perceived inefficiency of the system. Water is wasted, as many people commented to me, when it returns to a few plots of land in sectors that have already been watered by the other water mayor (figs. 2.8 and 2.9). Because of this waste, exchanges between fields classified as anansaya and urinsaya have occurred since at least the 1920s. In the years 1926, 1934, 1949, 1952, 1979, 1981, 1985, and 1987, fields were exchanged between anansaya and urinsaya primarily because of the damages inflicted by water entering into sectors already irrigated by the water mayor of the other saya.[12]

Because these land transfers threaten to upset the balance of the saya fields and the competition between the two water mayors, efforts were made to ensure that these land trades are evenly done. In 1926 and 1934, for example, there was a transfer of plots, and the fields were "balanced out" (BMC). On December 3, 1952, the urinsaya water mayor accepted a transfer from anansaya to urinsaya because there had been "an increase in the anansaya sector in Etinishu" (BIC). More recent transfers have also been carefully calculated so that the rounds of the water mayors will take an equal amount of time. Referring to the amount of land each water mayor must irrigate, one person voiced a common opinion: "Our ancestors really studied the situation. The lands are evenly distributed."

The anansaya/urinsaya system of water management in Cabanaconde—like the tinku battles and moiety divisions found in other Andean regions—clearly embodies an indigenous logic of dualism and production. Each water mayor distributes water to the fields of his saya and prepares ritual offerings to secure an abundance of water and personal safety. The competition between the two water mayors constitutes another ritual level in which their social and spiritual selves are publicly displayed and in which the rapid advancement of irrigation water is sought through alternation. Through these activities, Hualca-Hualca's raw and potentially harmful water is domesticated and literally channeled into the human realm.

However, the pages that follow demonstrate that moieties and the cultural logic of dualism have another side, one that is extractive and colonial in nature. A close reading of the saya divisions and the office of water mayor should allow us to understand not only the cultural logic they embody, but the power relationships that have conditioned this logic.

THE HISTORICAL ROOTS OF THE SAYA SYSTEM

The Moieties of Inka Cuzco and Inka Hegemony in the Provinces

Dualism, as mentioned at the beginning of this chapter, permeated the organization of the Inka state. In addition to the anansaya/urinsaya division, Inka civilization was conditioned by other concepts such as suyu and *ceqe* (see Urton 1984, 10–16). Together, saya, suyu, and ceqe were the fundamental building blocks for the elaborate ceqe system, a conceptual model that helped order the social, ritual, and political organization of the Inka empire (Sherbondy 1982b, 1994; Urton 1984, 1990; Zuidema 1964, 1989, 1990a, 1990b). The ceqe system was made up of forty-one ceqes or sightlines radiating like the spokes in a bicycle wheel from Cuzco's Temple of the Sun. On each of these sightlines there were several sacred sites, each of which received ritual service from a particular social group. The forty-one sightlines were conceptually arranged into four groups called suyu: Kuntisuyu, Qullasuyu, Chinchaysuyu, and Antisuyu. This fourfold division was bisected to form halves or moieties known as sayas: Chinchaysuyu and Antisuyu constituted anansaya, and Kuntisuyu and Qullasuyu made up urinsaya.[13] The saya divide was the central axis of the ceqe model (fig. 4.2).

The valley, city, and populace of Cuzco were divided into the moieties of anansaya and urinsaya (Zuidema 1990a, 1990b). There

FIGURE 4.2. Suyus and Sayas of the Inka State

was a clear separation of land and water rights in terms of this dual division (Sherbondy 1982a, 1986). Institutionalized duality was also expressed in the organization of the royal court (Moore 1958, 117) and Inka troops (Rostworowski 1983, 16). More important for our analysis is the fact that the Inka used the saya division as a model for organizing subject groups throughout the empire.

Dualism was a symbolic and institutional form that preceded the Inka empire and which the latter developed as a tool of empire.[14] Under the Inka, dual organization found its most widespread, elaborate, and well-defined expression as an administrative principle. The Inka attempted to reproduce the complex ceqe system, which integrated and delineated the social, spatial, and temporal relations of the imperial capital of Cuzco, in each city of the Inka empire (Urton 1984, 15). In this way, "The replication of the pattern of the sacred center appears to have proceeded outward in space and downward into levels of ever smaller social scale" (Salomon 1986, 216, 217). However, the ceqe model was only partially reproduced as it spread across the periphery, and it was the anansaya/urinsaya component that had the greatest social and political impact on the nations reorganized by the Inka.[15]

Two kurakas, or ethnic lords, were appointed to each conquered group, the leader of anansaya superior in command to that of urinsaya.[16] From what is present-day Bolivia throughout the highlands and coastal areas of Peru, and as far away as Ecuador (see, e.g., Rostworowski 1983, 116; Salomon 1986, 174), the many peoples and nations that fell under Inka rule were arranged in accord with anansaya/urinsaya division (fig. 4.3), hierarchically ordering the chain of authority and institutionalizing social dualism for political purposes.

Inka dual organization converted the heterogeneity of the conquered polities into "other Cuzcos," and the saya division became the conduit through which labor was drafted, tribute was organized, and surpluses were extracted from peasants by the state. Further, I would argue that the deliberate diffusion of the saya model throughout the empire was one of the principal means by which the Inka state attempted to "saturate and homogenize certain aspects of consciousness . . . [making] it difficult or impossible for subject peoples to construct alternative understandings" (Williams 1980, cited in Patterson 1991, 70). Moreover, because different social and cultural dualisms were present in many pre-Columbian polities and peoples, Inka dual organization restructured the resources and people of the conquered areas in a way that was consonant with preexisting worldviews, thus claiming "to serve universal human interests while actually serving the controlling interests of the imperial state" (Patterson 1991, 70).

The current anansaya/urinsaya system of water management in Cabanaconde surely originated in the expansionist policies, administrative structures, and political economy of the Inka state.[17] The Inka presence, as we saw in chapter 1, was especially strong in what is the present-day site of Cabanaconde (de la Vera Cruz 1987). The anansaya/urinsaya division, mapped onto the agricultural lands, high pastures, and warm valleys by the Inka, continued after the Spanish conquest.

Dual Organization under Spanish Colonial Rule

There are references to the encomiendas of Cabana anansaya and Cabana urinsaya as early as 1549 (Cook 1982, 4). The dual administrative system was appropriated and redirected to serve the Spanish

FIGURE 4.3. The Extent of the Inka State and Saya Divisions

Crown and encomienda system, and large tributes were exacted from each saya (Barriga 1955; Benavides 1988b; Cook 1982). Encomiendas were grants of "Indian" labor given to certain Spaniards in the sixteenth century for their service to the Crown. The grants were not the labor of the "Indians" per se, but the very kurakas, or ethnic lords, who controlled this labor (Trelles 1983, 158). A system of indirect rule through the kurakas, "based on lines of authority that existed during the later Inka empire" (Julien 1991, 124), was maintained by the Spaniards. That is, since the different kurakas were apportioned to different *encomenderos* (encomienda owners), the dual administrative system was kept in place. Labor and tribute to the encomenderos were extracted through this renovated form of dual organization.[18]

In the 1570s the anansaya/urinsaya moiety division became further institutionalized when the population of the area was reordered into a nucleated settlement (reducción) as part of the programs introduced by Viceroy Toledo. We can assume that the subjects of the two kurakas (these in turn subjected to two different Spanish encomenderos) became spatially localized as endogamous moieties within the newly formed town (fig. 4.4). As such, it is probable that each moiety continued to have its own set of resources, including agricultural land.[19] I believe that saya endogamy was a concomitant of the tribute system; that is, kurakas and encomenderos sought to keep their tributees and productive resources separate by forbidding intermarriage.

Spatially localized moieties of Inka origin were joined to the Iberian plaza, church, town hall, and gridlike residential pattern. The two sayas apparently functioned as two autonomous communities within the same town, each with its own set of resources. Each saya also had its own priest, and the large fields dedicated to each of the many saints honored by the town were also divided by saya lines. The dual organization of church lands and the alternation of the moieties in sponsoring the major fiestas of the community suggest that, as with the Inka, dualism was inextricably tied to religious practice and continued to naturalize the control and extraction of local labor and resources within a longstanding ideological framework.

After the encomiendas faded, dual organization continued to

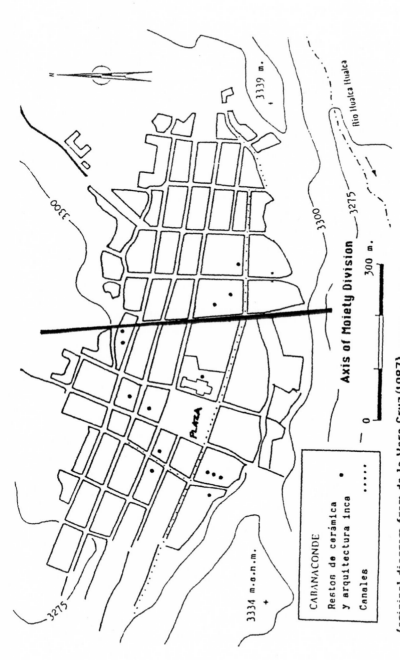

CABANACONDE

Restos de cerámica
y arquitectura Inca •

Canales ·····

Axis of Moiety Division

0

300 m.

(original diagram from de la Vera Cruz (1987)

FIGURE 4.4. Old Saya Division of Town of Cabanaconde (altitudes given in meters). Taken from de la Vera Cruz 1987.

promote the interests of the Crown and the large number of Spaniards who settled in the region (Benavides 1991). The moiety division continued to serve an administrative purpose in Cabanaconde even after independence: there were tribute collectors for each saya or parcialidad well into the mid-nineteenth century, and pressure from state officials to maintain moiety endogamy may well have continued until then.[20] The breakdown of endogamy between the moieties is thus correlated to the breakdown of colonial authority. The scattered nature of each saya's land, then, mirrors the process of endogamy breakdown during the nineteenth and twentieth centuries as landholdings in anansaya and urinsaya were brought together through intersaya marriages.[21]

Withering Structures and Cultural Categories in the Twentieth Century

The anansaya/urinsaya system of administration, instituted by the Inka and later adopted by the Spanish state, has affected contemporary cultural categories and the organization of social space and natural resources in many ways. The saya division remained a key institution for organizing people and varied activities, including the sponsorship of fiestas and communal work projects, until the 1920s. The moieties also continued as a means for exploiting the local populace; they were still used, among other things, to organize labor for "public works" such as sowing the fields of the town authorities and those of the church. In the 1930s a new system of four "cuarteles," or quarters (spatially bisected by the old dividing line of anansaya and urinsaya), was instituted, delivering a final blow to the already waning segregation of people into distinct moieties.[22]

Many of the social and cultural dualisms found in the community today—in addition to the anansaya/urinsaya system of water management—are residuals of the defunct moiety system of organizing people and resources for administrative purposes. Others are not. For example, the division of the high pastures into "upper" and "lower" (anaq altus and uray altus) on either side of the Hualca-Hualca River (see fig. 4.1) was part of the old moiety division whereby each moiety had a designated pastoral area for grazing its cattle. The people who live in the lower end of town still tend to have their cattle in the lower pastures, and those of the upper end of town have their cattle in the upper pastures. It is evident that the high pasture is another productive domain conditioned by Inka and Spanish imperialism, that the rigidity of the imposed divisions has now eroded, and that the current conceptual model and organization of the pastures follows a social classification (the division of the populace into moieties) that has ceased to exist.

But with this historical disjunction we also find ritual action based on duality in the high pastures, which, like the alternation of the water mayors, is oriented to the attainment of fertility and abundance. In the major fiesta of the community, the Virgin of Carmen, there are two competing sponsors.[23] In the bullfight, one of the fiesta's central events, the bullring and the two holding pens on either side of it become centers of ritual activity. Ritual specialists employed by the two sponsors make offerings and libations for the bulls so that they will fight valiantly.

So, too, there were ritualized sling fights (wititi) in Cabanaconde between the upper and lower moieties during the annual celebrations of Carnival. As in the tinkus of other Andean regions, people sometimes died in these battles, which ended in the 1960s when they were prohibited by regional authorities. The wititi has today been transformed into a competitive dance in which two groups dance for days on end during Carnival. In sum, the dualism displayed in the bullfights and the wititi originated in the ancient moiety system and today embodies the same cultural logic of competition and alternation as that of the water mayors.

Another way to examine the tension between historical process and cultural modeling is to contrast different applications of the categories of "upper" and "lower." The cultural categories of *anaq* and *uray* (upper and lower, respectively), on which the old moieties were originally based, encompass many semantic domains that are *not* directly related to production and are not concomitants of the moiety system. A clear example of the conceptual differences between the imperial saya model and contemporary categories of high and low is found in the classification of agricultural land. The geography of the cultivated fields leads to a conceptual division that is different from the anansaya/urinsaya mapping followed by the water mayors. A strictly altitudinal distinction is made between the "upper" fields (*anaq chakra*) and the "lower" fields (*uray chakra*) (fig. 4.1).[24]

Thus, we have a situation in which dual categories are mapped onto the same fields in different ways. The one that is institutionalized and spatially localized and that guides social practice—anansaya/urinsaya—is marked by the word saya. The other, marked only by the roots *anaq* and *uray*, remains at the level of geographic conceptualization. But while we may discern the disjunction between contemporary cultural categories and the social practices linked to the old moieties, the Cabaneños do not. In the case of the water mayors, the wititis, and the bullfights, dual organization embodies a cultural logic that obtains equilibrium and fertility through ritualized competition.

EQUILIBRIUM AND EXTRACTION

The dual saya model embodies a communicative rationality that structures social practice, ritual, and production in Cabanaconde. The carefully measured saya divisions are the water mayors' game board; they establish a rhythm and a set path for ritually assuring, and for distributing, irrigation water. The cultural logic of dualism is related to a wide range of semantic and social fields concerned with fertility, complementary opposition, and the ritual efficacy of alternating sides.

At the same time, the physically demanding, time-consuming, and dangerous job of water mayor is a legacy of Inka and Spanish colonialism, that is, a carry-over of an exploitive system that required poor peasants—formerly illiterate "Indians" from each moiety—to oversee water distribution. So, although the saya division is today "a fundamental tenet of native Andean cosmology" (Sallnow 1987, 217), it was also the "sociological blueprint" (Geertz 1980) used by the Inka state to organize and standardize the political geography, social relations, and natural resources of the empire and its subject peoples. Indigenous moieties often received further impetus through Spanish resettlement policies, whereby they became spatially localized within reducciónes.

In comparing the different uses and histories of dual organization and mountain ritual, the two key components of the local model of irrigation, we find important similarities and differences. In the last chapter I suggested that local mountain cults, such as that directed to Hualca-Hualca, were consecrated and symbolically appropriated by the Inka through state-sponsored human sacrifice on the highest peaks. So, too, pre-Inka forms of cultural and social dualism were also appropriated and used in Inka statecraft.

But unlike mountain cults, which the Spanish considered "idolatrous" and completely antithetical to their monotheistic Christian beliefs, dual organization was not readily identifiable as religious belief or ritual practice. The Spaniards suppressed the worship of mountains and sacred landscapes, and these beliefs and rituals went underground, becoming a form of resistance during the Spanish colonial period. However, because of the saya system's close links to the organization of production and because it even had some affinity with preexisting Spanish models of social and political organization, dual organization was appropriated by the Spanish state for its own extractive purposes.

We see, then, that mountain cults, equilibrium ideologies, cultural categories based on dualism, and hegemonic models of production and administration have conditioned each other in complex and variable ways over the last five hundred years. Dualism as cultural logic is concerned with obtaining abundance and fertility through complementary opposition and the social practice of alternation. As an imperial administrative model and ideology of control, dualism is concerned with regulating the production and flow of resources, as well as the reproduction of tribute payers. Both forms of dualism, then, are concerned with social equilibrium. While dualism as cultural logic is geared toward successfully producing and sustaining the natural and human world, dualism as an administrative model uses the idioms of fertility, alternation, and equilibrium to institute and maintain social inequality.

Today, however, the Peruvian state has other means of extracting surplus production at a cheap cost and has other models for organizing irrigation. Contemporary dual organization, as we see in the next chapters, serves counterhegemonic purposes in Cabanaconde and many other highland communities. The "state" model of yesteryear has become the "local" model today.

5

THE POWER OF
THE PEN
Patriarchs, Pudientes, and the
State Model of Irrigation

"*And I hear you've been telling people you're an engineer!*" *Eugenio Buitrón,
the district water engineer, said mockingly to his second in command,
Extension Agent Héctor Villar. His threatening tone brought a chill over
the emergency meeting of the Irrigators Commission, which was being
held in the town plaza. It was February 1988, and some fifty irrigators,
many with shovels in hand, watched the exchange intently. Buitrón, the
highest-ranking official of the state's irrigation bureaucracy in the province, had just made the two-hour drive down from Chivay. He looked
away and cursed again under his breath before silently turning to glare
at his subordinate. Villar, who had been stationed in Cabanaconde for
the last six months, just stared at his own feet. "I could screw you with
pen and paper right now if I wanted to," Buitrón hissed angrily.*

Although Buitrón and Villar later patched things up, Buitrón's
statement underscores the centrality of the written word to the state
model of irrigation. Just as a certain cultural orientation to power,
authority, and fertility is represented by alternating sayas and the
water mayors' snake-headed staffs in the local model, the state's
legitimacy and symbology of power reside in its written decrees,
official stamps, and seals of authority. However, in the archives of
Cabanaconde's Irrigators Commission, side by side with resolutions

and directives sent by state officials, one finds Minute Books dating from the 1940s that were penned by *local elites*, not state officials.

Over the last fifty years, local elites and state officials have attempted to supplant the staff-bearing water authorities and ritualized dual model of irrigation with a thoroughly different set of norms and institutions, a supposedly more rational and efficient model of distribution. The development of the secular state model of de canto distribution and the transformation of the dual saya system from an extractive mechanism of Inka and Spanish hegemony to a form of cultural resistance against the contemporary Peruvian state must be studied within the context of the sweeping changes in the community's authority structures over the last century. This chapter explores links between local elites, the state, and the introduction of new forms of water distribution.

RAINY SEASON INDETERMINACY AND THE INFORMAL SYSTEM

As mentioned in chapter 2, the local saya model and system of water mayors ends with the first heavy rains in late December or January, and then other models of distribution are applied to the same fields (fig. 2.6). From January through March, water management is less ritualized, involves fewer social activities, and ignores the anansaya/urinsaya classification, following one of two systems. The first of these is the state's de canto system (i.e., the system of irrigating sequentially, from "one end to the other"), which, as mentioned in chapter 2, is overseen by controllers, community members like the water mayors who receive a monetary payment to oversee water distribution. The second is the anarchic informal system (*sistema informal*), also known as "every man for himself" (el que pueda).

Although they differ in fundamental ways, both the local and state models have "repartitioners" (called *repartidores* or *regidores*), the water mayors and controllers, respectively, who oversee irrigation. However, after the first strong rains, an entirely anarchic period begins in which there is no repartitioner or political authority and water is "up for grabs." In this informal system of distribution, water goes to the person who gets it first or who has the most social

or physical muscle. During prolonged dry spells in the rainy season, struggle over water reaches a chaotic pitch.

After the advent of the rains and the water mayors' fourth
round of water (*hallmayu*), everyone irrigates at least once so that
the maize fully matures. Although there is an overall abundance
of water and several canals are in use during this time of year, dry
spells are especially scorching and people anxiously vie for water
so that their plants do not "get burned." If it is a year with little
precipitation, several waterings may be necessary just to keep the
plants alive during these hot months. And with the exception of
the heaviest and most sustained downpours, rainwater is viewed
by the Cabañeños as being insufficient to thoroughly soak the
fields. Even on rainy days, farmers will often irrigate their fields to
ensure maximum saturation of the soil.[1]

As soon as the rains let up even temporarily, conflicts can
emerge. To prevent them, families or groups of irrigators band together to take water down different canals, using water guards
(*tiyaq*) and patrollers (*muyuq*)—family members, hired day-laborers,
or irrigators taking turns among themselves—so that no one inter-
feres. The tiyaq guards the large intakes where the main canals meet
the river or the secondary canals, making sure that no one redirects the water. The muyuq does the rounds, walking briskly up
and down the length of the canals to secure smaller intakes and to
wave off other irrigators. Effective cooperative arrangements often
emerge informally among families, friends, and neighbors.[2]

Nevertheless, the absence of any water official provokes many
conflicts and even physical violence. Women sometimes enter into
scuffles. At times, they sit defiantly on top of the intake rocks channeling water to their fields, their long skirts getting completely
soaked.[3] Although it is thought improper for a man to dislodge a
woman from the intake, they sometimes do. As one woman told
me, "Oh, they really go to it! Sometimes the women grab shovels
and threaten anyone who tries to take the water. Every year it's
the same—constant fights." This vying and negotiating for water
continues into the night; from a hill above town one can see many
small irrigator's lamps flickering like fireflies against the darkness
of the fields. The lack of any order is wasteful and inefficient ac-

cording to the Cabaneños; as one person said, "People are cutting off water here, shifting it there, and nobody ends up irrigating."

The chaos and conflict that accompany the informal system have plagued the community since at least the 1920s (BMC), and this discord was in part responsible for the establishment of a police station in the community in the 1940s. A 1956 entry in the books of the Irrigators Commission shows that the local authorities tried to do away with the informal system at that time: "For the moralization of administration in the agrarian fields, to escape from the very old and steadfast custom of Tiacc and Muycco ... with the good will of the irrigators, this custom is now done away with" (BIC). Yet, despite this resolution and repeated attempts to abolish this system, the anarchic informal system remains part of Cabanaconde's annual irrigation cycle.

CONTROLLERS AND THE STATE MODEL OF DISTRIBUTION

The de canto state model of distribution is put into use as soon as the Irrigators Commission or the resident extension agent (sectorista) from the Ministry of Agriculture decrees it. Although the Irrigators Commission, the local link to the state's irrigation bureaucracy, is technically operative throughout the year, it is only during the "emergency" dry spells in the rainy season that it implements the state model of de canto or "rotational" distribution as found in the General Water Law (*Ley General de Aguas*). The extension agent—who has the authority to make decisions regarding distribution during these dry spells, as these fall under the "Emergency Measures" of the Water Law—can also decree the use of the state model during this time.[4]

In the state model, the Irrigators Commission names controllers to oversee water distribution until about mid-April, when the maize is mature and does not require more water. At this point, the informal system is again set into motion, though most of the water goes to the Colca River as in many upper valley villages (Denevan 1987, 34). In the past, the water mayors would take over during these dry spells. Today, the controllers are physically in charge of distribution and provide the functional equivalent of the water mayors during this period.

The state model of irrigation has radically different historical roots than the local model. A good deal of Peruvian water legislation originated from Spanish practices and their antecedents in the Arab world, and de canto distribution is no exception (Glick 1970; Lynch 1988). Colonial water legislation, which dates from as early as 1556 (Costa y Cavero 1939, 155), was directed toward the coastal and highland cities of Peru. Even when the Water Code of 1902 declared all water the property of the state (Andaluz and Valdéz 1987), Peruvian authorities rarely intervened in the distribution practices of the rural highlands. State intervention in highland irrigation received a strong push in 1969, when the Velasco regime initiated its general reordering of agrarian social structures. The Water Laws and the other policies of the regime incorporated institutions, norms, and values similar to those of state-financed irrigation systems throughout the world (Lynch 1988).

The controllers and de canto distribution put into practice a radically different set of cultural orientations than those of the local model. Although the controllers alternate in four-day cycles as do the water mayors, they do not follow the anansaya/urinsaya classification of the plots; rather, they distribute water sequentially (de canto) from one plot to the next (fig. 2.7). They receive money, instead of coca leaf and liquor, from the irrigators. Unlike the water mayors, the controllers are not fulfilling a major cargo, but a minor civic duty. Instead of a snake-headed staff to legitimate their authority, the controllers have an official decree from the Irrigators Commission. They neither perform elaborate rituals nor sponsor large social events as the water mayors do. Moreover, holding the office of controller does not exempt one from assuming the office of water mayor at a later date.

The water mayor is a major cargo held only once in a lifetime, with well-defined social and symbolic correlates; the snake-headed staffs, elaborate rituals, and tinkachus are firmly linked to many important aspects of community life. The controllers, on the other hand, are seen as employees of the Irrigators Commission, the Ministry of Agriculture, and the Peruvian state; those who hold this office are fulfilling a minor civic duty. As one controller put it, "The people would laugh if they saw me carrying a staff. They'd ask, 'What—are you passing a cargo?' No, Pablo, I'm working for the Ministry."

A final fundamental difference is that the controllers do not compete. Although competition is seen as the motor for the saya system, it is not important in the state model. People will comment on which controller is doing a better job and on the relative advancement of the water, but this is not phrased in the same terms as when they are speaking of the water mayors. Rather, with the anansaya/urinsaya conceptual grid and playing board conceptually erased, the "motor" for advancing water in the state model is a monetary payment to the controllers. Here, the idea is that irrigators must pay for the "state's water" and the controllers advance the water quickly to collect more money.

But how did this supposedly more efficient and rational model first come to be implemented in the community? Whereas distribution based on the de canto system and controller-managed irrigation certainly are part and parcel of the institutions, norms, and values found in irrigation bureaucracies and state-financed irrigation systems throughout the world, the "state" model in fact has local origins.

PATRIARCHS, POWER, AND IRRIGATION, 1821–1933

As we saw in chapter 1, the large number of Spaniards who settled in Cabanaconde paved the way for a different type of physical miscegenation and ethnic composition than other Colca Valley communities. This also created the conditions for the survival of a small enclave of literate, powerful criollo families—called "españoles" (Spanish), "blancos" (white), and "mistis" locally—who ruled Cabanaconde and continued to intermarry. The Fuentes and the Salinas families were two of the most important of these.[5]

The reassignment of a large tract of land to Felipe Fuentes seven years after Peruvian independence demonstrates how little things had changed. Fuentes had been a Spanish military captain who helped rebuild the church of Cabanaconde after the 1784 earthquake (Málaga 1987). In 1828, regional officials of the fledgling Peruvian state legally assigned his family a large area of pastures, one that the family had possessed "for many years."[6] That same year, one Jacinto Salinas, who represented another powerful Spanish family, was named to the position of tribute collector for Cabanaconde anansaya.[7]

More than a century later, the descendants of Salinas and Fuentes, as well as those of a few other powerful "Spanish" families continued to grip the reins of power. But the nature of domination, the institutional forms by which it was achieved, had changed. During this period, the saya system of exacting tribute along moiety lines gave way to other organizational forms such as the municipal district, which was established in 1857. This office later oversaw the change from two localized sayas to four localized *barrios* or cuarteles, each of which had its own staff-carrying barrio mayor or *comisario* (*alcalde de barrio* or *comisario de barrio*).

The municipal authorities also oversaw the water mayors and other irrigation-related matters, such as the annual trips to Mount Hualca-Hualca and repairs to the Huataq Canal, until the early 1940s when the Irrigators Council was formed.[8] Positions in the municipality were reserved for the literate and powerful descendants of the Spanish families who settled in Cabanaconde. In contrast, the position of water mayor and barrio mayor were filled by illiterate and relatively powerless "indios."[9]

Five families emerged as a central power clique during this period. Yet other wealthy families, many of them "Indian," have always existed; these five powerful families, then, never held a complete monopoly over power and wealth. There were also many poor "Spaniards," including members of these five families. Yet there remained a small group of powerful mistis who, while assimilating themselves into the local culture in many respects, maintained an ethnic boundary by claiming direct descent to Spanish families and by intermarriage. These powerful misti families, which had ties to a larger regional elite (see, e.g., Manrique 1985; Benavides 1988b; Femenias 1997; Paerregaard 1997), continued to dominate the political life of the community until the 1960s.[10]

The men who were the "most abusive" or who "installed order," depending on who one talks to, were Antonio Fuentes Salinas, José Vázquez Fuentes, and Geraldo Domínguez Fuentes. These were "the three big ones" ("los tres grandes"), who I will call the Patriarchs. These powerful figures are very present in the official documents and historical consciousness of the Cabaneños. Some remember them as representing a time of order and progress, and others blame them for the divisiveness in the community today.

Fuentes was a descendant of both Felipe Fuentes and Jacinto Salinas, the powerful Spaniards mentioned before. One man remembered him as "a gringo, just like you, Pablo, tall and what a voice! His voice was frightening and people obeyed him." He had been in the service and had even traveled abroad to Panama—some say that his discipline grew out of this experience. Others told how as governor he would climb the church bell tower and shout out orders to the community. Walking with a whip in hand, he would smack any young man who did not greet him properly. Many older Cabaneños spoke to me of his overbearing manner and almost dictatorial command of the townspeople. "He was governor the whole time," one man explained. Community documents reveal his signature in hundreds of entries in the books of different political offices for the years 1920–1970, attesting to his position as a constant authority figure for half a century.[11]

That Antonio Fuentes and other Patriarchs were perpetuating colonial institutions in Cabanaconde during the early twentieth century is evidenced by many facts. As late as the 1930s, Governor Fuentes had the four barrio comisarios irrigate and cultivate his personal fields as well as those of the other authorities; the comisarios also organized a banquet for the authorities on January 1. These activities were all in keeping with the colonial heritage of dual organization and other institutions in which powerful Spaniards and local priests had "their servants and canal water according to the customs of the Town" (BPA 1882). An 1813 ecclesiastical report reveals that during the late colonial period these same services had been afforded to the priest, mayors, and kurakas of Cabanaconde (Málaga 1987), some of whom were Antonio Fuentes's ancestors. He was continuing a family tradition.

The complicity of ecclesiastical and civic authority in perpetuating these colonial "customs" is apparent in other ways. The parish archive, for example, kept marriage, baptismal, and death records by "race" into the 1920s and beyond, and the barrio comisarios, who were administered by the governor, carried silver-plated staffs of authority. Unlike the water mayors' snake-headed staffs, they were associated with the religious authority of the Catholic Church.[12] A small silver crucifix hung from these staffs, and the comisario had only to lift the staff to silence any dispute and to impose order.

Another colonial holdover were the *altares*. On Good Friday the comisarios would organize the collection of palms, and the governor and the comisarios would present a palm to each family. The priest would then collect altares, each family bringing fruit, maize, and other produce in return for his blessing; he would later market this produce at great profit. After the Easter Mass, the priest, accompanied by the "eternal authorities" (*las autoridades de siempre*), as the Patriarchs are often referred to today, would be served a feast while the townspeople looked on.

Nevertheless, there is also a history of resistance to this power. In 1915, Francisco Huamán, a self-identified *indígena* (indigenous person), petitioned the prefect of the Department of Arequipa (the highest ranking official at the level of Department) to be exonerated from the "obligatory and unpaid office" of *alcalde envarado*, or mayor, of one of the four quarters. He denounced the "illegal customs that are used in the highlands where the law signifies nothing. . . . This unpaid and obligatory service is prohibited by several decrees" (personal document of the Huamán family, 1915). Huamán, seventy years old at the time, was a wealthy "Indian" who loaned money and left a long testament to his children. In a reply from the prefect he was exonerated from this service. One can imagine that most "Indians" were not as resourceful and were forced to fulfill these roles.

Most central to the conflict between local and state models of irrigation is the fact that both Antonio Fuentes and Geraldo Domínguez were from two of the powerful families, discussed in chapter 2, who took advantage of the community's political structure to sell and purchase among themselves legally uncultivable fields (*eriazos*) in a fertile area during the years 1925–1955.[13] These lands were ostensibly sold by the municipal council for improvements for the common good, such as the construction of the boys' school in 1926 and the purchase of sluice gates in 1927 (BMC). Antonio Fuentes required the entire community to work in faena (a system of obligatory communal labor) to build stone walls around his large extensions.[14] Several men still remember their fathers working for Fuentes. One man said, "Just like a dictator, he made them work that wall in Liway around his fields."

In certain entries in the books of the municipal council it is declared that these newly purchased lands would have access to irrigation water; in other entries, that they would be dry-farmed. This would become the subject of much debate. In 1928, Geraldo Domínguez declared that, to raise funds for the school, more eriazo land should be sold and that it should receive irrigation water (BMC). What is revealing here is that it was agreed that "these fields should be irrigated, but by *one Water Mayor*" (emphasis added). The first attempt to use de canto distribution did not come from the state, then, but from the Patriarchs' desire to water their ill-acquired fields.

PATRIARCHS, IRRIGATION, AND THE STATE, 1934–1964

The creation of an independent Irrigators Council, state intervention, and the changing water distribution regimes during the 1940s must be understood in terms of the Patriarchs' continued abuses, as well as the challenges to their power and to the colonial forms by which they ruled. The growth of state involvement in Cabanaconde moved at a snail's pace until the 1940s. In the late 1920s the arrival of a state official was still a special event; a cow was slaughtered to honor such visits.[15] The state had little direct influence in communal irrigation practices other than legitimating the de facto power of the Patriarchs through the municipal council and receiving the "rustic contributions" (a kind of tax levied on rural indigenous communities), which the community continued to pay until at least 1936. The Patriarchs in turn used their power to receive unpaid services from the "Indians," to illicitly acquire lands through political office, and to control irrigation. But this was to change.

On November 12, 1934, following a drought year, a representative of the state arrived "to organize the Irrigators of this District." Presiding over this meeting were Antonio Fuentes and Geraldo Domínguez. Fuentes and Domínguez complained about the deficient state of agriculture and irrigation water and how despite these problems they still had to pay "the Industrial and Rustic

Contributions." They went on to tell the representative that "since time immemorial, the State has never helped subsidize the increase of water." Appealing to the representative, the authorities told of the dangerous annual efforts to increase the waters of Hualca-Hualca and the need for "the intervention of a qualified engineer" (BMC).

Here we see a different side of these two Patriarchs. They were mistis and the members of the community that were most culturally similar to the state official, but they were also acting as representatives for the community. However, their interest in increasing the water was also motivated by their desire to water their own recently usurped lands. To complicate the picture even further, these two Patriarchs were themselves factionalized—on some counts Domínguez and Fuentes were united, on others, bitterly opposed.

In fact, according to both the historical record and many Cabaneños today, it was Domínguez who was responsible for soliciting the aid of provincial authorities to stop the feudal ways of Fuentes and company. This progressive Patriarch helped the community by using his own education to enhance that of his townspeople, and he made substantial contributions to political reform. These included replacing the dual division of the populace into sayas with a quadripartite one (barrios or cuarteles) and discontinuing the altares. He was the first director of the boys' school in 1926; he later helped establish the girls' school around 1945 and the high school two decades later.

When Domínguez helped introduce the Irrigators Council in the early 1940s, then, it was just one of his attempts to modernize the town and to do away with archaic colonial forms.[16] On May 4, 1940, Cabanaconde saw "the Creation of a Water Tribunal [*Juzgado de Aguas*] . . . under the Presidency of the Municipal Mayor," Geraldo Domínguez. In this first act, the "Administrator of the Sayas" wanted to raise the fine for stealing water to fifty soles or a month in prison. Hundreds of signatures at the end of the proposal for this act supported the creation of the new tribunal and authorized it to set fines, rebuild and clean canals, and administer distribution.

A year later, on April 8, 1941, the tribunal was officially recognized in the provincial capital, Chivay. It was approved by "all the townspeople of Cabanaconde" and the "Authorities of the Province" that the water of Cabanaconde "shall be distributed evenly among all of the agriculturists *excluding any preferences like those that have been used until today*" (BIC 1941, emphasis added). Similarly, a year later, on April 26, 1942, when the "Community of Irrigators" was formed, the irrigation officials—which included a water administrator, two water mayors, and four committee members (vocales) evenly divided between anansaya and urinsaya (BIC)—were implored to carry out their jobs "without favoritisms of any kind."[17]

The creation of the Water Tribunal and Irrigators Council is also directly linked to the chaos generated by the informal system during the rainy season. In February 1943, conflicts over water escalated to the point at which the Irrigators Council solicited "two policemen for the services of the Irrigators Council . . . because of urgent necessity. . . . Without the support of the respective authorities there will be complete anarchy among the irrigators." Two policemen did arrive, and the establishment of a permanent police station followed in 1944.

As the state began to take an active role in asserting ownership of irrigation water at a national level, the community used this action of the state to limit the Patriarchs' irrigation of the legally uncultivable eriazo lands. An entry from January 24, 1944, reveals that "the Directorate of Waters" was against irrigation water being used for eriazo lands, stating that the owners could be criminally tried "for usurping eriazo lands since the State is the only one who can dispose of these" (BIC).

Yet, in spite of the changes made in irrigation administration and in the general political authority of the community, the abuses of Antonio Fuentes and other Patriarchs continued. A letter from the subprefect of the province of Caylloma, H. Zúñiga Gamero, to the mayor of the community, Fuentes, was read publicly in the plaza of Cabanaconde on November 27, 1945.

> Frankly, it is shameful that until now there has been a platoon of unpaid servants attending the authorities of this district under the pretext of repartitioners, constables, commissaries, distributors of water, and water guards, that all that is lacking is that the authorities make them serve as cooks and

dishwashers. . . . You should know, if you do not already, that free
services have been completely abolished and are punishable by
law. . . . Make this prohibition public. . . . By the same token, the
altares are prohibited . . . unnecessary expenses that hinder those
poor of spirit and of few means who are the ones obliged to fulfill these cargos . . . so that you might take one step forward towards progress, leaving behind or suppressing the customs and
habits that have always worked against and hurt those who have
been forced to or have voluntarily fulfilled them. (BIC 1945)[18]

The subprefect's exasperated letter goes on to insist that the
communal authorities name a comisario "who will oversee the water of the preparation and sowing rounds, who will look after the
potable water, and who will be in charge of administering the irrigation waters. Of course he will be paid a salary of at least 30 *soles*
a month" (BIC 1945). It was also decided to measure the size of
the fields that each comunero had. Fuentes responded to the subprefect, and on June 7, 1946, it was agreed that the water mayors
would receive twenty *centavos* per *tupu*, an agrarian measure of land
that is approximately eighty-eight by forty-four yards.

We find here clear precedents for the monetarization of irrigation that today is associated with the de canto model of distribution. But at the same time, the subprefect's letter and other entries
in the books of minutes of the Irrigators Council indicate that neither communal nor state officials had a consistent view of how irrigation should be organized.[19] In May 1949, for example, when
the saya system resumed, the water mayors were not being paid
(BIC). In contrast to the strong stand taken by the subprefect four
years earlier, on July 5, 1949, the general water administrator of
the province wrote to the communal authorities that the water
mayors should continue in their cargo "Ad Honorem." On August
11, the water mayors promised "to fulfill the sacred mission without charging a single cent" (BIC). Although this statement probably reflects opposition to the monetarization of irrigation by
poorer peasants, these inconsistent legal and administrative policies and directives are typical of Peruvian state intervention (see,
e.g., Davies 1974).

The Patriarchs continued experimenting with the de canto
form of distribution well before the state instituted it. In 1947 the

members of the Irrigators Council, led by Geraldo Domínguez, decided to irrigate during the preparation and sowing rounds "without distinction of moieties [parcialidades]" (BIC). Instead of the saya model, the water should go "from head to tail" (de cabeza a culata). An entry from November 1, 1947, reads, "The rotative irrigation that is being performed has been proven successful . . . the water having commenced July 23rd and having finished the agricultural fields September 28th. . . a gain of six days . . . a triumph for irrigation" (BIC).

But despite its success, the de canto system did not catch on at this point. This was probably because the community perceived that the six days of irrigation water gained was not only for communal benefit, but also for the Patriarchs' newly acquired eriazo fields. Changing water distribution regimes was in fact just one way that the Patriarchs attempted to expand the "availability" of water for communal and personal gain.

For example, a teacher in Cabanaconde who was a relative of Antonio Fuentes, published an article in *El Comercio*, Lima's most prestigious newspaper, appealing to the Peruvian state. In "The District of Cabanaconde and Its Water Problems" (December 31, 1948), the author stated that the "District of Cabanaconde, Province of Caylloma [Arequipa] has asked the Public Powers on many occasions for economic and technical help for the urgent and primordial need to increase the liquid element; but, unfortunately, this has not been heard, possibly because of a lack of political connections."[20] That the author of this piece is seeking water not only for the good of the community is suggested by his purchase of eight tupus of eriazo land from the municipal council the previous year.

When the Directorate of Waters prohibited the irrigation of eriazo land in 1944, the Patriarchs apparently realized that the only way these lands would be irrigated was if the community could increase its overall water supply and overall area of cultivated lands. In 1945 the Patriarchs were at the head of an effort to recover land for the entire community. However, because of the fighting over land titles occasioned by the municipal sale of land earlier in the century, this land-recovery project and subsequent ones in 1948 and 1953 ended in failure.[21]

But both Fuentes and Domínguez used these efforts to justify accessing water for their own ill-acquired lands. On July 22, 1954, after years of conflict with the community, and only after the two Patriarchs had appealed to higher provincial authorities, a compromise was reached on their lands and a decision was handed down by the state.[22] Because of "their service to the community," it was agreed that "don Geraldo Domínguez and don Antonio Fuentes will take the water to [the eriazo fields of] Liway for only two hours." We see, then, that the state was manipulated by these Patriarchs and again contradicted its former decrees. But the two hours of water that Domínguez and Fuentes were awarded allowed them to irrigate just a small fraction of their eriazo land.

PEASANT COMMUNITY, CHANGING CYCLES OF DISTRIBUTION, AND THE STATE

The mid-1960s was a period of rapid social change in Cabanaconde, one that accelerated through the 1970s with the Majes Project. When, in 1965, the high school was opened and the road reached the community, the time of travel to the city of Arequipa became a matter of one day instead of three days. The school increased the townspeople's literacy in Spanish, and university-trained teachers introduced new political ideologies and worldviews. By the same token, Cabanaconde and different state offices became more mutually accessible. This enhanced connectedness with the outside world, the greater presence of the state, and internal politics caused further changes in the authority structure of the community. Entirely new institutions were created and fundamental changes in irrigation practices took place.

Although the perennial figures of the Patriarchs refused to relinquish their control completely, power became more diffuse. A group of powerful peasants known as *pudientes* (the "well-to-do") that extended beyond the Patriarchs had always existed, and now positions of authority became more widely distributed among them. The dozen or so pudientes, whose status as such was based solely on their land and cattle holdings as opposed to being based on ethnicity (as with the Patriarchs), was comprised of families with both Spanish and "Indian" surnames. As the power of the Patriarchs waned, and as literacy among the general populace increased, it was the pudientes who were at the center of the political conflicts in the community after 1965.

Communal attempts to gain official recognition as an "indigenous community" (comunidad indígena) and later as a peasant community (comunidad campesina) were begun in 1950 (BMC). Officially recognized communities have legal charters demarking their territories, jurisdiction over natural resources and customary law on these territories, and the power to act legally as a corporate body to defend communal interests from external or internal threats. The Patriarchs and many pudientes, fearing a democratic forum that could be used to oppose their power, had blocked Cabanaconde's recognition as an indigenous community, the institutional precursor to the peasant community.[23] During the 1970s, there was more need for corporate legal status as the community was threatened by both the Majes Canal and internal power plays.[24] After almost thirty years of trying, Cabanaconde was officially recognized as a peasant community in 1979.

State intervention in Andean irrigation also received a strong push during the 1970s, when the military government reorganized highland water management as part of a general reordering of Peru's agrarian and social structures (see, e.g., Bolin 1994; Caballero 1980; Lowenthal 1975; Lynch 1988; Philip 1978; Seligmann 1987, 1995; Guillet 1985, 1992, 1994). The most important innovations included the establishment of "local level, special purpose irrigation associations . . . [and] a corpus of regulations to more efficiently manage water resources" (Guillet 1994, 45). The Ministry of Agriculture created irrigation districts and commissions to administer highland waters.[25]

The new institutions, Water Laws, and good intentions of the revolutionary government did not always translate into practice.[26] One of the state's major objectives was to "rationalize" irrigation use in highland communities; that is, to strip it of "inefficient" practices. But when the state attempted to impose the de canto model of controller-directed distribution in many communities, it encountered resistance. To understand this resistance, we must understand the local uses of de canto distribution that preceded state intervention.

Until the 1970s, the water mayors were required not only to

supervise the three or four rounds of water that precede the rainy season but also to resume their duties as soon as the rains ceased. Their tenure lasted the *entire nine-month cycle*, not the seven-week round that it does today. The usual annual irrigation sequence used to be local model/informal system/local model. In short, the saya system was generally used throughout the year, except when interrupted by the rains, when the informal system then took hold.

The Patriarchs' attempts to implement the de canto method in the 1940s and 1950s (and even earlier in 1928) were always short lived. For example, during the preparation round of 1955, it was decided to return to the dual system "for the reason that in the rotative form the Repartitioners become careless . . . [we must do this] for the quicker advancement of water" (BIC). Yet there are intermittent references to the de canto model being used in the rainy season throughout the 1960s and 1970s, which suggests that the pattern we have today—local model/informal system/state model—was slowly forming.

There are several possible explanations for the recurrent use of the de canto system before the Velasco years.[27] Most importantly, experimentation with different distribution regimes was linked to attempts, both by ambitious individuals and the community as a whole, to secure more water for new lands. In the case of the Patriarchs, doing away with the saya divisions would allow the inclusion of eriazo lands into the distribution cycle. And with the communal initiatives to recover land in the 1940s and 1950s, it was recognized that the new lands would affect distribution patterns for the cultivated area as a whole and that distribution would have to be efficient. There was discussion as to which system, that of the sayas or de canto, would be used if land was recovered.[28] Land recovery failed, however, making such a decision unnecessary.

The firm consolidation of the de canto or rotative system as *the* system to be used in Cabanaconde during the dry spells of the rainy season, and of the current distribution cycle of local model/ informal system/state model, was brought about by state intervention and changes in the office of the water mayors. The Peruvian state pushed hard for the de canto system in the early 1970s, a system that it deemed the most efficient. On June 26, 1971, for example, Ministry of Agriculture officials sent a memo to "congratulate the members of the Irrigators Council for the rotative system, the system of irrigating by parcialidades having now disappeared" (BIC). However, it was the de canto system that soon disappeared. De canto only becomes a fixture of the irrigation cycle—and then only during the rainy season—around 1980, when the extension agent began to visit the community regularly.

However, the democratization of the office of water mayor through the 1969 Water Laws is also responsible for the permanent introduction of de canto distribution during part of the annual irrigation cycle. Just as the Velasco reforms allowed a larger group of peasants to accede to positions of authority within the community, so, too, powerful peasants were forced to fulfill cargos formerly reserved for illiterate "Indians," such as that of water mayor. Specifically, the Water Laws insisted that canal maintenance and other such obligations, such as irrigation-related cargos, be proportionate to individual landholdings.

The Patriarchs and the pudientes resisted this requirement. For example, when a major landholder, a misti, was elected to the position of water mayor in 1969, Antonio Fuentes, who was governor at the time, appealed to the subprefect of the province—the landholder was released from his obligation. The president of the Irrigators Commission publicly denounced the governor and declared him responsible for finding another water mayor. Nevertheless, the owners of large plots of land were increasingly obliged to take this office. One of Antonio Fuentes's nephews, for example, was obliged to be water mayor in 1980.

By that time, however, the tenure of the office had been reduced from the entire year to one round. This change occurred in 1977, most likely because the pudientes were then being obliged to undertake this onerous cargo.[29] Controllers were appointed after the rainy season instead of water mayors, and irrigation during this time was by the de canto method. This is the same sequence used today.

LOCAL AND STATE USES OF DE CANTO

The establishment of a water users' association and formalized irrigation authority in Cabanaconde resulted from popular efforts headed by Geraldo Domínguez to end the colonial practices still enjoyed by elite families, including his own. But the evidence also demonstrates that the introduction of the supposedly more progressive form of de canto distribution is directly linked to his and other mistis' desire to water their ill-gained personal fields.

Additionally, the historical evidence shows how these local ethnic differences were tied to regional power structures. The Patriarchs, as the Cabaneños most culturally similar to members of the dominant society (i.e., literate, Spanish-speaking, with many criollo orientations), were those who worked most directly with state officials on the community's behalf. They were at the forefront of communal initiatives to get aid from the Peruvian state, rebuild the Huataq Canal, improve the waters of the Hualca-Hualca River basin, and expand cultivable lands for all. There is no doubt that these men had a strong sense of communal pride and often worked for the common good. This was especially the case with Geraldo Domínguez, an educator who greatly increased the literacy of the community and lobbied for the suppression of altares (the forced collection of produce on Good Friday) and other forms of servitude benefiting the local priest and municipal authorities.

Yet it is clearly the Spanish heritage of Domínguez and other Patriarchs and their links to a regional "white," "criollo," "Spanish," and "misti" elite that also led them to adopt the organizational forms of the "Hispanic" tradition, which included de canto distribution and the creation of the Water Tribunal. The Patriarchs' uses of the de canto system in the 1940s—to "rationalize" the archaic colonial saya system and to increase the available water supply for personal gain—anticipated the state's introduction of this same model in the late 1960s and early 1970s.

In sum, the 1940s saw a general reordering of society and political authority, and these changes ushered in a special purpose body for irrigation. In the 1970s the power of the Patriarchs and pudientes was greatly reduced through the increased literacy of the populace, the ascendancy of the Peasant Community, and the democratization of political office. Clearly the state's intervention made the assumption of the hazardous cargo of water mayor much more democratic, and this in turn affected not just the office itself but the irrigation cycle as a whole.

The entry of de canto distribution into the rainy-season part of the annual irrigation cycle is thus correlated with the breakdown of the most exploitative features of the cargo of water mayor and the colonial saya system. However, the institution of de canto distribution and state intervention since the 1970s has not always had positive effects in distribution and has in fact allowed for further abuses by powerful individuals and challenges to communal control in many instances.[30]

Today, for example, Geraldo Domínguez's daughter, Amanda, exceeds the one hour of water that provincial authorities granted her father in 1954. She does this by paying off the controllers or stealing the water (sometimes with the son-in-law of Antonio Salinas). She is also still seeking a decree from the extension agent and provincial authorities that would grant her more "official" water for her eriazo fields. Yet, even if Amanda Domínguez were to obtain a resolution allowing her to irrigate a larger extension of land, it is doubtful that the community would allow it. In fact, one night in the mid-1980s, a group of people under the cover of dark destroyed the canal that leads to her field. She has since rebuilt it.

6

WATER POLITICS AND DISTRIBUTION ON THE GROUND

"We're going to ignore him," Ricardo said, referring to Extension Agent Héctor Villar. "He's nobody to be ordering community officials around here." Ricardo García, the water mayor of urinsaya during the third round, had just been presented with an official order by an irrigator in the fields. Signed by the extension agent, the local representative of the Ministry of Agriculture and the Peruvian state, the oficio granted the irrigator water for legally uncultivable eriazo fields in Achachiwa sector. Ricardo refused him, stating that it was common knowledge that they were eriazo—the irrigator strode away cursing and threatening legal action. The water mayor, his hand resting on his snake-headed staff, just shook his head.

Villar had already challenged Ricardo's authority and that of other water mayors several times now, ordering them to water lands that were clearly out of the irrigation sequence—that is, those designated as eriazo or as dry-farming land (de secano) and which had no saya affiliation. A few days later, Villar again tried to decree water to a particular individual because the man had received a loan from the state's Agrarian Bank. Adan, Ricardo's son-in-law and sidekick in the irrigation round, confronted Villar when he showed up in the fields, telling him, "You're nobody here. The maximum authority in the fields is the water mayor—stay in your office!"

Having looked at the differing cultural rationales and historical roots of local and state models of irrigation in the preceding
three chapters, we now turn to the on-the-ground application of
these models. This chapter concentrates on the effects, both positive and negative, of state officials during the "emergency periods"
of the rainy season. Using ethnographic vignettes that illustrate the
actions and strategies of a varied cast of characters (fig. 6.1), I try
to evoke the chaos of the informal system.[1] I also show how, in
implementing the de canto model, state officials manipulate and
are manipulated by powerful individuals and interest groups, and
how state officials resolve and engender conflict. I then discuss the
interpenetration of local and state models and the varied reasons
that the dual saya model persists.

RAINY-SEASON SYSTEMS

When Héctor Villar took up residence in Cabanaconde, it had been
over two years since Cabanaconde had last had a permanent extension agent in town. Because of the Majes conflict in 1983 and
the way in which extension agents and other government officials
were occasionally run out of town, Cabanaconde was known to
Ministry of Agriculture officials as being a "difficult," uncoopera-
tive community. Villar, who had lived most of his life on the coast,
was enthusiastic and hardworking when he first arrived. Traveling
far by foot and on horseback, he created irrigator commissions and
irrigator lists in the nearby villages of Tapay, Llanca, and Acpi. In
Cabanaconde, however, the work was not so easy, and before Villar
could create a list, he fell prey to powerful individuals, some of
whom were controlling the Irrigators Commission.

*The president of the commission, Celino Anaya, had passed other
cargos in the community and was generally respected. He had recently
experienced a few personal setbacks, however, and had turned to drink,
which was the reason people gave in private to explain the corrupt and
irresponsible way he was handling his role as president. He had neither
done much in the way of organizing canal cleanings nor convoked a single
Irrigators Assembly or fined those caught stealing water. It was common
knowledge that he was selling estancadas, water from the one small reservoir in town, to the highest bidder. Supposedly for the "expenses" of*

Figure 6.1   Cast of Characters (in order of appearance)

Ricardo García	water mayor of urinsaya
Héctor Villar	extension agent
Celino Anaya	president of the Irrigators Commission
Eugenio Buitrón	state water engineer
Carlos Canseco	interim president of Irrigators Commission
Felipe Galdos	controller
Hugo Rosaldo	irrigator
Other characters	town mayor
	president of the Peasant Community
	interesados: the interested parties of particular sectors, canals; those that cultivate a certain crop (alfalfa); recipients of loans from the Agrarian Bank

---

the commission (paper, pens, and the like), the money was going, as one person put it, "straight into his pocket and to drink." Anaya was relieved of his duties in February and finally expelled from office in March, when a new commission was appointed.[2]

Many people felt that Extension Agent Villar was complicitous in some of these abuses. He not only had failed to intervene earlier to supplant Anaya but also had tried to challenge the water mayors' authority; some accused him of lining his pockets as he generated the oficios ceding water to eriazo and secano lands. Luckily for the majority of peasants, the saya system of water mayors—invested with local authority and legitimacy—had effectively limited the range of his interventions. But this was not the case during the rainy season.

During the rainy season, which has "emergency periods" when the extension agent is ostensibly in charge of irrigation, the manipulation of Villar by certain families and groups greatly increased. Not only was it Villar's job to appoint controllers, but he also had the legal power to decide which sectors would receive irrigation water. But Villar had neither the authority nor the local knowledge to regulate water during this period; in addition, the boundary between his duties and those of the president of the Irrigators Commission was not clear.

Possession of a loan from the Agrarian Bank was one criterion used by Villar to direct irrigation water or to grant reservoir water to certain sectors or plots of land. These loans, which began in 1986 and through which the APRA (Alianza Popular Revolucionaria Americana) regime (1985–1990) established zero-interest credit for small farmers, usually served the wealthiest and most criollo peasants, often only those with a large amount of land or a high number of cattle to be used as a guarantee for repayment. It was common knowledge that to secure a loan one had to bribe the bank officer with several beers, a large meal, and possibly a sheep—approximately 10 percent of the loan. This is, of course, a situation in which having a criollo attitude is an asset. Loan officers and Ministry of Agriculture officials are more willing to endorse loans to highlanders with cultural orientations similar to their own (see Herzfeld 1992), that is, those peasants who are more "progressive" and "criollo" and less "indio," in the bureaucrats' terms.

At the same time, the Agrarian Bank did not monitor the lands that peasants presented as mortgages for the loans, which sometimes resulted in Villar granting water to eriazo and secano fields. The loan recipients thus used Villar to bypass the local Irrigators Commission. Villar's lack of local knowledge, his inability to provide a coherent irrigation plan, and his susceptibility to different factions soon became manifest to all. These flaws were especially apparent when the first prolonged dry spell of the rainy season arrived. When the rains had let up even slightly, a number of fights over water had broken out in the fields. Even though many irrigators suggested that Villar put the controllers to work and the de canto model of distribution into effect, he neglected to do so. Finally, after more than two weeks, an emergency meeting was held in the extension agent's office to put the de canto model into effect and to decide which agricultural sectors would receive water first.

Villar was inundated with petitions from individuals and from the interested parties (interesados) of different canals and agricultural sectors. While some argued for the need to provide water for the recently sowed alfalfa (majuelos), broadbeans, and potatoes, others declared that water should proceed without reference to plant. Still others invoked their status as Agrarian Bank loan recipients. After the way he had been generally disregarded during the first several months at his post, Villar was clearly thrilled with his newly recognized authority as the state representative in charge of this "emergency period." People in town were now acknowledging and catering to his power, and he appeared ready to grant any request. Villar granted water to one particular sector just because owners from that sector happened to be present. He then granted estancadas to the dry-farmed fields of Achachiwa because their owners had loans from the Agrarian Bank.[3]

Many people were upset by Villar's arbitrary and contradictory decisions as well as his favoritism to those who had loans from the Agrarian Bank. One man declared,"Why do they give us government officials who divide the people? He's no authority here. What, are the borrowers the only ones who need to eat around here? Besides, they've already got plenty!" Several others went on to criticize the Agrarian Bank for allowing peasants to mortgage eriazo lands and for their failure to inspect boundaries to see if they were legally held. After the meeting, a group of irrigators complained to the president of the Peasant Community, and he solicited a visit from the water engineer.

On February 23, Water Engineer Eugenio Buitrón, the highest irrigation authority of the province, presided over an Irrigators Assembly in the town plaza. He had driven two hours from Chivay to straighten out the mess that Villar and the Irrigators Commission had made of distribution. Haranguing the communal authorities for refusing to pay for his gas or meals, Buitrón further complained because few people were in attendance.

Buitrón exclaimed that Villar had overstepped the powers of his office, a crime punishable by law. Buitrón had also come to investigate the accusations that the president of the commission had sold water from the reservoir and that the extension agent had turned a blind eye to it and perhaps profited by it. He shook his head angrily when several people complained that the extension agent had done nothing to intervene in the chaos of the informal system, when he should have activated the controllers and the de canto state model. One man insisted, "Over here, over there, the water's everywhere. It has to become regularized now!" Buitrón concurred, and then directed some harsh words to Villar, threatening him with demotion.

Buitrón's presence was welcomed by the crowd, which was angry at how the water had been mismanaged. At the same time, the conspicuous differences in the cultural orientation and the relative power of Buitrón were apparent. A tall man with fairly light skin, Hispanic features, and dark sunglasses, Buitrón sometimes lapsed into the condescending demeanor of a visiting dignitary. The Cabaneños initially catered to his authority, holding hats submissively in hand when addressing him, but

their body language changed as the discussion heated up. When his as-
sertions were challenged at one point, Buitrón used a sarcastic, insulting
tone and the word "caballerito," saying, "Listen here, little fellow."

This and other sneering comments made it clear that Buitrón viewed
himself as culturally and racially superior to the Cabaneños and that it
was something of a burden for him to have to suffer their lowly com-
pany. This was also reflected in his disdain for the backward irrigation
practices in the community and the unwillingness of the irrigators to pay
the controllers: "If they don't pay, no water. Everybody's got to pay for
water. Cabanaconde is irrigating like in the days of little old grandpa. . . .
Today nothing's free. In grandpa's time, sure, it was free. What do we
gain changing officials if we don't change the system?"

One municipal official, pandering to Buitrón's presence, asserted,
"We're living in a mythological state, where there's money to make of-
ferings to the mountains and do the cortamonte *[a ritual tree-felling*
during Carnival], but there's no money to pay the poor repartitioners,
humble people with children." Buitrón suggested that the controllers re-
ceive forty intis *per tupu; others suggested twenty, to which he agreed.*
He also agreed that one canal be used to irrigate the upper fields and
one the lower, with four controllers overseeing them. There would be two
controllers to a canal, and they would alternate every four days.

Complaints about the current state of chaos in the informal system
then followed. "The strongest are irrigating." "People are selling water."
One man exclaimed, "There shouldn't be preferences! Those who get
estancadas receive better harvests and that creates envy. This disorgani-
zation favors the most cunning, not the humble." They then read the
Peasant Community's denunciation of Anaya, the president of the Irri-
gators Commission, and a discussion ensued about the abuses incurred
through selling the estancadas. It turned out that those who had bought
the estancadas had sold water to third parties, including members of the
Irrigators Commission itself!

Buitrón then demanded that a List of Irrigators be drawn up to pro-
vide a means for enforcing fines for water theft, nonpayment of fees, ca-
nal-cleaning absenteeism, and the illicit irrigation of eriazos. He pleaded,
"Why not be like other communities, like Yanque, Coporaque, and
Huambo, where people attend assemblies and canal cleanings, where
there's order and control?" High fines were then agreed upon to discourage
water theft. Since Anaya was to be discharged from office, an interim

*commission was named to serve until the next Irrigator's Assembly, a
week later, when a new commission would be elected.*

*It was decided that the controller would start and the de canto sys-
tem would go into effect immediately and that payment would be calculated by the hour instead of by tupu, the amount of land irrigated. It
was assumed that the hourly rate would motivate the irrigators to prepare their feeder canals and irrigate quickly and efficiently in order to
pay less. Moreover, payment would be made before irrigating; otherwise,
as everyone concurred, people would water and run. The price was set at
twenty intis per hour or fraction thereof.*

The effects that the engineer and the extension agent have on
irrigation are not limited to the Irrigators Assemblies: the positive
influence that they have on organizing distribution is often nulli-
fied by their actions outside of these forums, and there are dis-
crepancies between what is agreed upon in the assembly and what
is often decreed informally.

When government officials like the water engineer visit town,
they generally linger for the afternoon and occasionally overnight,
having a few beers—often, more than a few. Usually accompanied
by the extension agent and perhaps a member or two of the Irrigators Commission, as well as by some of the more politically adept
and more criollo young authorities, the engineer holds court in a
local store. Others seeking favors or wanting to catch the gossip
enter or listen from outside.

*Right after the meeting, Engineer Buitrón went with a group to drink
beer. Ex-president Anaya was trying to curry favor with him so that he
would not be prosecuted. He bought several rounds of beer and deferred
to Buitrón in each sentence with, "Yes, yes, Engineer. Yes, boss." After
the scolding he had received, Extension Agent Villar was also being ap-
propriately obsequious. Other irrigators approached Buitrón to curry favor.*

*After all of his talk about the need for responsible irrigation man-
agement, Buitrón got extremely drunk and forgot to—or was persuaded
not to—provide the certificate that would transfer power from Anaya to
the interim president and would give the controllers legitimacy. The next
day it was also revealed that Villar had granted water to four powerful
individuals, including communal authorities, despite the decision that
the water was going to enter into the supervised rounds. To further com-*

plicate the situation, outgoing president Anaya was still authorizing water to select individuals. Carlos Canseco, who had been unwillingly appointed as interim president of the Irrigators Commission, declared, "Gentlemen, between these authorities, each hand is washing the other. We can't let this continue. The preferences have just ended."

Carlos organized a meeting of the interim commission for the next night (February 24) to put the state model of de canto and controller-supervised distribution into action. The next night, before the meeting, he suffered yet another setback: Villar had held a meeting and had been persuaded to start the round in a different sector than had been agreed upon in the assembly. There was confusion as to which mandate to follow: that of the engineer, that of the extension agent, or that of the interim president. The latter was besieged with petitions, and, not wanting to make enemies, he had been hiding out. Yet people found out about the meeting and came to argue for their potatoes and majuelos, for their particular sector, or for estancadas.

Women, sometimes crying, pleaded for a little water for their dying fields. Anarchy reigned, and the interim commission could not reach an agreement on where the controllers should initiate the round. So that everyone could avoid responsibility, it was decided that Carlos would travel the two hours to Chivay to seek the engineer's decision. In the meantime, the members of the commission concurred that the controllers would start the round in the sectors that the engineer had designated and Villar's orders would be ignored. Irrigators were waiting outside as the session adjourned. "You can only gain enemies with this cargo," Carlos told me as we left the office.

Although Buitrón is supposed to intervene in order to organize distribution and manage this emergency period in a rational and equitable fashion, he and Villar, at an informal level, manipulate and allow themselves to be manipulated by powerful peasants, usually the most criollo. Members of the Irrigators Commission as well as other communal officials also use their authority to secure water for their own fields during this crucial period. Each player in the irrigation drama, then, pursues his or her best interests and manipulates local and state officials to this end.

One of the individuals who accepted the onerous job of controller, Felipe Galdos, did so, as he later confided to me, not just

because of the twenty intis an hour it paid, but because he wanted
to get some water for his mother's field. "That's why I want to take
the water down to the lower fields. On the way I'll give my potatoes a little shot," he said. I accompanied Felipe for the next few
days to observe the switch from the informal system to the state
model of de canto distribution.

*That night there was much jostling around as many people tried to
get in a last watering before the controllers took charge at six A.M. In-
credibly, one of the members of the interim commission, the vice president, had used his authority to obstruct Felipe from starting the round
so that he could irrigate his own potato fields!*

*The town mayor had also appeared in the early morning hours, tell-
ing Felipe, "I'm an authority, too. Let me just water this little piece here."
Even as Felipe was telling me this, the mayor walked by, irrigator's lamp
in hand, praising his good work. Felipe did not appreciate the compliment. "He's my neighbor, but I'm not going to be so friendly anymore. I
won't be lending him my plow again." Still another man had secured
water with an order from the extension agent. All of these "lawbreakers" (infractores) had tiyaq guarding the intakes to ensure that they could
irrigate freely. Other irrigators had refused to pay Felipe and had insisted
that distribution should follow the old system, in which no payment was
received. And those from another area were protesting the move to the
lower fields. It had been a rough morning for the controller.*[4]

*Another disheartening fact for Felipe was that Villar had left for
Chivay on the early morning bus and had neglected to give Felipe the
formal decree to control water. So, too, Anaya had gone to the high pastures to check his cattle, taking with him the seals of the Irrigators Commission so that there could be no transferal of authority. The governor
had gone to the orchards, so there was no one to "provide guarantees"
for the controllers. No signs had been posted, nor had the musical criers
been solicited by the authorities to announce the end of the anarchic informal system. In short, there was no official authorization for the shift
from the informal model to de canto distribution.*

*Without seals or certified papers, Felipe wondered if anyone would
respect his authority. He was especially afraid to administer the water
at night, explaining, "People, desperate for water, might try and do something to me." Yet after the initial problems that first day, people generally respected his authority and were relieved that the water "was finally*

in place." Popular support for regularizing the cycle was high. As one man told him, "If we'd done this three weeks ago we'd be through most of the fields by now."

Felipe was also having a certain amount of success charging by the hour. Many were paying less than the stipulated amount, but any money was much better than just coca and trago and was a real incentive for a cash-poor peasant. During the first twenty-four-hour period he made 260 intis, as opposed to the 480 he would have made if he had been paid in full. Even so, this was two and a half times as much as a peón or work hand normally earned for a day's work in the community.

In the next few days, the state model was implemented more resolutely. Other members of the commission helped patrol the canals, measured the river water, and divided it equally between the two canals so that the controllers would have equal shares. The sluice gates on two of the upper canals were padlocked, and a notice was posted at the Irrigators Commission office with the names of the controllers and the designated sectors. That night Villar returned from Chivay with certifications for the controllers. A list of the eighteen lawbreakers, including the town mayor and the authorities who had stolen water during the first morning, was brought forward. Several protested that the controller had not been a legally constituted authority at the time, and in the end no fines were administered.

Although the total anarchy of the informal system was ended, infractions continued to occur. People began to comment that if it did not rain within a week or so, there would be only one "good" canal of water instead of two. Many realized that it would soon be more difficult to secure water for their fields, and water theft continued. On Felipe's third night, the canal he was supervising dried up completely because a woman had stolen water for her potato fields. She had escaped into the maize plants and Felipe had been afraid to chase her, fearing that she might hit him with a rock. Two sluice gates in the upper canals had also been destroyed, and there had been a lot of water theft.

Felipe's fourth and last night of the round was even worse. He was exhausted after four days and nights, and it was foggy. Many irrigators had not prepared their intakes properly, and others would not pay, quickly disappearing into the fog after irrigating. There had been a lot of water theft, and Felipe had spent the night running up and down the canals, trying to redirect the water and catch the thieves. "But they know all the *little paths that go up and down to their fields, and it's no use trying to catch them," he complained. One of the other controllers had over fifty infractions during the four-day period. Yet both controllers had made an average of 250 intis a day and were pleased to have profited from the generally thankless office of controller.*

Pressure on Villar and Felipe from the irrigators of different canals soon became more intense. The interesados of Auqui, Airanpo, and Liway sectors presented petitions, each with fifteen or more signatures. Villar was persuaded that the water should be shifted from the Cusqi Canal to the majuelos and potatoes of the Liway sector.[5] It was announced that the shift would take place on March 1 and that the irrigators should "preserve order" and prepare their canals. Some said that Villar had again exceeded his authority, and rumors began to spread of a possible confrontation at the Liway intake between the irrigators of Liway and those of Cusqi. Others said that the irrigators of Cusqi were going to amass in the night and take the water by force. Fortunately, it rained during the night and a conflict was avoided.

STATE INTERVENTION IN LOCAL DISTRIBUTION

We see that the de canto model, enforced by official decrees, is sometimes an effective means of installing order during the chaotic dry spells of the rainy season. But when the state attempts to extend its control further into the local irrigation practices of the community, there is resistance. The Irrigators Assembly that took place a few days later (on March 3) to name a new Irrigators Commission illustrates many of the tensions that typify the state's attempts to determine the entire annual distribution cycle of water in Cabanaconde.

The assembly was again poorly attended. Many people stayed away for fear of being named to the new commission. Buitrón had again driven from Chivay, but this time the Peasant Community paid for his gas. He addressed the growing crowd by saying, "It used to be that the elders were in charge of irrigation, but since the Water Laws have been drawn up, things have changed. Having studied in the university, I haven't come here to preside over the customs of the community." He was angry about sluice gates being destroyed and sternly admonished the townspeople, saying that water belonged to the state and that this crime was punishable

by law. He then recited several statutes of the Water Laws, emphasiz-
ing that maintenance had to be equitable: "He who has ten tupus must
provide ten times as many laborers for the canal cleanings as the person
who has only one tupu. The law hasn't yet arrived to this town. . . . The
large landowners don't provide workers for the faenas, and we've got of-
ficials selling water. No, no, this has to end."

Buitrón then asked that the list of water thieves and canal-cleaning
absentees be sent to him. "I'll see they're deprived of water," he said.
Several people snickered at the thought of Buitrón depriving people of
water from his office in Chivay. He then explained that those nominated
for the new commission had to be irrigators who were up to date in their
faena obligations and were of moral solvency. Nominations and elec-
tions were then held. Many people were anxious to avoid being named
to the new commission; others were intent on fulfilling these cargos.

After the meeting, several people pointed out to me that the newly
elected president had a large quantity of dry-farmed fields and was surely
going to use his office to irrigate these. Moreover, one of his godchildren
had been elected secretary, and another man who was known to be cul-
tivating eriazo land had been elected alderman. But Hugo Rosaldo, an-
other person elected to the commission, was known to be honest, and it
was thought that he would oppose any abuses by the others.

Hugo was also known to be a hardworking and "progressive" agri-
culturist who had successfully experimented with new and different crops.
In the past, he had also attempted, unsuccessfully, to exchange what he
viewed as the outdated saya system of water mayors for the de canto
system. After taking the oath of office, which Buitrón administered, Hugo
broached the subject of the water mayors. "Why should we have to lis-
ten to some drunk slouched up against a terrace shouting at us, 'Hurry
up, hurry up'? No señores, we have to be open to new forms of irrigat-
ing." He then suggested that the de canto system be extended through-
out the year to completely replace the local saya model. Buitrón fully
agreed, and it was written into the books of the Irrigators Commission
that the controllers and the payment of twenty intis an hour would con-
tinue throughout the year. Buitrón declared, "Adiós to anansaya. That
old tale just passed into history."

I had my doubts that the de canto system would entirely replace the dual system. My compadre Cansio, a former water mayor,
referring to the saya system, told me, "The old ones studied the

system well—there was no talk of our traditions in the assembly today." He was voicing, I believe, an unspoken sentiment that many Cabaneños shared. In the assembly, Hugo Rosaldo had been the only comunero to support a permanent change in distribution patterns, and there had been an uneasy silence when Buitrón declared an end to the saya system.

When the irrigation cycle was renewed after the harvest, I awaited a major change in distribution, the water mayors and centuries-old saya model finally giving way to the monetary de canto state model. But no such change was forthcoming.

LOCAL MEDIATIONS OF THE STATE

To understand why the saya model did not yield to the de canto state model, we must go back to the nature of the local water users association, the Irrigators Commission, and to the way that the state model is mediated by local understandings. The most obvious example of how the local model conditions the state model is that the controllers, like the water mayors, follow a dual sequence in which they trade shifts of four days and nights.

Such mediations can be accounted for by the fact that the members of the Irrigators Commission are townspeople fully immersed in the local culture and social mores of the community. Although the water mayors are legally under the jurisdiction of the Irrigators Commission, the water mayors' ritual activity takes place outside the formal aegis of the commission. In the following instance, one of the few in which I observed members of the Irrigators Commission enter the ritual activities of the water mayors, it was evident that the cultural orientations of the local model absorbed and overrode those of the state.

The vice president of the Irrigators Commission, Pablo Calderón, showed up with two other irrigators at the yakutinkay. After coca and trago were passed around and we each prayed with incense to Mount Hualca-Hualca, the vice president ceremonially presented the staffs to the water mayor, Adan. First, he took them from where they were resting and dunked them in the water. He then declared: "You're now the mayor of the fields; we're the mayors of the irrigator's locale. Our dear little mother Hualca-Hualca has chosen you, don Adan. On behalf of the Irrigators Commission, I congratulate you and your wife." He then handed the staffs to the water mayor, who placed them in the ground, facing downriver. When Pablo left, one man said, "Cheap bastard," which got a laugh. Everybody felt he should have brought some trago and cigarettes at a bare minimum.

We see that the vice president, by ceremonially delivering the staffs to the water mayors and invoking Hualca-Hualca, appeals to the water mayors' symbology of power. Although he has the institutional backing of the state, it is the higher authority of the snake-headed staffs and Hualca-Hualca Mountain that the vice president invokes here to legitimate his authority.

But while the Irrigators Commission is made up of community members who fully participate in the religious ideas and practices embodied in the office of water mayor, the books of the Irrigators Commission—subject to review by future office holders and state officials—are written in official tones and virtually ignore the discourse and rationale found in the local model. Nevertheless, occasional entries, such as that found from 1955 that mentions the "companions" of each saya who help "with the customs of idolatry" (BIC), show that local belief penetrates even the privileged realm of literacy and official discourse.[6] The power of indigenous belief and practice is most clear, however, in the way the local saya model refuses to yield to the state model of distribution.

RATIONALITY AND RITUAL ASSURANCE

Local elites and state officials, we have seen, have attempted to "rationalize" water distribution by instituting the de canto system of controllers for the entire annual irrigation cycle, thus completely doing away with the saya model of distribution. The de canto model is supposedly more rational and efficient since it avoids the loss of water that occurs when one water mayor has to irrigate a few plots of his saya's land in fields predominantly classified as belonging to the other saya, which the opposing water mayor has already irrigated.

Although townspeople are well aware of this water loss, they say that the state model is less efficient and less equitable. The motor of this system, a monetary payment and the sequential watering of the fields, is supposed to hurry water along. The rationale here is that people will more effectively use water to avoid paying more and that sequential watering is more efficient.

People admit that water is lost and at other times causes damage with the saya system. However, the unvoiced sentiment is that these inconveniences are made up for by the competition between the two water mayors and the well-established circuit that water follows. Because it is a once-in-a-lifetime cargo, there is also greater pressure for the water mayor to be conscientious and fair in distribution. As one man put it, "The controllers don't give a damn, they don't care if the water moves along, as long as they get paid. They'll even slow it down to collect more money, and they leave their posts without a thought." Moreover, the office of water mayor is underwritten by indigenous cultural logics about efficacy, availability, and the ritual means by which to secure an abundance of water and fertility, which are fundamentally opposed to the secular, monetary model of the state. Finally, the dual model provides a cognitive map and a fixed sequence of distribution not found in the state model; local elites can more easily manipulate the latter as a means to irrigate unauthorized fields.

It is evident that although state intervention after 1969 challenged the most abusive colonial holdovers of the saya system by making the cargo of water mayor less onerous and more democratic, state officials failed to understand the local model's cultural rationale and ritual logic and the way that this system effectively classifies irrigable land and equitably distributes water. Rather, the state has attempted to completely replace this model with its own bureaucratic one, a model that ignores Andean cultural orientations and reproduces the cultural hegemony of the dominant criollo culture.

The power of the local model, and its capacity for resisting and absorbing the state model, is quite remarkable. Since the 1940s, there have been repeated attempts—first by local elites and later by state officials—to completely replace the saya model with that of the de canto model. As we just saw, Engineer Buítron, the highest-ranking water official in the region, supported by a local member of the Irrigators Commission, again made the irrevocable decision to abolish the local saya model and to install a monetary payment for the water mayors. As in 1947, 1955, 1960, 1971, 1980, and 1984, this decision was officially entered into the minutes of the meeting, which were signed by Buitrón, Villar, and most of those present, including the water mayors.

However, when the new irrigation cycle began, it was the water mayors who ignored the decree. Despite official pressure to adopt the de canto system and to charge for their services as the controllers had done during the rainy season, the water mayors continued to follow the dual model and to receive only coca and trago. One water mayor explained, "If I try to charge, people will talk," adding that there was also a great deal of social pressure to follow the saya classifications. Yet, according to a member of the Irrigators Commission, it was the water mayors themselves who were most opposed to changing the system, a system that not only assures communal control of distribution and the continued fertility of the fields but also ritually obtains the safety of the water mayors.

CONCLUSION
The Cultural Politics of Irrigation, Community, and Development in the Andes

The main problems [of the Colca Valley villages]
are the low cultural level of the irrigators...[and]
a certain resistance of the agriculturist to rational work methods.

ORDEA, Ministry of Agriculture,
1980

In this book, I have studied the different histories, models of water distribution, and fields of contention found in Cabanaconde's irrigation system. The first chapters explored "community" and the political ecology of irrigation, showing that water availability and land recovery are mediated by communal, regional, national, and international political and economic forces. The second half of the book delved deeper into the cultural politics of water and power by peeling back different layers of meaning and history found in state and local models of water distribution.

The division of Cabanaconde's agricultural land into anansaya and urinsaya, with corresponding water mayors, was at one time part of an all-encompassing moiety system used by the Inka and Spanish states for extraction, that is, to organize and siphon off the labor and productive resources of the community.[1] Time-worn vestiges of state hegemony, the alternating water mayors and dual divisions today constitute the local "indigenous" model of irrigation. Each water mayor makes ritual offerings to Mount Hualca-Hualca, Earth Mother, and Water Mother to secure an abundance of water, the fertility of the fields, and his family's safety.

Taken together, the practices of the two water mayors constitute another ritual level, one that seeks fertility and abundance through ritual alternation and alternating rituals. The local model of dual organization not only establishes a pace of distribution along a set path, but also provides a game board for the water mayors. The ritual competition between them, in which their social and spiritual selves are publicly displayed, advances the water quickly. The entire community observes and participates in this other ritual level. The local model, then, has its own communicative rationality, one that suggests designs for living and structures social practice.[2]

Peruvian state officials are generally oblivious to the instrumental nature of indigenous ritual practices. Rather, the latter are viewed with contempt. This is part of the mixed legacy of the Velasco regime. On the one hand, the greater state intervention in highland communities and their irrigation practices that began with the Velasco reforms of the late 1960s and early 1970s, as in many other domains of rural life, broke the concentrated power of local elites, power that was already being challenged from within communities (see, e.g., Guillet 1992; Long and Roberts 1978; Seligmann 1995). In Cabanaconde, the requirement that the landed misti elite, not just poor "Indians," fulfill the cargo of water mayor and the subsequent modification of this office from a full year's service to one round of water is part of a larger democratization of political office in the community.

But, on the other hand, the Velasco regime, largely because of its class-based orientation and the way it "peasantized" most of rural Peru (see, e.g., Mayer 1994), also sidelined indigenous models that were effective for distributing water. Indeed, in its attempt to modernize highland political structures, the regime imposed bureaucratic norms taken from an international irrigation tradition (Lynch 1993), norms that challenged longstanding, non-Western cultural frameworks for organizing water management, production, and ethnic identity. I have shown that in Cabanaconde, the water mayors and the local model of irrigation embody a fundamentally different rationale concerning power, authority, efficiency, and water availability than that of the controllers and de canto state model. The latter, which are informed by a secular, bureaucratic, and supposedly more rational and efficient approach to water management, have a hard time displacing the local saya model.

Rather, the meanings and cultural forms of the saya model, which have been intimately tied to local identity, political practice, and successful production for the last five hundred years, mediate the state model of distribution and shape it in idiosyncratic ways. It is the cultural staying power of duality and mountain ritual—that is, the instrumental meanings and ritual efficacy of the saya system in relation to irrigation and other productive activities—that has allowed the saya model to change from a conduit of Inka and Spanish extraction to a form of resistance against interference by local elites and the contemporary Peruvian state.

I have also argued that the ongoing clash between state and local models of irrigation, furthered by post-Velasco irrigation bureaucracies in Peru, is conditioned by a racist colonial legacy and by a larger cultural politics in Peruvian society today. National power-holders who determine the state's policy toward Andean communities live an urban criollo lifestyle in coastal cities with Western lifeways. Andean peasants often resist new forms of distribution not only because they have the potential of creating greater inequalities in water use, but because they constitute a form of cultural hegemony by a nation-state that neither shares nor respects highland cultural values. The micropolitics of water in Cabanaconde provides a window, then, into a struggle that is taking place in countless hundreds of highland communities.

ANDEAN CULTURE, HISTORY, AND IDENTITY

My study of irrigation and community has also demonstrated that there are a broad number of "indigenous," "Andean" cultural orientations that are fundamental to rural life in the highlands. I have shown that the religious beliefs and practices tied to production are just one piece of Cabanaconde's cultural mosaic and that Cabanaconde has always been firmly linked to larger political and cultural forces. Today, the Cabaneños use many different cultural frameworks as they transit communities, towns, and cities in Peru and other countries. My analysis has also insisted that the cultural orientation found in local production remains an important and vital framework within highland society.[3] Indeed, the orientation that joins people, place, and production transcends the boundaries of community and lies at the heart of a culture that extends to urban and transnational spheres.

By studying the imperial and communal uses of mountain ritual and dual organization as forms of extraction and resistance, we gain a new understanding of "Andean" culture. Indigenous peoples throughout the Americas, past and present, revere that which sustains life, and, therefore, mountains, water, and the earth have been at the center of their religious systems. But in the case of the Andean region, where there was a highly centralized indigenous empire, mountain cults and dual organization were local forms that the Inka state appropriated and used for its own expansionist purposes. These two components of Cabanaconde's local model of irrigation were at odds during the Spanish colonial period. Unlike dual organization, which continued to be used to organize production and tribute by the Spaniards, mountain ritual was completely antithetical to the Spaniards' belief system and was suppressed. We have seen that today these two components of the local model of irrigation are inextricably linked to each other and to local identity, and that this potent mix challenges cultural imports from the coast.

The local ethnic dynamics of Cabanaconde have also conditioned state intervention. I have shown that, in contrast to neighboring towns, there was a large concentration of Spaniards in this community in the colonial period and a small group of powerful criollos maintained power in the community until the 1960s. The de canto state model of distribution was first used by local elites in Cabanaconde long before the 1969 Water Laws spread this type of organization and distribution throughout the highlands. It is the differentiated nature of community life and the way that class and ethnicity get racialized and culturally elaborated that explain the cultural affinity between local elites and state actors and the irrigation models that they employ.

For example, in the last two chapters, we saw that today it is the most "criollo" individuals within the community who succeed with bureaucracies and development agencies. They do so "by persuading the bureaucrats that they, the clients, are insiders: kinsfolk, fellow patriots, spiritual kin, coreligionists—in short, one blood" (Herzfeld 1992, 181).[4] This is true at different moments in

Cabanaconde's history, whether we are talking of the Patriarchs convincing state officials to give water to their ill-acquired eriazo lands in the 1950s or of Agrarian Bank loan recipients who do the same today.

But at another level, that of the regional system of economic and ethnic stratification, the Cabaneños as a whole are perceived by other indigenous peoples in the region as "whiter," aggressive, powerful, and more criollo.[5] I would suggest that, indeed, the Cabaneños' possession of a greater cultural literacy in national discourse partly explains why it was Cabanaconde, and not another community, that challenged the Majes Project.

WATER, POWER, AND THE STATE

The hydrology, topography, rich soils, and microclimate of the lower Hualca-Hualca River basin made this area ideal for agriculture and dense settlement, and indigenous states fought to control it as early as the seventh century A.D. In the expansion and contraction of indigenous state control, thousands of terraces and dozens of canals were built over Cabanaconde's current territory. With the great population decline following the Spanish invasion, the better part of this infrastructure was abandoned. Today, because of the Cabaneños' resolve, the state-sponsored Majes Canal has been used to recover part of Cabanaconde's lost infrastructure.

But what have been the political means by which this infrastructure has been harnessed by different states, and what is the relationship of irrigation to power? This brings us back to the question of "development," be this the agricultural intensification and centralization of political authority in pre-Columbian times or the ways that contemporary national and international development initiatives attempt to intensify agriculture and centralize authority today.

It is undeniable that irrigation, by intensifying agriculture, was one of the great technological revolutions in the history of humanity. As Wittfogel (1957) argued, the densely populated settlements, food surpluses, and social coordination that irrigation brought about played an important role in the evolution of sociopolitical complexity in early polities around the globe.[6] But there is nothing inherent in this technology that demands or necessarily produces highly centralized control and "Oriental despotism," an unsympathetic caricature of political order that Wittfogel extends to many other non-Western contexts, including that of the Inka state.

On the contrary, the Inka, like many other precolonial indigenous polities the world over (see, e.g., Tambiah 1976; Geertz 1980; Wheatley 1971), attempted to reproduce their cosmological and political center in miniature throughout the provinces of the empire. The anansaya/urinsaya model embodied a "symbology of power" that was used to spatially, socially, and productively organize subject peoples and nations. So, too, local mountain cults were symbolically incorporated into the imperial cult by means of state-directed human sacrifice on the highest peaks. These cultural orientations—not the political exigencies of irrigation—were active agents in the development and organization of centralized political authority under the Inka.

Wittfogel's model of water and power, which resonates with the objectivist and ethnocentric orientations of many development initiatives of today, is the quintessential expression of "Orientalism," a literary and academic discourse in which the histories and cultures of non-Western "others" are homogenized, defined in opposition to the West, and viewed as static and ultimately inferior (Said 1978). Unfortunately, because of its affinities with modernization theory, this kind of generalizing and worldview finds its way into irrigation development and state bureaucracies, which put more faith in supposedly cross-culturally valid formulas than in contextualizing analyses.

Irrigation politics in widely diverse settings such as Peru and Bali must be understood in terms of conflicts between bureaucratic and local forms of understanding. As we saw in the Introduction, local ritual practices are also "an integral part of the technology of farming" (Lansing 1991, 6) in Bali. They, too, are challenged by state bureaucracies and development organizations that are opposed to seeing agriculture as meaningful except in the most utilitarian way. The conflict between state and local models in both Peru and Bali thus illustrates a larger process whereby "non-European areas have been systematically organized into, and transformed according to, European constructs" (Escobar 1995, 7).[7]

The deployment of secular, "rational" irrigation models is clearly a powerful means by which many contemporary nation-states around the world extend their control over their peripheries. In Inka times, dual organization and mountain ritual were extremely effective as means of extending and legitimating state authority. Catholicism did the same during Spanish colonial rule. Today, the secular, monetary de canto model is part of a new symbology of power—espoused in modernization theory and diffused through development—that claims to provide universal benefits while in fact extending state control and the cultural orientations of national and international power-holders.

But these state-sponsored cultural imports from the coast and beyond find not only covert resistance through the continued use of local models of irrigation, but also overt resistance. Cabanaconde, by the way it challenged the Majes Project, recovered abandoned terraced fields, and democratically divided these for the greater prosperity of the townspeople, provides a dramatic case study of open resistance to Peru's coastally oriented political economy of development.

The historical and interpretive understanding of water, ethnicity, and power in Peru developed here can be applied to the politics of community, irrigation, common property, and development in other culturally plural countries. This is especially the case in the Andean nations of Bolivia and Ecuador and in Guatemala and Mexico in Mesoamerica, where pre-Columbian empires flourished and established extensive farming systems and infrastructure (e.g., raised fields, chinampas, terraces, irrigation works) and where indigenous peoples today continue to constitute a large percentage, often the majority, of the population. The study of indigenous models of resource management in these other nations, I believe, will reveal that these models were also forged through indigenous and Iberian colonial processes and that they today face similar challenges from secular state models of resource management, which supposedly advance the "national interest" but in fact often do the exact opposite.

Implicit in most ideologies of national development throughout the Americas is the assumption that indigenous peoples must renounce their cultural orientations and ethnic identities to progress. But things are changing. Although the Cabañeños and other indigenous people increasingly transit regional, national, and international frontiers, discovering new worlds, adopting new technologies, and prospering, they do so without necessarily having to sacrifice their cultural orientations. Rather, indigenous peoples in Cabanaconde and elsewhere are demonstrating that their cultural distinctiveness is entirely compatible with "modernity," urban spaces, transnational migration, and social mobility. Indeed, during their occasional visits to their community, many Washington-based Cabañeños make q'apa payments to Mount Hualca-Hualca, provider of water, life, and identity.

EPILOGUE

Things have changed considerably in Cabanaconde since the mid-1990s, the town greatly transformed by land recovery, the rapidly increasing pace of transnational migration, and new information technologies. For example, television first became available with the installation of a parabolic antenna in 1993, and as of 1998 televisions are found in approximately half of the homes in Cabanaconde. Four radio stations have sprung up in town, broadcasting information to the lower Colca Valley. And in 1998 two telephones were installed, directly linking Cabanaconde to its colonies and the outside world. The town will soon be connected to the Internet.

These new technologies are being used not just to spread the cultural images and products of the dominant society but also to reproduce Andean culture and communal identity. An increasing number of the Cabaneño transmigrants in Washington, D.C, whose numbers have increased fourfold since the early 1990s and who today amount to approximately six hundred individuals, use video technology to record local customs ("la costumbre") on their return visits. There is a voluminous flow of cultural goods between Washington and Cabanaconde that includes everything from the latest musical exports from the United States to videos of the most recent fiestas in Cabanaconde. Many of the Washington-based

Cabaneños have video libraries of these fiestas and other local rituals, and there are several video versions of the Virgin of Carmen
patron saint fiesta—increasingly sponsored by migrants now living in Washington—circulating throughout households in Mary-
land, Virginia, and Washington, D.C., as well as in Cabanaconde
itself.[1]

Land recovery has also brought about major changes in the
town's cultural landscape. As mentioned in chapter 2, Cabanaconde
successfully used the Huataq water as a bargaining chip for more
water from the Majes Canal, which has been used to recover over
eight hundred hectares of land as of 1998. This new land has meant
greater prosperity for the townspeople, a good deal of return migration, and an increasingly dispersed settlement pattern (as people
build secondary residences in their new fields). Land recovery has
also resulted in a large influx of immigrants from the upper Colca
Valley, Puno, and Cuzco. Many of the "caballeritos," the herders
who formerly worked as migrant farm laborers for the Cabaneños
in the harvest season, are seeking and receiving comunero status
and access to newly recovered land. Cabanaconde is thus both ex-
porting and importing laborers and residents, and new forms of
class and ethnic differentiation are arising in the community.[2]

In the last few years, land recovery has also affected the local
model of irrigation, features of which have given way to those of
the state model. Most importantly, in 1997 the cargo of water
mayor ceased to exist as such. The water of the main fields is now
distributed by the controllers (who are still often referred to as
"water mayors" by the irrigators), paid employees of the Irrigators
Commission who collect fees from the irrigators in the fields. The
Cabaneños on the whole now accept that they have to pay for water, and since the mid-1990s a water tariff has been imposed by
the Irrigators Commission on the water of the main fields.[3] In 1997
I found a herder from a different community passing this paid office. In 1998 it was being filled by cash-poor Cabaneños. Some controllers carry the snake-headed staffs, but most do not, and instead
carry a shovel or a walking stick.

How to explain these abrupt changes? First, the new offtake
valves and the land recovered in other sectors of Cabanaconde's
territory signify that the main fields and the irrigation complex

studied in this book do not have the same importance that they did before. Moreover, since the mid-1990s, the water of the Hualca-Hualca River has been redirected to one of the newly recovered sectors, Joyas, and only a small amount of Mount Hualca-Hualca's sacred water now nourishes the main fields. The latter are now dependent upon the Majes water from the Tomanta offtake. For the main fields, then, Hualca-Hualca's life-giving water is not as economically or symbolically important as before.[4]

Nevertheless, important features of the local model, such as the age-old saya system, still persist. The controllers alternate in four-day shifts and still distribute water in terms of the anansaya/urinsaya classification. Although they do not make q'apa offerings throughout the irrigation round as did the water mayors, most controllers still perform the major yakutinkay ritual, q'apa offerings and all, at the beginning of the round. But today, the controllers of anansaya and urinsaya invoke both Hualca-Hualca and the Majes Canal in their offerings.

The final outcome of the clash and interpenetration of local and state models of irrigation is far from decided, and there is an ongoing debate about which system is the most effective and the most equitable. Some Cabaneños argue that with monetarization and the loss of competition in the new system, the water advances more slowly—this group wants to bring back the water mayors. Others are still calling for the abolishment of the saya divisions and the local model altogether. In any case, Cabanaconde is now firmly linked to the state's irrigation bureaucracies through water tariffs and through the town's increased dependence on the water from the Majes Canal.[5] As one friend, referring to the local irrigation authorities, put it, "It's not like before, Pablo—they're paid employees. The mayor's got his hand out when you get to the fields." "But," he assured me with a grin, "not everyone pays."

Appendices

My own involvement with Earth Mother began almost immediately after arriving to the community. The severe upper back pains I felt after the first few days (due to an old back problem aggravated by sleeping on a dirt floor with little padding for several days), which grew worse to the point that I could not sleep, were attributed to tierra, or the illness caused by the earth. Exalta, the mother of the family that had adopted us, asked me if I had dreamt lately of a woman other than my wife. I told her no, I had not, wondering why she asked. She and her daughter Marcela laughed at my obvious embarrassment, then explained that the earth is a woman and often appears in dreams as such. Even with no such foreboding, she was sure I had tierra. Although I had had positive experiences with Andean and Amazonian healers in the past, I waited several days before visiting a ritual specialist, taking aspirin and hoping the pain would go away. When it worsened, causing me greater pain and little sleep, I took Exalta's advice and called on the paqu.

I had heard that Federico Chocano was a good paqu; he told me the same right after we shook hands. He fairly bragged about how he was solicited from all over the province and could cure many ills, make men who had left their wives return, and locate lost cattle. "If you're in really bad shape, I'll tell you, 'There's nothing that can save you now.' I see everything."

He was lame and walked with a stick, his left foot grotesquely twisted to one side. Fetching his coca from the other side of his house, he hobbled slowly, bent over his knobby little walking stick, his wildly out-of-kilter leg and hip sticking out to one side. He spoke through almost toothless gums. He was very animated, with crinkly, bright eyes and a wry smile, obviously more comfortable speaking Quechua, but proficient nonetheless in Spanish. His little son and daughter, the latter a strange-looking girl (I later learned she was epileptic; this disease is interpreted differently by the people there), looked on as we talked. I asked him what had happened to his leg, and he told me of his bad luck as of late, and began weeping as he recounted the accident and his wife's death three months before. He wiped away the tears and almost immediately regained his composure. He would read coca to find out what was wrong with me; he told me it would cost 5,000 soles (five intis).

He needed a piece of my clothing to divine what my illness was and I had brought a T-shirt, which he spread out on a table. He then put several handfuls of coca on top and placed among the leaves the 5,000 sol bill and a coin. Gathering the shirt up in his wrinkled hands, he handed it to me and instructed me to breathe heavily onto it three times; I did this and gave it back to him. He asked me my name again, and, after making a brief prayer, he dropped the shirt onto the ground. He opened it slowly and carefully, and, picking up a few nicely rounded leaves on top of the pile and near the bill and the coin, he declared, "You have earth— you've been afflicted by white earth." He then divined two more times, finding the same leaves and the same answer. We decided that he would cure me that very night by making a q'apa. I would have to get together some of the necessary thirteen ingredients, including a pig fetus. The cure would cost me three hundred intis.

"Three hundred intis! Too much," said Mr. Mamani, who I visited after the divining session. "They're expensive but it shouldn't be more than 150 intis, two hundred at the most." It had seemed expensive to me (about ten dollars) after the relatively cheap divination (about seventeen cents), especially since I would have to procure some of the ingredients. This proved to be problematic. Exalta had decided that she too wished to have the paqu treat her leg with a q'apa (she also had tierra) and informed me that one of her relatives might have a pig's fetus, but, like many people in the community, this relative was very envious of Exalta and might not want to give anything that might help her.

Don Federico arrived at around 7:30 P.M. with his son, his apprentice. Federico explained that he had been born with his gift, indicated by his being born with one of his hands and one of his feet larger than the other, "strong and weak at the same time." Nobody had taught him his trade; he had learned it by himself. He lowered his price to two hundred intis, and we then began the curing ceremony.

First, he rubbed the sore part of my back and shoulder with llama fat (pechowira), and then rubbed it with the pig fetus and a cigarette. While Federico prepared the q'apa, Exalta continued to rub my back gently with the fetus, repeating several times, "Return, return, from foreign lands, from California" ("kuti, kuti, extranjirumanta, califurniamanta"). She then named off the places around the community where I had been: Auquiqucha, Liwayqucha, Huanqequcha, Cabra, Puquio, and so on; these were the places I may have picked up tierra or where it might have worsened since, according to Federico, I had already caught tierra in California and it had gotten worse upon my arrival to Cabanaconde. Meanwhile, Federico prepared the q'apa. On top of a coca bag (ista) he laid out small, long twigs of kunuka, an aromatic plant, followed by small pieces of the llama fat. Then Exalta gave him the fat, fetus, and cigarette that she had been passing over the afflicted part of my back, and he covered the fetus with llama fat.

He then took small pieces of silver- and gold-colored paper (qulqilibru, qurilibru) and placed them into the small pieces of fat and onto the fat-covered fetus. His son helped him with these delicate operations. Then six coca seeds were placed into the fat of the fetus, followed by twelve nicely rounded coca leaves. He then placed the decorated fetus over the ista and sprinkled gold powder (oro pimiento), a bit of confetti, and incense on top. A plant called kañiwa followed, then a few grains of special corn, "return corn" and "sacred corn" (kuti sara and misa sara, respectively), and cigarettes. He breathed heavily on many of these ingredients, saying short prayers, before placing each one on the coca bag. Federico told me that the pig fetus was especially good for curing illnesses, whereas the vicuña fetus was good for water-related offerings.

The curing ritual took about one and a half hours. Federico told me, "Yes, yes, you are going to get well. We're offering to the Earth Mother, to your place, to California, and, just like that, it will get there!" Exalta went out to grind up some of the return corn to make toasted corn flour. At one point the three of us gathered together and made, in a wooden cup, libations with trago to the earth. I then had to leave the others and alone ask forgiveness of the soil from where I had come, of Lima, and of the different places I had visited in the communal territory, pleading that I might be cured.

Oscar then made Exalta's q'apa over a small piece of brown paper, using a guinea pig fetus; her q'apa was smaller than mine. Exalta went out to the cooking fire burning outside and returned with some flat stones covered with burning embers, which we used to burn incense. Each of us in turn walked around the room and outside into the patio with our offering raised, making prayers and asking for good health and forgiveness. We then went outside to where Exalta had begun burning cow dung on top of some broken clay vessels. Federico's child took my q'apa carefully off of the coca bag and placed it in the fire. We made yet another libation to Earth Mother with *pitu* (corn beer with the flour of "return corn" mixed in) and trago, and we said another round of prayers as we stood around the burning offering. Federico again mentioned the twelve mountain gods (cabildos), and invoked my godfather and god-mother mountains. He fanned the fire with the coca bag so that it would burn; the sweet smell of the kunuka and animal fat filled the air, and parts of the q'apa popped, which was considered a good sign. "You see, it's being received," he told me. With each crackle and pop, we would say, "Thank you, thank you" to Earth Mother for receiving our offering.

It was important that the q'apa burn properly, that the smoke disappear, and that the embers end up white. Federico carefully observed how it was burning, and he fanned it until the smoke dis-appeared. He told me that it had been received and that I would be cured.

Exalta's q'apa, however, was not received—black smoke floated up and the offering did not pop. Worse still, it continually burst into flame (the q'apa should burn slowly without igniting) and Federico had to fan it hard until it smoked again. "It's really strong—there's a lot of talk." "Runaq simin?" asked Exalta. "Yes, strong gossip. You have this nice house, lots of cattle, and now this gringo living with you [he nodded over at me]. Strong envy, very strong." Envy, pervading the atmosphere, was blocking the offering from reaching its destination.

At the time, it seemed to me that Exalta had suggested this possibility and that the paqu had seized upon it as a nice way out of his inefficacy; it was a compliment of sorts to tell her she was strongly envied. Because the cure did not work, Exalta did not pay him, except with trago and cigarettes. I could tell she was miffed.

When Exalta's q'apa had finished, we heated the "return corn" flour. We put it in two small cloths, tying up each one to form a small tightly filled little cloth bag; one was for me and the other for Exalta. Rubbing the warm bag over my back several times, Exalta repeated, "Return, return, return" ("kuti, kuti, kuti"). We then gave the bags to Federico's son and Federico instructed him to put them in two different corners of the house, so that "they wouldn't cross." Federico told me to remember what I dreamt that night and to tell him the next day. I was also told (by him as well as other people) that I should repeat the q'apa at least once and preferably twice more for it to be really efficacious. A neighbor added, "It really only works if you have faith."

For whatever reason, I slept well for the first time in two weeks, and the pain steadily decreased in the next days—I was cured. "You see?" was the common response when I related this to my acquaintances in the community. Many people confessed that they too had at one point been skeptical until, because of some trespass against the earth, they had enjoyed a similar cure. The next day I went to seek out don Federico, but when I arrived to his house I heard drunken singing inside. I realized he was so drunk that it was pointless to tell him of my dreams, which he had requested the day before.

"Of course. Who wouldn't have gotten drunk with all that money!" Mr. Mamani exclaimed when I spoke with him later, referring to what he considered the still exorbitant price I had paid.

APPENDIX B: THE VENGEANCE OF HUALCA-HUALCA

I had come to know Amalia Cutipa, the wife of water mayor Braulio Fernández, quite well, and I had helped her over several weeks by taking food, ponchos, irrigator lamps, and other supplies from her house to her husband in the fields. After his tenure, we remained friends, and I would visit their house regularly. A couple of months after Braulio finished his cargo, Amalia became ill. Her legs and back ached and she felt weak all over.

In the next months, she received several different types of medical treatment. She was even taken to Arequipa, where a doctor diagnosed her with cancer. This diagnosis was not accepted by her family or others in the community, and she was taken to and treated by different healers in town. These healers diagnosed it as different things: shock (*susto*), a curse (*boca de la gente, maldición*), earth illness (tierra), ill wind (*machuwayra*). Many of these conditions were supposed to be related to her duties as the wife of the water mayor. In the end, it was her relationship with Hualca-Hualca that came to be viewed as responsible.

After trying several healers, Amalia went to one man who was reputed to be the best. He read a crystal and coca; these revealed to him that two men and two women had tried to cure her, but they "hadn't been able to understand the illness properly." "There is something missing," he said. He went on to explain that what was missing was the "forgotten q'apa." It was because *she had not gone to make the payment to Hualca-Hualca.* Her husband and her sons-in law, who had also "accompanied" the water, had all made their farewell q'apa payments, but she had not and was now paying the consequences.

That was why I was awoken by don Braulio early one morning; he knew that I had rented a mule from the paqu Marcela and that I was on good terms with her. "Please don Pablo, do me this favor . . . we need the fetus of an alpaca to feed the virgin [Hualca-Hualca]." He went on to tell me that the earth "is addicted. She has become so accustomed during the many years that people have made offerings to her that she becomes resentful and vengeful if you don't deliver. When she doesn't receive her trago, fetuses, and her payments delivered properly, she gets angry. That's what happened." As another family member put it, "Because she wasn't paid, Hualca-Hualca is eating Amalia instead."

I obtained the fetus, and Braulio performed the q'apa for her. She was better the next day and remained so for a week. Over the next several months, however, her condition worsened. Other offerings were made, but to no avail. I would visit her regularly, bringing food or some photographs I had taken of her and her children and grandchildren. She became more and more ill, and eventually she looked like a frail little mummy. Her family kept her wrapped up in blankets on top of a pile of sheepskins on one side of a small, dark, depressing room. A few months later, she died.

APPENDIX C: NAMING THE WATER MAYORS

The process of naming the water mayors is capricious. Sometimes, individuals will be named to the post as a type of petty revenge by a member of the Irrigators Commission; in these cases the irrigator will take a trip to Chivay and appeal to higher authorities. Other times a middle-aged man will welcome the opportunity to undertake this office while he is still relatively young and in good health. Even when named to the office of water mayor, many of the wealthier peasants avoid actually distributing the water by paying peons to replace them. The following is a vignette taken from my field notes.

There was a tremendous amount of discussion today at the Irrigation Commission office. The eight water mayors who had been named for the coming year, as well as several of their sons, were present—several were disputing their appointments. "Many large landholders haven't yet passed the cargo!" one man complained to the president of the commission. "Who named us—who elected us?" The secretary of the commission threw up his hands in disgust, saying, "In a disorganized town like ours, which doesn't cooperate on anything, people don't come to the communal work parties and they steal water right and left. They're no good for working, but when it comes to complaining, they're real good."

As it turned out, the water mayors had been named in a meeting of the Irrigation Commission and not in Assembly, as had been decreed. This led to greater protestation, and several people were fairly shouting, "Why me? What about so and so?" naming off people who had larger landholdings. One old, monolingual Quechua-speaking woman, who had been named water mayor of anansaya, was crying and protesting in Quechua, saying that her fields were small and that she had little land in anansaya. Another man protested, "You all don't even know if I'm the owner of the fields I'm irrigating. What if they're sharecropped?" The vice president responded, "You're in charge of that field; you're the one who irrigates it. That's all there is to it!"

The secretary then launched into a long harangue, at the end of which everyone was silent except the old woman who continued to mutter furiously to herself in Quechua. "Oh, big fields, sure!" ("hatun chakra, aah!"). She was livid, and she started crying again. Her son argued with the authorities a while longer, and finally it was decided that since he would be doing the actual distribution and fulfilling the cargo, they would count his participation as fulfilling both his mother's and his own cargo obligations. Other agreements were arrived at, and the meeting was adjourned.

Notes

The hualina in the epigraph was written by Mr. Mokollunca during the Water Fiesta of Huachupampa in the year 1983. The original reads: "Si los mares fueron tinta y el cielo un papelito blanco y mi puño un pincelito para escribir la hualina."

1. For my master's research I studied the relationship between ritual, irrigation, and political power in Huarochirí and other Andean regions (Gelles 1984a, 1984b, 1986a).

INTRODUCTION

1. While *indigenous* and *peasant* do not encompass all of the diverse cultural, economic, and political processes and identities found among rural peoples in the Andean nations, these terms do highlight important features of highland society. The United Nations defines *indigenous* in the following way: "Indigenous communities, peoples, and nations are those which, having a historical continuity with pre-invasion and pre-colonial societies that developed on their own territories, consider themselves distinct from other sectors of the societies now prevailing in those territories, or parts of them. They form at present non-dominant sectors of society and are determined to preserve, develop, and transmit to future generations their ancestral territories, and their ethnic identity, as the basis of their continued existence as peoples, in accordance with their own cultural patterns, social institutions, and legal systems" (in Van Cott 1994, 23). There are more than forty million indigenous people in Latin America, and they constitute over half of the population in some countries (e.g., Peru, Bolivia, Guatemala) and less than 1 percent in others (e.g., Brazil).

I use the term *peasant* to highlight the following relationships: "[the] peasant family as the basic multidimensional unit of social organization, land husbandry as the main means of livelihood, specific cultural patterns linked to the way of life of a small rural community/neighborhood, and the underdog position, the domination of the peasantry by outsiders" (Outhwaite and Bottomore 1993, 454–455). This does *not* mean that peasants are economically undifferentiated, that their communities are isolated or there are not other economic processes occuring in them, or that rural dwellers do not transit many other social worlds in which they assume other identities; it is quite the opposite (see, e.g., Colloredo-Mansfeld 1999; Gelles and Martínez 1993; Kearney 1996;

Starn 1991). Nevertheless, the term does link identity with the key form of livelihood (land husbandry) and its economic domination by relatively powerful outsiders. It has special salience in Peru, as discussed below, in that the Velasco regime (1968–1975) largely "peasantized" the highlands of Peru (see, e.g., Mayer 1994), that is, made this the predominant idiom for discussing rural dwellers; the regime replaced an ethnic designation, "indigenous communities" (comunidades indígenas), with a socioeconomic one, "peasant communities" (comunidades campesinas). See Van Cott 1994, Brysk 1994, and Urban and Sherzer 1991 for insightful discussion of the conflicting goals and ambivalent ties between ethnicity-based indigenous movements and peasant organizations, labor unions, and armed revolutionaries in Latin America.

2. In Sherbondy's words, "Ancient Andean peoples did not only possess practical knowledge concerning subterranean hydrology, developing techniques for using these subterranean waters, but also elaborated a cosmology based on this knowledge which was useful for expressing concepts about ethnicity and political units" (1982b, 24). This explains why the Inka nobility claimed the largest body of water in the Andes, Lake Titicaca, as the source of their imperial origins. See also Urton 1990; Salomon 1991; Bastien 1985.

3. Many anthropologists, following Kosok (1965) and Wittfogel (1957), have explored the role that irrigation played in the development of pre-Columbian social formations (see, e.g., Astete 1984; Espinoza Soriano 1971; Kus 1980; Mitchell 1981; Netherly 1984; Rostworowski 1977, 1978; Sherbondy 1982a, 1994; Spalding 1984; Zuidema 1986). Others have focused on the symbolic and ritual dimensions of water (Arguedas 1964; Bastien 1985; Isbell 1974; Ossio 1976; Osterling and Llanos 1981; Paerregaard 1994; Sherbondy 1982b, 1986, 1994; Tello and Miranda 1923; Urton 1981; Valderrama and Escalante 1988). Still others have studied the ecological, social, and political facets of contemporary irrigation (Bolin 1994; Boelens 1998; Bunker and Seligmann 1986; Seligmann and Bunker 1994; Denevan 1986; Echeandia 1981; Fock 1981; Fonseca 1983; Fonseca and Mayer 1979; Gelles 1996b; Gose 1994; Guillet 1985, 1987, 1992; Guillet and Mitchell 1994; Gutiérrez and Gerbrandy 1998; Hoogendam 1998; Lynch 1988, 1993; Mayer 1985; Mitchell 1981, 1994; Montoya et al. 1979; Oré 1998; Seligmann 1987; Treacy 1989, 1994a, 1994b; Winterhalder 1994; Zimmerer 1994). The twenty-seventh and twenty-eighth issues of the journal *Allpanchis* from 1986 feature articles on highland irrigation. Other recent publications on the subject include Altamirano 1992; Boelens and Dávila 1998; Gandarillas et al. 1994; Gose 1994; Huallpa 1992; Lynch 1993; Mitchell and Guillet 1994; Trawick 1994; Treacy 1994a; Sherbondy 1994.

4. See Valeri 1991, Lansing 1991, and Pfaffenberger 1988 for discussions of Marx's concept of "humanized nature."

5. Critiquing Wittfogel's portrait of the Balinese state as an example of hydraulic bureaucracies "run by Asiatic Despots" pursuing "Total Power," Geertz demonstrates how a "symbology of power" and an "administratively decentralized and morally coercive body of regulations" (1980, 77) conditioned precolonial Balinese political formations and the management of their irrigation systems. Geertz in turn has been critiqued for being inattentive to political economy (see, e.g., Roseberry 1989; Tambiah 1985).

6. Just as the state is not a single monolithic entity but made up of individuals and semiautonomous groups vying for resources and institutional survival (see, e.g., Bunker 1985; Orlove et al. 1989; Herzfeld 1992), so too the state's policies and organizational models will be refigured at the local level.

7. Unmasking the "myths" that underlie the "bureaucratic tradition," Lynch (1993) denaturalizes the male biases that make women invisible in irrigation bureaucracies, development agencies, and the fields. For critical studies of natural resource management and development, see, among many others, Altieri 1987; Anderson 1996; Apffel-Marglin 1998; Cronon 1983; Escobar 1995; Fortmann 1989; Mabry 1996; McCay and Acheson 1990; Norgaard 1994; Peluso 1992.

8. Lansing's written work and his film, *The Computer and the Goddess* (1989), keenly illustrate how the productive significance of the ritual water temple system in Bali lay "in the ability to synchronize the productive activities of large numbers of farmers" (1991, 123). This was thoroughly disrupted when the modernizing Balinese state's bureaucracies took control of water. The degree to which irrigation bureaucracies help or hinder

local water management is debated (see, e.g., Hunt 1976; Landau 1990; Melville 1994; Viqueira and Torre 1994; Mabry and Cleveland 1996).

9. The strong cultural and geographic divide between the coast and highlands in Peru is unique among the Andean nations in its intensity, and it is reflected in language, music, dance, dress, food, education, and many other cultural domains. See, e.g., Lombardi 1988; Gelles and Martínez 1993; Mannheim 1991; Albó 1973; Ackerman 1991; Gelles 1996a; Cohen 1979; Martínez 1994; Weismantel 1988; Turino 1991; Orlove 1991; Mendoza-Walker 1993; Van Den Berghe and Primov 1977; Zorn 1987; Femenias 1997. For some of the late colonial and republican historical and political processes that condition this divide, see, among others, Davies 1974; Mallon 1995; Flores Galindo 1987a, 1987b; Walker 1992; Manrique 1988; Méndez 1991; Wolf 1982; Thurner 1997. Peru has been compared to South Africa in terms of the "differential incorporation" (Smith 1982) of its indigenous Andean majority.

10. As Abercrombie says, "Centuries of colonial domination (and resistance to it) have produced many hundreds of small, community sized 'ethnic groups,' centered on 'county seats,' towns in which pre-Columbian populations were forced to settle. . . . [They] generally define themselves as members of a local group, coterminous with town-territory, and beyond it, as citizens of the province and department defined by the nation-state to which they also pertain" (1991, 95, 96). Many of the communities found throughout the highlands today were established in the late fifteenth century as nucleated settlements (reducciónes) for the purposes of tribute assessment, social control, and religious indoctrination. Since that time there has been a seesawing back and forth between "emancipating," that is, severing indigenous populations from their communal identities and collective forms of organization, and a system that recognizes and affords legal protection to communities.

   In the early Republican period, progressive thought in Latin America held that "Indians" should be incorporated as citizens into the country and that intermediary forms of association—such as ethnic groups, communal identities—should be done away with. By the same token, communal ownership and organization were seen as obstacles to progress. This mindset led to reforms, which often took away the only safeguards peasants had against predatory haciendas, mines, and so on. In the 1920s, under the Leguia government, several hundred communities gained the title to their lands and became incorporated as legally recognized "indigenous communities" (comunidades indígenas). This number steadily increased through the century, receiving an even larger impulse in 1969, through the massive land reforms and reorganization of rural life by the Military Radicals; it was at this time that they were renamed "peasant communities" (comunidades campesinas). See, e.g., Allen 1988; Long and Roberts 1978; Molinié-Fioravanti 1986; Ossio 1992a, 1992b; Remy 1994. The peasant communities in Peru are similar in many respects to the "comunas" of Ecuador (see Selverston 1994) and the "resguardos" of Colombia (see Rappaport 1994).

11. In the Andean nations of Ecuador and Bolivia, indigenous peoples have made significant political gains (see, e.g., Albó 1994; Selverston 1994). While we must not exaggerate these gains—their resources, leaders, and organizations are still very much under attack—the way that activists have organized along ethnic-based lines in these other Andean nations is virtually inconceivable in Peru, where indigenous organizations have only recently begun to have some impact on national politics (see, e.g., Remy 1994).

12. All ethnographies, and the presentation of self within them, are partial accounts, selectively dealing with certain issues and excluding others. The "arrival trope," through which the ethnographer demonstrates how she or he establishes the necessary "rapport" and "complicity" to carry out research, is one of the rhetorical devices used to establish ethnographic authority. My narrative is no exception. Yet, it also gives the reader a sense of the conditions under which I conducted research and introduces important dimensions of community life and water politics that I develop in later chapters. A more complete account would also include my friends and activities in Arequipa and Lima, a bout with hepatitis, massive hangovers induced by ritual drinking, and the slow and sometimes frustrating process of being socialized into Cabaneño lifeways. For discussion of ethnography as a form of writing see, e.g., Pratt 1986; Rosaldo 1986, 1989; Marcus 1997; Clifford and Marcus 1986; Marcus and Fisher 1986; Kondo 1990.

13. By 1998, this number had quadrupled. The Washington-based Cabaneño community is the culmination of a larger process. By the 1930s, there were colonies of Cabaneños in Arequipa and Lima, and during the 1940s a migrant association called the Center for Cabanaconde's Progress was established in these cities. The Cabaneño diaspora gained a foothold in the United States in the early 1970s. In the mid-1980s the Cabanaconde City Association, one of the only officially recognized Peruvian migrant associations in the Washington, D.C., area, was established. The Cabaneños in Washington actively participate in their home community (see Gelles and Martínez 1993), as do migrants in many other transnational communities (see, e.g., Altamirano 1984, 1990; Palerm 1994; Kearney 1996; Walker 1988; Vélez-Ibáñez 1996),

14. Tinkay and q'apa offerings are made in most parts of the Andes today. See, e.g., Candler 1993; Valderrama and Escalante 1976, 1977; Valderrama et al. 1996; Allen 1988; Gose 1994; Bastien 1978; Paerregaard 1989. Q'apa also goes by the name "despacho" in other regions; q'apa means "to reek well" or "to stink pleasantly" and it is thought that the deities smell and enjoy the sweet and pungent odor of the burning kunuka plant and llama fat. Tinkay libations are often accompanied by the invocation, "Santa Tierra, Pachamama," or by flicking it in the direction of a mountain, and invoking the mountain's name. For related concepts, see, among others, Gelles and Martínez 1996, 161; Allen 1988, 262; Harrison 1989, 94; Treacy 1989, 266; Bastien 1978.

15. Once people realized that we were there to stay for a while, rumors flowed; these sometimes got back to us through our growing network of friends. "Students, sure! They're CIA," was one of these. Others said we were spies of the revolutionary Shining Path. Others versions had it that we were poor indigents who had come to bum corn off the locals, that we were evangelists, or that we had come for economic profit, as had most misti outsiders. When we left a year and a half later, the impressions people had of us had changed considerably. For more on this fieldwork experience, see Gelles 1990.

16. See, e.g., Rudolph 1992. To give just one indicator of the disintegration of the Peruvian economy, the cumulative inflation between 1985 and 1990 was over 2 million percent. A geometric rise in gasoline and food prices throughout the country in 1988 hit Cabanaconde especially hard; seeing their savings deteriorate in value, many peasants were quick to buy appliances that would not devalue, while others fell back on barter relations. Although Cabanaconde is a relatively prosperous and affluent community, it has the same high rate of infant mortality that characterizes other Andean regions. In Peru, half of all deaths are children under five years of age (Roddick 1988, 167).

17. Shining Path entered communities and a mine just a few valleys over from Cabanaconde, and a Shining Path incursion or the deployment of trigger-happy military police in Cabanaconde was always a possibility. But Shining Path kept a low profile in the Colca Valley itself during our stay, and life in town continued as if the war were being fought in another country. For the violence and social dislocations generated by this war, see, e.g., Lombardi 1988; Starn 1991; Kirk 1992, 1997; Mitchell 1991; Starn et al. 1995; Bourque and Warren 1989; Mayer 1991; Stern 1998.

18. Sabankaya became active in early 1987 but posed no threat to the Huataq pastures or surrounding communities until June 1990, when the volcano began to spew lava, poisonous gases, and ash. The latter killed off pastures and livestock in the area, and there has also been a great deal of seismic activity in the region; at one point the communities of Maca and Achoma were evacuated.

19. These included teaching in the high school, as well as helping to establish a library and a cultural association (Asociación Cultural Magisterial Claudio Tinta Feria) that sponsored community events. I believe that anthropologists have an obligation to reciprocate the individuals, communities, and countries that they study. At the communal level, I also distributed copies of a short history, "Los Hijos de Hualca-Hualca: Historia de Cabanaconde," that I wrote for the Cabaneños (Gelles 1988). At an individual level, I reciprocated the information and knowledge provided by my friends and informants by giving them family photographs that I had taken, as well as giving them other goods and services. And by publishing my research findings in Spanish and giving talks to colleagues at universities and nongovernmental organizations in Peru and the Andean nations, I reciprocate at the national level. Return visits and the fact that Cabanaconde is a transnational community allow me to stay in touch with the community and its changes.

20. See also Gelles and Martínez 1993. One of the Aguilar children is now a truck driver in the United States; another is a cosmetologist. Some of the Mamani children are pursuing college educations, and others work by installing air conditioning and by baby-sitting. The Aguilars and Mamanis maintain close contact with kin back home, get news from the community on a regular basis, and travel back regularly. From a phone call to Washington, I can find out everything from recent deaths and new gossip to the particular pastures where Toribio's cattle are presently feeding. And now, I can call the community directly—two phones were installed in Cabanaconde in 1998.

ONE. CABANACONDE

1. Although all of these communities share much of the same regional culture, the Cabaneños are viewed as a distinct people within the valley. In addition to differences in dress, ritual, and even language, fundamental differences in production between the upper and lower valley are also associated with this ethnic differentiation. The history of the area is well documented (see, e.g., Pease 1977; Cock 1978; Cook 1982; Denevan 1986, 1987, 1988; Málaga 1987; Galdos 1985; Tord 1983; Benavides 1983, 1987, 1988a, 1988b; de la Vera Cruz 1987; Manrique 1985; Neira 1961). So, too, ethnographic works by David Guillet (1987, 1992), Enrique Delgado (1988), Karsten Paerregaard (1997), Blenda Femenias (1991, 1997), Bradley Stoner (1989), Herman Sven (1986), Ricardo Valderrama and Carmen Escalante (1988) and by the late John Treacy (1989, 1994a) have also produced a wealth of information about the valley. But most studies have focused exclusively on communities that were formerly part of the Collaguas polity and occupy the upper Colca Valley. Cabanaconde, the largest and most densely settled community in the Colca Valley (see Bridges 1991, 28), has been the subject of few studies in addition to my own; see de la Vera Cruz 1987; Ismodes and Salinas 1985; Abril 1979. See Gelles 1990 for more detail on the history and on different social domains discussed in this chapter.
2. According to local inhabitants and archeological evidence (de la Vera Cruz 1987), the places known today as Umahuasi, Tukuwasi, Huchuy Qallimarca, and Antesana were some of the important settlements of the Cavanas. The early Spanish accounts refer to these people as Cahuana, Caguana, or Cavana. Cabanaconde probably comes from the adaptation to Spanish of the words *qawana* (Quechua for "lookout" or "vantage point") and *kunti*, the latter from *kuntisuyo*, one of the four quarters of the Inka empire. This change from *kunti* to *conde* is also found in the way the Spaniards changed the name of *kuntisuyu* to *Condesuyo*.
3. This polity, like many others in the Andes, was formed during the process of state expansion and contraction in pre-Inka times (see Schreiber 1992). The Cavana were a classic example of the "archipelago" formation (Murra 1975), with productive colonies in the Majes Valley, in what are the present-day communities of Pinchullo, Huambo, Lluta, Lluclla, Guacan, Tajarqui, and Pitay, which are in the valleys of Siguas, Yura, Tiabaya, and even in La Chimba of Arequipa (Galdos 1985, 138, 147).
4. The studies of Johan Reinhard, one of the two men who found the Ice Maiden, have gone far in contextualizing this sacrifice and in explaining a vast array of symbols, shrines, and rituals found over thousands of miles of territory, and hundreds of years of history. He has shed light on the Nazca lines (Reinhard 1986) and has shown how the ceremonial centers of Chavin and Tiahuanaco "were selected because of their positions relative to the most sacred mountains in each region" (Reinhard 1985, 395). The Inka ascended, consecrated, and symbolically appropriated many mountains over the 17,000–foot mark, reaching heights in the fifteenth century that were not again reached until the second half of this century (see Reinhard 1998).
5. The importance of the Cavana polity is also evidenced by the fact that Juan de la Torre, one of the original Conquistadores and the mayor of the city of Arequipa, was granted one of the Cavana encomiendas (Barriga 1955, 1). See Gelles (1990, 88–90, 123–124) for the encomiendas of the early colonial period.
6. For example, in 1549, a thirty-three-year-old Spanish woman, Ginessa Guillen, was accused of having "burned two caciques . . . to get gold out of them." A witness once saw her hang an "Indian" by his feet and torture him to death with smoke and peppers, another kuraka was starved to death, and yet another committed suicide (Barriga 1955,

278, 279). The Cavana polity suffered greatly in the civil wars between Spaniards after the conquest. Gonzalo Pizarro, who led a rebellion against the Crown, possessed an encomienda in the upper Collagua part of the Colca Valley. Juan de Arbes, one of the original encomenderos of Cavana, was killed in this war.

7. The encomendero of anansaya forced his subjects to sell lands to him in that year (ADA 1562). However, the loss of outlying territory was not completed until the late eighteenth century, following general trends in Andean history outlined by Murra (1982). The lords of Cavana eventually lost control over lands in places such as Pitay, Tiabaya, Lluta, and Siguas, which had belonged to them since time immemorial.

8. In 1813, there were 359 "Spaniards," 2,311 "Indians," and two "Blacks" in both Cabanaconde anansaya and urinsaya (Málaga et al. 1987, 170). The large presence of Spaniards in Cabanaconde is probably due to its high maize and grain production, access to a wider range of production zones, and the presence of small mines in the lower reaches of the community. It is possible that many of the Spaniards who worked in the mines of Caylloma preferred to keep their families in Cabanaconde because of its lower elevation and more benign climate. As the great grandson of the tribute collector of Cabanaconde anansaya told me, "this was always a center of operations for the Spaniards."

9. These rituals and religious observations, key to the social life of Cabanaconde, also affect the rhythms of transnational migration. The Virgin of Carmen patron saint fiesta is the key ritual event of the year in Cabanaconde, and the population doubles as migrants return from Arequipa, Lima, and Washington, D.C. (Gelles and Martínez 1993).

10. We find the population rising from 1,796 inhabitants in 1876, to 2,960 in 1940, to 3,421 in 1981 (Cook 1982, 41, 84; Denevan 1987, 17). Ministry of Agriculture officials estimated that there were eight hundred families and a total population of 4,000 in 1987 (Ministry of Agriculture 1987). A report by the resident doctor in 1988 found a population of 3,985. See Gelles (1990, 92, 124) for more on the demography of Cabanaconde.

11. However, most of the men over forty have had only grade school education, and some 59 percent of the individuals listed on the Peasant Community's Members List never finished grade school. Only 18 percent of the community members finished high school, and 5 percent of these continued their studies at the university level. Of these twenty-one individuals at the university level, only three were women.

12. According to many Cabaneños, political parties first appeared in the late 1970s and greatly changed the political dynamics of the community. Different parties often control particular political institutions, thus making it difficult for the community to create a unified policy. The governor is appointed by the prefect of the province and is partisan to the party in power. Municipal council and Peasant Community officials, on the other hand, are elected by the townspeople. In the late 1980s, the municipal council and governor's office were controlled by APRA (Alianza Popular Revolucionaria Americana), the political party then in power in Peru, whereas the Peasant Community was affiliated with United Left, an opposition party. The community is an arena of conflict, where wealthy and powerful individuals exploit communal institutions for their benefit and profit, and poorer peasants seek protection and subsistence in these same institutions (see, e.g., Long and Roberts 1978; Mallon 1983; Erasmus 1977; Alberti and Mayer 1974).

13. The women enrolled in the Members List (*Padrón Comunal*) are either single mothers, "daughters of the community" who have married outsiders, women whose husbands have migrated and are involved in wage labor, others whose husbands have left them and who have children in their charge, or women who are simply trying to gain access to the rights that community members enjoy, such as eligibility for new lands being recovered. The Members List includes some 1,956 people, including members, spouses, and children in their charge. If we accept the 1981 population figure of 3,421, over one-third of the population is not enrolled as community members. See Gelles (1990) for more detail on how this list illuminates the composition of the community.

14. Ninety-one percent of the people on the Members List declared agriculture as their "primary activity," and 3 percent listed cattle; 77 percent of people listed cattle as their secondary activity, and 4 percent, agriculture.

15. In a list drawn up by the Ministry of Agriculture, there were some thirty-seven stores

that carried rice, noodles, sugar, and condensed milk. Most stores also sell soft drinks, bread, trago, aspirin, and an assortment of other goods. These stores are generally run out of a small room of one's home and are often open only during the early morning and the evening hours.

16. One of these hotels has been around for over twenty years and is oriented to travelers from the local communities (e.g., Tapay, Choco, Llanca), people doing business in town, and people who come for the fiestas or during the harvest season. The other hotel has been accommodating the backpacking tourists who increasingly began to visit the valley in the mid-eighties. The doctor and a locally trained nurse were the only nontraditional health specialists available for Cabanaconde and the surrounding towns, and they served an estimated population of 8,500 people (Cuba 1988).

17. Once, when I greeted a friend with "Hello, brother" ("Hola, hermano"), I was told it was an insult. My friend was referring to the fact that siblings are often pitted against each other over family resources. At the opposite extreme is the term *quri layllasi*, which refers to the relationship between the two sets of parents of a married couple as being "golden" (see also Webster 1977; Ossio 1980; Bolton and Mayer 1977). See Gelles 1990 for more information on kinship, marriage rituals, and godparenthood in Cabanaconde.

18. The first day the "loved ones" (munaqkuna) of each spouse go to the house of the groom's parents; on the second, the festivities take place in the house of the bride's family; and on the last day, in the house of the newlyweds. The munaqkuna are friends, family, and admirers. One's entire group of loved ones (entero munaqkuna) is manifest at key events in one's life: at marriage, at the passing of a cargo, and at wakes.

19. By "ideology" I refer to the political nature of cultural frameworks and dominant ideas, ideas that are are largely determined by those who exercise control over society. As Scheper-Hughes (1992, 171) explains, "Specific forms of consciousness may be called 'ideological' whenever they are invoked to sustain, legitimate, or stabilize particular institutions or social practices." For insightful discussions of ideology and hegemony, and the different ways these get instituted, see Bourgois 1995; Kertzer 1988; Scott 1985; J. W. Scott 1988; Scheper-Hughes 1992; Comoroff and Comoroff 1992.

While in this book I generally use the terms *ideology* and *hegemony* to discuss the ways in which different states exercise power over Cabanaconde and its irrigation system, I believe that local gender constructs constitute an ideology that generally benefit men more than women. For example, in the aphrutinkay marriage ritual, there is symbolism and a ritual that again exalts the role and the position of the male. Here, the newlywed husband receives money and the wife receives primarily maize, as well as pots, pans, and chickens. The woman's gifts are placed on the ground; the man's are placed on a table. This symbolism also indexes the greater contact that males have with the wage-paying urban and rural labor markets (see, e.g., de la Cadena 1991; Collins 1986; Weismantel 1988). For an overview of changing gender ideologies during the Inka and colonial periods, see Silverblatt 1987. For descriptions of Andean women and the patriarchal nature of Andean society for the modern period, see, among others, Andreas 1985; Babb 1989; Belote and Belote 1988; Bourque and Warren 1981; Chungara de Barrios and Viezzer 1979; de la Cadena 1991; Femenias 1991, 1997; Harrison 1989; Harvey 1994; Kirk 1992; Weismantel 1988; Lynch 1991; Seligmann 1989; Skar 1981; Sikkink 1994; Sindicato de Trabajadoras del Hogar 1982; Wasserstrom 1985; Valderrama and Escalante 1996; Weismantel 1988.

20. Special licenses are granted to take such funeral processions around the plaza instead of just up the main street. The authorities attend important funerals and the procession that accompanies these can swell up to more than a hundred people. In contrast, the death of a poor peasant receives scant notice.

21. For example, the term *misti* does not connote a well-defined group of powerful individuals within Cabanaconde as it does in the upper valley (Valderrama and Escalante 1988; Femenias 1997). See Gelles 1990 for more on misti and other ethnic categories in Cabanaconde. See Gose 1994 for an insightful study of class and ethnic identity in another highland region.

22. The words *Callallino* or *Yaurino* (a person from the herding communities of Callalli and Yauri), as well as *llamero* (llama herder), are used as insults between the people of Cabanaconde. Llama herders from Cabanaconde are also seen as less civilized.

23. Maize is valued for its nutritious and ritual value, as well as for making corn beer. More-

over, the Cabaneños have alpaca and llamas; the herders do not, however, cultivate maize. This in part explains why the Cabaneños are in a position to hire the herders as migrant laborers (see Gelles 1992).

24. The Peruvian system of stratification racializes class and ethnicity, and it is quite fluid (Bourricaud 1975). As Fuenzalida (1971, 20) puts it, "The higher one is on the social ladder, the whiter one appears; the lower one is, the darker." As an individual moves from rural to urban areas or ascends socially, different racial classifications will be applied. Unfortunately, such a system mandates that indigenous persons must sacrifice their cultural identity to gain social mobility.

25. Ironically, a dynamic similar to the one that takes place between the Cabaneños and the herders takes place between herders that live in villages or communities such as Callalli and those who live in the surrounding herders hamlets. Yet the latter in turn view the people of the neighboring Yauri region as even more savage! As Taussig (1987) has found elsewhere, savagery is also associated with a greater capacity for healing and spiritualism.

TWO. IRRIGATION AND LAND RECOVERY

1. Disease, civil war, exploitation, and the opening of the mines of Caylloma in 1627 led to a tremendous demographic loss in Cabanaconde, reaching an extreme in the late seventeenth century. From the 1570s until the 1680s, the tributary population declined from 1,345 to 256 (Cook 1982, 17, 25). For discussions of terraces in the Colca Valley, see, among others, Denevan 1986; Guillet 1987; Treacy 1994a.

2. My usage of the term *political ecology* borrows from those who view political ecology as combining the concerns of ecology and political economy (e.g., Blakie and Brookfield 1987; Cruz Torres 1992; Schmink and Wood 1992; Sheridan 1988, 1996; Peluso 1992), but differs in its emphasis on the way that politics and natural resources are culturally modeled (see also Gelles 1993, 1996b).

3. This wildlife includes puma, fox, deer, ducks, flamingos, condors, vicuña, viscacha, opossum, and trout. In addition to the animals and plants described in this chapter, families raise pigs, chickens, and guinea pigs for consumption. The Cabaneños have a detailed and wide-ranging knowledge of the wild herbs of the area, and many have house gardens and plants used for a variety of medicinal and culinary purposes.

4. These areas of terraced fields are approximately three miles in length with varying widths and are situated on a gentler slope than many of the upper-valley villages, allowing a much higher incidence of "broadfield" terraces (Denevan 1986). Because of the rich volcanic soils and warm microclimate, land in Cabanaconde is more valuable than that of many neighboring communities. This fertile land accounts in part for the relative prosperity of Cabanaconde.

5. There are a lot of sharecropping and rental arrangements, as well as constant maneuvering to gain access to more land. According to the land census that correlates with the 1980 water users list, 865 people owned 3,820 parcels of land. In 1987, the Ministry of Agriculture found that 27 percent of the population were smallholders and possessed between one-third to two-thirds of a hectare, 70 percent possessed between two-thirds to one hectare, and 3 percent possessed between one and one and one-half hectares (Ministry of Agriculture 1987). This data is unreliable, but it points to a general trend.

6. Cabanaconde's territory encompasses the "natural regions" of Yunga, Quechua, Suni, and Puna, also known as Jallca (see Pulgar Vidal 1987). The Cabaneños exploit a greater range of "ecological floors" (see Brush 1977; Murra 1975) than do upper-valley communities (see Gelles 1990, 97–98, 125–126, for more detail on the products and social arrangements of the orchards).

7. In the high pastures there are many herd steads (estancias) where herders live year round. According to the 1980 statistics of the National Planning Institute, Cabanaconde and Pinchullo together had eight hundred bovine cattle, 5,800 sheep, 2,250 llamas, 4,600 alpacas, and sixty goats (Denevan 1987, 20).

8. Frequent trips up the mountainside to the pastures to check on one's animals are the counterpart to the steep descent into the valley to check on one's orchard. People know the habits of their animals, such as which small lakes or water holes they tend to frequent. Villagers keep an eye on one another's animals, but there is nevertheless a lot of

cattle rustling. Many people cultivate alfalfa and keep their animals in corrals in town to avoid this. Community members, as well as those from neighboring and even distant communities, were apprehended for rustling cattle during my stay in the community. The most notorious case involved several men from the Chumbivilcas area, which is known for its cattle-rustling culture (Aguirre and Walker 1990; Poole 1987; Valderrama and Escalante 1992). The community has not formed vigilante groups to patrol for rustlers as do communities in other parts of the Andes (see, e.g., Starn 1992). According to the 1988 head count by the communal authorities, there were ten estancias with a total of 1,924 alpacas and llamas, 650 sheep, and sixty-four goats divided among 141 owners. It is difficult to get precise figures concerning cattle holdings (see Gelles 1990, 98–100, 126–127, for more detail on the social arrangements surrounding cattle and the high pastures). For the importance of cattle to Andean society, see, e.g., Martínez Escobar 1983; Flores Ochoa 1977, 1985.

9. Although heavy rainfall is important for the proper maturation of maize, precipitation also increases the snowpack on Hualca-Hualca and the volume of snowmelt. The changing flow of the river during the year (and during the course of the day as more snow melts) is indicated by the number of irrigation canals in use at any one moment, from one to four. Irrigation extends the growing season, permitting sowing four months before the rainy season and ensuring the plants' maturation before frost sets in, which is usually in May or June. This allows farmers to raise the upper limits of certain crops, such as maize (Mitchell 1981; Mayer 1985). The river water from Mount Hualca-Hualca travels over ten miles and more than 6,000 vertical feet to the fields below. In fact, the Hualca-Hualca River could be considered a stream during most of the year. In the rainy season, however, its volume can reach over 1,500 liters per second during periods of intense precipitation (Abril Benavides 1979, 14). Because it is considered a river by the Cabaneños and maps of the region, I retain the word *river*. In rain-abundant years, a few farmers try to dry-farm additional fields (usually fodder crops).

10. Reservoirs for storing water at night, which are used by most other Colca Valley communities, are not an important feature of Cabanaconde's irrigation system. A small spring, used mainly for the potable water of the community, also irrigates a few plots of land near its source and occasionally fills the one small reservoir in the community. It takes eight days' flow of spring water to fill the reservoir that is used for "extras" (additional water given to fields outside the regular irrigating schedule). Because reservoirs are not a regular or systematic feature of the irrigation system, reservoirs full of water (estancadas) are often a domain of manipulation and contention (see chapter 6). The absence of functioning reservoirs in Cabanaconde distinguishes it from many of the upper-valley communities such as Coporaque (Treacy 1988, 1989, 1994a), Lari (Guillet 1987), and Yanque (Valderrama and Escalante 1988), as well as nearby Tapay (Paerregaard 1994).

11. There is some flexibility in that the individual has complete power over which crop he or she will plant, and can decide to plant on the second or even third round of irrigation water. Fenced lands, small in number, may be harvested when their owners see fit. Although the community restrains the agricultural activities of the individual to a large degree in Cabanaconde, this is less so than in other areas, such as some communities in Huarochirí, which determine which crops will be planted, and which sectors will be cultivated (Gelles 1984b, 1986a). Sectoral fallowing systems, which highly constrain individual behavior, have been discussed at considerable length in the literature (e.g., Camino 1980; Godoy 1984; Orlove and Godoy 1986). There is no sectoral fallowing system in Cabanaconde. Rich volcanic soils and the high mineral content of the water from the Hualca-Hualca River permit an intensive use of land. In most fields, maize is cultivated year after year.

12. Water is obtained from small springs that emerge from the sides of the steep cliffs of the Colca Canyon, close to the base of the canyon. Because the orchards are in a warmer climate, irrigation has to take place every ten to fifteen days (as opposed to every forty or fifty days for the upper fields).

13. Large, communally sponsored, ritualized canal cleanings in other highland communities are known as the "Water Fiesta" or "Canal Scraping" (Fiesta de Agua or *champería* in Spanish, *yarqá aspíy* in Quechua). In Cabanaconde, as seen here, irrigation water is perceived as feminine, whereas in many other Andean communities, irrigation water is

conceptualized as a male force (see, e.g., Arguedas 1985; Isbell 1974; Ossio 1976; Gelles 1986a; Valderrama and Escalante 1988).

14. The Huataq Canal appears to have been built by the Inkas. In 1916, the people of Cabanaconde were trying to recover lands by rebuilding the Huataq Canal; the municipality was providing the workers with sugar, trago, and coca (BMC). Work continued in October and December of 1919, and again in 1920 and 1921. Engineers inspected Huataq in 1926 and 1932 (BMC). The name *Huataq* (wataq), which means "tied down" in Quechua, suggests the difficulty the community has had with this water source.

15. The new saint was the Virgin of Chapi. On May 4, 1981, they moved the image of this virgin from the camp at Castropampa to Antesana, a hill above town. Today this saint has a dedicated following among misti schoolteachers and some community members.

16. On October 18, 1977, the Irrigators Commission complained that the Majes Consortium was "using water of Cabanaconde without authorization, and there is a considerable diminution in the volume of water" (BIC). Canals were also severely damaged, and subterranean tunnels built by the Majes Project interfered with underground sources of water, causing several springs to dry up.

17. Official sources assert that, for 1979 and 1980, the cultivated area was 10 percent below the average for the period from 1975 to 1981, and 25 percent smaller than the most productive of these years (see Denevan 1987, 17). Many Cabaneños assured me that it was much worse.

18. In 1978, for example, the Majes Consortium pledged to send an engineer and help Cabanaconde obtain more water from the Hualca-Hualca River. Two years later they repeated their promise, stating that machines were available for improving the waters of Hualca-Hualca. They also promised assistance to recover the Huataq Canal, as well as water from the Majes Canal "for three thousand hectares in Cabanaconde and Huambo." In 1979, 1980, and 1981, the consortium again promised to help recover 1,000 hectares of cultivable lands in Cabanaconde—it never carried through with its promises.

19. There were failed communal attempts to recover land in 1945, 1948, and 1953, but the titles to these newly recovered lands have been legally secured. See chapter 5 for the early history of land recovery. In the case of Auquilote, despite food aid, tools, and other support by a German development agency (Cooperación Peruana Alemana de Seguridad Alimentaria [COPASA]), attendance at faena work parties was about 50 percent. This was largely because the different lots varied in quality, which meant different incentives, levels of enthusiasm, and work commitment.

20. This money was acquired largely through government funds distributed to peasant communities throughout the highlands in 1987 (the "Rimanakuy" program) and through communal funds generated from such things as grazing taxes.

21. Six hundred liters per second is the minimum. During the rainy season, this volume is much greater and can reach 1,120 liters per second (Estudio de Huataq 1985).

22. By February 1990, several hundred more hectares of land in the areas of Joyas, Huanque, Valve 18, and elsewhere had been allotted. This project, while initiated by the community, has received the support of COPASA, a nongovernmental organization that helped to subsidize canal construction to the new fields. The recovery of abandoned terraced fields and other indigenous technologies for cultivation, such as raised fields (see, e.g., Denevan 1987; Portocarreo 1986; De la Torre and Burga 1986; Smith 1989; Malpass 1986; Trawick 1994; Treacy 1989, 1994a; Erickson 1988; Erickson and Candler 1989), is increasingly being taken seriously by scholars and nongovernmental organizations. Masson (1987, 191) estimates that there are a million hectares of terraced fields in the Peruvian highlands and that only 25 percent of these are currently in use (see also Masson 1982). Cabanaconde, with its recovery of almost a thousand hectares of abandoned terraces, shows the potential that land recovery has in the highlands; this, of course, depends on tapping greater supplies of water. In 1994, the amount of water that had been allotted from the Majes Canal to the different agricultural sectors was as follows: Main fields (*campiña agricola*) receive 150 liters per second; Pirachapampa, Auqui, and Ukru-Ukru receive 115 liters per second; Villa del Colca (Valve 18) receives 155 liters per second; and Ccalhuani receives fifteen liters per second (see also COPASA 1997; Gelles 1994).

23. Water mayors are also called *alcaldes de agua*, *alcaldes de campo*, as well as *regidores* or

repartidores de agua. There are four rounds of water, each of which is handled by two water mayors. The four rounds are tied to the following agricultural activities: preparation of the land (*barbecho*); sowing (solay); weeding and reinforcing the stalks (*lampeo* or *qallqay*); and a second reinforcing and weeding known as *hallmayu.* The actual appointment of the water mayors occurs in April, well before the first round of water begins at the end of May. The snake-headed staffs of authority used by the water mayors are passed down through different families. For a wonderful account of the chores, hazards, and rewards associated with an irrigation cargo in New Mexico, see Crawford 1988.

THREE. WATER RITUAL

1. This description of a yakutinkay is based on my field notes, October 1987.
2. During my stay in the years 1987–1988, as many as three of these theaters (each seating twenty-five to seventy-five people) would be packed several nights a week. Young people, some of whom had never been to Arequipa, were now exposed to Bruce Lee, Arnold Schwarzenegger, and a wide assortment of kung fu movies. The movies appeared to have the greatest impact on the youth of the community, as most adults were fairly oblivious to the Hollywood imports. Several people branded these movies as destructive of communal values and even pornographic. At that time, the main street and the plaza were the only places with electricity and streetlights and were the center of the town's "modernity." In 1993, the town installed a parabolic antenna and now receives television broadcasts (albeit one station at a time); several private homes now have video cassette recorders.
3. Cabanaconde was suddenly on the front page of the *San Francisco Chronicle* and other major newspapers. Rather than serving to educate the public about the complexities of the Inka empire or contemporary Andean society, the Ice Maiden was to be sacrificed on many other altars. Peruvian President Alberto Fujimori sacrificed her on the altar of Peruvian nationalism, declaring in an address to the National Geographic Society that "Juanita has awoken to find her country united in a common purpose." President Clinton sacrificed her on the altar of bad taste, declaring, "If I was a single man I would ask that mummy out. . . . I am telling ya, that's the best-looking mummy I've ever seen." *National Geographic* sacrificed her to the West's insatiable desire for exotica from the "mysterious" third world. And no less a source than the *National Enquirer* got involved, expressing concern that the perfectly preserved ovaries of the Ice Maiden might be used to create a test-tube baby. "Imagine growing up knowing your mother was a 500 year old Inca girl. There is no good reason to go ahead with this procedure," a "reliable" source told the magazine.
4. The sides are embroidered as well and have little pouches used to store coca seeds, which are used only in ritual. Coca bags are used often to honor the earth and Hualca-Hualca, and to protect oneself from these and other potentially harmful spirits. Istas can also be used to secure enchanted objects (*encantos*) and treasures (*tapados*), which the mountains will sometimes give forth.
5. There are also other healing specialists, such as bone doctors (*hueseros*), midwives (*parteros*), and the nurse and doctor of the medical outpost.
6. The verb *karpay* means "to instruct initiates in spiritism, to give them lessons and learning" (Lira 1982). Karpayuq acquire their skill to communicate with the mountain deities by being struck by lightning, usually three times. The karpayuq, who almost always have come from other towns, are sometimes "charlatans" who bilk people out of money. But even those who had been bilked continue their faith in the existence of true karpayuq.
7. This is especially the case for distant pastures, such as Huataq, which Toribio compared to a wild deer, not yet domesticated. When he first started going there in 1966, few people used Huataq and few q'apas had been made. As he put it, "The earth used to move. It's become sturdier since people started to arrive. When I first started coming, I wouldn't even spend the night. I'd ride eight hours, check the cattle, and then about-face." See Allen (1988, 37–67) for a rich discussion of Earth Mother and her distinct manifestations. For an insider's view, see Gregorio Condori's narrative (Valderrama and Escalante 1996).
8. The descriptions of cabildos by paqus are far more detailed and explicit than that of

most Cabaneños, as well as less circumscribed to the mountains immediately surrounding Cabanaconde. One particular paqu views these powerful mountains as a series of concentric circles, which broaden out from the community. According to the description of one paqu, the principal cabildos that follow Hualca-Hualca in the hierarchy are Sabankaya (male), Waynillo (male volcano currently spewing smoke), Ampato (male), Warangande (male, near Chivay), Qotallaysi (male), Escirbano (male), Seprigina (female), Coripuna (female), Qoranqima (female), and Kuyaq (male). Surrounding the town of Cabanaconde are four male cabildos, the cabildos of the town itself: Antesana, Taqayqima, Ichergate, and Umahuasi. Serving these principal cabildos are the next in command which the paqu (and others) referred to as "seconds in command" or "commission members" ("siguientes" or "comisarios"). He told me, "Just as the treasurer or secretary of a town council will have a commission under his office [people to whom he delegates], so too do the principal cabildos." These "helpers" or "seconds" include the mountains of Big and Little Sarajoto, Big and Little Qallimarka, and Auqui.

9. In these ritual contexts, the distinct family units become apparent. The marking of bovine cattle happens twice a year, in July during the patron saint's fiesta and in February during Candelaria. Before marking the calf, the q'apa or iranta is offered to the cabildos to ensure protection of the cattle; blood from marked or slaughtered animals is also proffered. For the economic and symbolic importance of cattle, see, e.g., Zorn 1986; Flores Ochoa 1977, 1985; Martínez Escobar 1983; Starn 1992; Orlove 1980; Valderrama and Escalante 1992.

10. In discussing the meaning of *qayqa,* the Cabaneños mention other concepts such as *qamaqiy* and *layqar.* Whereas *layqar* is to bewitch or do harm to someone, *qamaqiy* is to attract, hypnotize, and subjugate.

11. The association between mountains, lakes, and the ocean is most explicit in the rituals surrounding cattle, when seashells (*mullu*) are employed to make offerings to the lakes, mountains, or water holes. Again, there is a great diversity of belief. This is exemplified in the case of Nilo Abril Benavides, a Cabaneño who participates in the traditional model but who also wrote a B.A. thesis on the hydrology of the Hualca-Hualca River basin (Abril Benavides 1979).

12. Water is an extension of Hualca-Hualca Mountain, which is sometimes referred to as a *mamadera,* a breast pump or milk bottle, from which one derives nourishment. Hualca-Hualca gives water to her children as a mother gives milk to her young.

13. According to Zuidema, the condor is conceptually linked to mountain gods, the snake to Earth Mother (1967, 50). At springs, water emerges from the ground in a snakelike fashion and, according to Zuidema, is associated with volcanoes in other areas of the Andes (1967, 49). This is also illustrated by a story in Cabanaconde that tells that, during the attempts to rebuild the ancient canal of Huataq, which originates in a large spring, the workers killed a two-headed snake. The snake was moving along in front of the recently released water, and, when they killed it, the water stopped and turned back. Seligmann (1987, 393) has found a similar explanation for an abandoned Inka canal in the Cuzco region.

14. The vicuña fetus is an especially powerful offering. Not only are they more difficult to obtain than alpaca or llama fetuses, but they are "of the mountain," that is, not domesticated.

15. See, e.g., Abercrombie 1998; Dillon and Abercrombie 1988; Dover et al. 1992; Salomon and Urioste 1991; MacCormack 1991; Ortiz 1973; Langer 1993; Stern 1987; Flores Galindo 1987a.

FOUR. DUAL ORGANIZATION

1. The word *moiety* derives from the French word *moitié* which simply means "half." The idea of particular societies rigidly organizing key activities—marriage, exchange, warfare, ritual, village and polity structure—along dual lines has held a special fascination for anthropologists. Studies of Andean dualism has followed two basic lines of scholarship, structuralist and culturalist, as found in the work of Lévi-Strauss (1949, 1963, 1976) and Maybury-Lewis (1960, 1974, 1979, 1989), respectively. For a critical review of the scholarship on dual organization in Andean studies, see Gelles 1995.

2. The saya division, whether used as a spatial classification or to distinguish socially

constituted moieties, always refers to a division in halves. In Quechua, the lingua franca of the Inka empire and the language of millions today, the words *anaq* and *uray* mean "upper" and "lower," respectively. Thus, when the derivative terms *anan* and *urin* are added to *saya*, they came to mean "upper moiety" and "lower moiety."

3. These activities range from symbolic classification in the aesthetics of weaving (see, e.g., Cereceda 1987; Harris 1985) to the rigid spatial division of social groups and their natural resources; it is the latter instance of dualism with which I am primarily concerned here. These moieties are often known generically as *sayas* (Quechua) or *parcialidades* (Spanish), and sometimes by other names, such as *barrio* (Spanish). For social dualism in pre-Inka polities, see, e.g, Cavallaro 1991; Duvoils 1973; Fonseca 1976; Julien 1983; Murra 1968; Netherly 1984, 1990; Rostworowski 1990; Salomon and Urioste 1991. For the moieties found in the Inka empire see, e.g., Bauer 1992; Julien 1982, 1983; Murra 1975, 1980; Murra and Wachtel 1986; Ossio 1973, 1980; Pease 1981; Platt 1986; Rostworowski 1981, 1983; Rowe 1946, 1982; Salomon 1986; Sherbondy 1986; Silverblatt 1987; Urton 1984, 1990; Zuidema 1964, 1989, 1990b. For dualism in the Spanish colonial period see, among others, Benavides 1987, 1988b, 1991; Fuenzalida 1970; Julien 1991; Hopkins 1982; Castelli, Paredes, and Pease 1981. For contemporary social dualism see, among others, Allen 1988; Bastien 1978; Bouysse-Cassagne and Harris 1987; Earls 1971; Fock 1981; Harrison 1989; Isbell 1978; Fonseca 1976; Gelles 1986b, 1995; Harris 1985; Isbell 1978; Molinie-Fiorvanti 1986; Ossio 1976; Palomino 1971, 1984; Paerregaard 1992; Platt 1986, 1987; Sallnow 1987; H. Skar 1982; S. Skar 1981; Treacy 1994a; Urton 1981, 1984, 1990; Valderrama and Escalante 1988.

4. Tinku, in this context, has been interpreted by Platt (1987) to mean "symmetric justice" and "equilibrium wars." Tinku has the more general connotation of "encounter," the meeting of two forces and "a commingling of energy" (Harrison 1989, 30) which ideally gives way to balance, order, and equilibrium. The notion of encounter and alternation is also related to the notion of "the center," known as *chaupi* in Quechua and *taypi* in Aymara (Harris 1985, 9), which is conceived of as a bisecting line, the place where two sides meet. This is true whether the line is dividing a weaving, a town, a cultivated field, or dueling moieties.

5. The relationship of oppositional complementarity to community-based moieties is also expressed in the fact that these are sometimes referred to as male and female, both in Cabanaconde and elsewhere (e.g. Platt 1987, 69; Skar 1982, 236). Sallnow (1987) finds that the alternation between moieties orders relations between human populations and the raw forces of nature. Palomino similarly finds many instances in which the rivalry and alternation between moieties function to "dynamize all types of communal labor and collective projects, accelerating action and obtaining positive results that benefit everyone equally" (1984, 61). Competition has been an important feature of Andean moieties for centuries (see, e.g., Hopkins 1982, 170; Murra 1980, 8).

6. Because Andean dual forms became part of the Spanish colonial apparatus, we have better historical documentation for it than for mountain worship. This allows us to explore, both theoretically and historically, the complex relationship between these two components of the local model of irrigation.

7. See Treacy (1989, 325) for a similar event in another Colca Valley community, where official political authority is present. Variants of anansaya/urinsaya model can be found in other Colca Valley villages (see, e.g., Benavides 1991; Guillet 1994; Valderrama and Escalante 1988; Paerregaard 1992; Treacy 1994a), and there is tremendous variation in how this model conditions irrigation and other social domains from town to town.

8. Each visitor approaches the water mayor and his wife, who first receive a light embrace and then have the qalqinchas placed on them. The most valued gift is the palm (*ramo*) that some very close relatives or friends bring. Both the qalqincha and the palms are given in different fiestas as a sign of love and high regard for the sponsors or cargo holders. The composition of a tinkachu includes a very diverse lot (see Gelles 1990, 217–222, 338–339).

9. As one woman put it, "The men accompany us, but that's separate from the women." Indeed, while men do not go alone to a tinkachu, women do. The water mayor and his family are also greatly assisted by their immediate female kin, who distribute food, corn beer, and liquor (see also Isbell 1974).

10. While the water mayors already know the irrigation sequence and the distribution of

anan/urin fields in the sectors where they have lands, they must learn the sequence for those areas with which they are unfamiliar. In these cases it is the irrigators waiting their turns who inform them about the proper sequence.

11. Some who missed their turn beg the water mayor to allow them to irrigate. He usually accedes as long as the person's field is not too far behind and belongs to his saya and the person has the canals and intakes properly prepared. All of this is highly negotiable and depends on the water mayor's relationship with the parties involved and on pressure from other waiting irrigators. Although they are supposed to be completely even-handed in meting out water, the water mayors will often favor family and friends with a more thorough flooding of their fields. They are watched closely in the distribution process, however, and are criticized if an inordinate amount of favoritism is perceived.

12. Although there are surely more, I found eight references to these transfers in the books of the Irrigation Commission and the municipal council. For example, in 1979, a man solicited a transfer of saya status because his field was "the only one in the middle of the fields of the other parcialidad" and he was doing damage to other plots during irrigation and sowing. In 1985, eight irrigators of one sector changed their lands' saya affiliation with ten people in another sector because of the damage inflicted. The latter includes water entering the recently sowed fields of the other saya and killing the seedlings; the presence of different saya fields in the same sector also leads to different planting schedules for that sector. The team of oxen necessary for the plowing enter the sectors at different times and sometimes trample the recently sprouting plants in adjacent fields.

13. The concept of *saya* differs from that of *suyu* in fundamental ways. Although *saya* means "half" or "moiety" and is inseparable from the notion of duality, *suyu* does not mean "quadrant" but rather something akin to "part" or "portion" and is often semantically related to the apportionment of space into units of variable size or number for work tasks (Urton 1984; Zuidema 1982). See Rostworowski 1981, Pease 1981, Harrison 1989, and especially Urton 1984 for analyses of the terms *parcialidad* and *saya* and the way that these are semantically differentiated from terms such as *suyu*. For the way in which "upper world" and "lower world" are conceptualized in contemporary Andean society in the Cuzco area, see Gelles and Martínez 1996, 149. Tripartition was also an important part of the ceqe model. The ceqes or sightlines within each of the four parts were ranked hierarchically in repeating sequences of *qullana, payan,* and *cayao.*

14. There is a large amount of literature on the prehistory of dualism, and it is probable that statecraft based on dualism is an ancient phenomenon in the Andes (see, e.g., Rostworowski 1983; Mosely 1990; Conklin 1990; Zuidema 1990b) and elsewhere in the Americas. Yet, as I have shown elsewhere, the ethnohistorical analogies used by many scholars studying pre-Columbian polities are often based on faulty premises (see Gelles 1995).

15. See Salomon (1986,178) and Cavallero (1991, 61) for statements regarding the partial realization of the ceqe model in the periphery of the empire. Of all the Inka's spatial and organizational concepts, the anansaya and urinsaya division appears to be the most important for understanding Inka administration (see, e.g., Julien 1991, 119). In Salomon's words, "The moiety system, applied on an imperial scale of organization, was a coherent and durable one with a clear formal likeness to that of Cuzco" (1986, 177).

16. Matienzo, a Spanish lawyer, found in the year 1567 that "in each district or province there were two sectors, one which is called hanansaya, and the other hurinsaya. Each sector has a chief who commands the subchiefs and "Indians" of his sector, and does not interfere in commanding the other, except that the native lord of the hanansaya sector is the leading personage of the whole province" (Matienzo [1567] 1967, 20, in Salomon 1986, 174; see also Rostworowski 1983, 115).

17. Although it is possible that the Cavana polity was divided into moieties before Inka times, the saya division *as such* was most likely an Inka imposition. The four-day rounds of each water mayor and the resultant eight-day week appear to be of Inka origin (Tom Zuidema, personal communication, 1991).

18. In his seminal article on the "colonial matrix," Fuenzalida mentions in passing that sayas were used for administrative purposes during the colonial period (1970, 249).

This certainly was the case for the Cavana polity, which in 1572 had a population of 5,846 (Cook 1982, 17). In the mid-sixteenth century, Juan de la Torre became encomendero of Cabana urinsaya and Hernando de la Cuba Maldonado became encomendero of Cabana anansaya (Barriga 1955). The Spaniards left other indigenous forms of administration in place: each of Cabanaconde's moieties was subdivided into three ayllus (see Zuidema 1964; Benavides 1988a). In the case of Cabanaconde, the ayllus and tripartite divisions were more fragile than the moieties, but some of these managed to last for over two centuries (Gelles 1990).

19. The use of dualism as an organizing model was not unfamiliar to the Spaniards (Stanley Brandes, personal communication, 1991; Juan Palerm, personal communication, 1999), and the moieties that the Spaniards encountered in the Andes were to a certain degree consonant with organizational forms in Spain.

20. I have found firm evidence of the continued tribute function of the sayas after independence in the personal documents of the great-grandson of the tribute collector of anansaya. Several Cabañeros recall being told by their elders that marriage between the sayas used to be prohibited. The moieties probably remained endogamous for purposes of tribute collection until the mid-nineteenth century, but it is possible that endogamy as a longstanding tradition associated with productive resources influenced this marriage prohibition. In another community of the area, moieties are still spatially localized and fairly endogamous (see, e.g.,Valderrama and Escalante 1988).

21. The fading of Cabanaconde's saya endogamy in the mid-nineteenth century followed a larger trend in the Colca Valley (Cook 1982). At about this time a new authority structure was mapped onto Cabanaconde, probably when it was made a municipal district in 1857. By the turn of the century there was an income trustee (*síndico de rentas*), an expense trustee (*síndico de gastos*), two aldermen (*regidores*), a mayor, and a governor. These new officials governed the town as a whole.

22. Yet even after the 1920s, when mention of the two moieties all but disappears from communal documents (except in relation to the irrigation system), the dual divisions remained a strong structuring force. A 1937 document is the first that I found which mentions the four "quarters," though the same year reference is made to the *toreros* (sponsors of the patron saint's fiesta) of anansaya and urinsaya (BMC). Each of the quarters was referred to as "barrios" in documents from the 1920s and earlier, and each had its own staffholder. In the 1930s this fourfold division was apparently formalized into the four "quarters" (cuarteles), and the staffholders changed their name from "mayor" (alcalde de barrio) or "commissary" (comisario) to "director" (*jefe*). Although the directors no longer carry staffs, and the importance of the quarter division has declined, this fourfold division is still used today for organizing communal work projects.

23. That the competition in the fiesta has its basis in the Spanish reappropriations of the moiety division is evidenced by the division along the lines of anansaya and urinsaya of the fields of the religious brotherhoods (*chakras cofradías*). Almost every saint has an anansaya and an urinsaya field in his or her name. Until about the 1940s, the sponsors of these fiestas came from the two sides of town. To a certain degree, the two sponsors continue to be conceptualized in terms of the sayas.

24. An example of this is the assertion that people make that anaq chakra receives more water than uray chakra during a drought. The agricultural fields of the two moieties were not divided between geographically higher and lower areas because, as Murra (1980) and many others (see, e.g., Shimada 1985) have shown, ecological complementarity and the vertical control of ecological niches is central to Andean society and civilization. Modeling the dual division by altitude would have created economic specialization between the moieties, with one moiety enjoying the warmer lands of the lower fields and controlling the source of water. The way duality was institutionalized guaranteed each moiety fairly equal access to ecological zones and irrigation water.

FIVE. THE POWER OF THE PEN

1. The Cabañeros perceive the mineral content of irrigation water as being at a premium at this time of year because of the landslides that occur in the upper reaches of the Hualca-Hualca River basin during the heavy rains. Irrigation water is valued over rain-

fall because it is viewed as protecting the plants: it is "cold," penetrates deeper in the ground than rainfall, and supports the roots of the plants, which otherwise "get burned" by the heavy rainfall or intense radiation during these summer months.

2. People who have their fields in the same sector may contact each other and say, "What about taking the water over to our fields in Cusqi sector?" Or an irrigator may see the water being taken down a canal off of which he or she owns land, or hears that so-and-so is taking water down a particular canal. *Tiyaq* refers the person sitting on and watching over the intakes; *muyuy* means to go around in circles (Lira 1982). Only one muyuq is needed to do the rounds, whereas several tiyaq are needed to guard the intakes. See Guillet (1992) and Treacy (1994a) for their analyses of irrigation clusters in Lari and Coporaque, upper valley communities. Cabanaconde's informal system is similar to what Mitchell (1981) has described for Quinua, Ayacucho.

3. Seligmann (1987) has described a similar situation for a community in the Cuzco region. In some parts of the Andes, women do not open or close intakes but assist in most other irrigation-related activities (Bourque and Warren 1981, 20).

4. See especially Articles 45–48 of the *Ley General de Aguas*. Article 45 states that those irrigation districts that have insufficient or widely fluctuating supplies of water should give preference to plants that have the largest and most direct benefit for the population, and they should employ "the most efficient irrigation structure" (*Ley General de Aguas* 1969, 11). The de canto system is also called *cantullamanta, canto a canto,* and *mita global* (Guillet 1994; Treacy 1989, 1994a).

5. As explained in the Note to the Reader, these and the other names used throughout the book are pseudonyms.

6. The title was given "in reward and recognition of the merits and other qualities which permit us to distinguish him with preferences and at his request we confer a good deal to him so that in the future he will not be needy" (Copy of a Possession given to Don Felipe Fuentes y Rojas, December 27, 1828, in the community of Cabanaconde, Intendent of Caylloma Province and the Commissioner of Contributions and Distribution of Lands).

7. In an 1841 letter to a provincial judge (*juez de la primera instancia*), Salinas demanded that a field be fenced and cultivated for the tribute collectors, arguing that "until the present time I have been entrusted with and have fulfilled the Collecting, at the service of the State." His demand was further justified by the fact that he had been the object of witchcraft and "diabolical acts" by one of the tributees, María Quespi, and was now having to spend money treating himself and pursuing a criminal suit against her. Beginning his account with,"It happened last year in the month of September," he proceeded to relate how he was bewitched by this woman. He ended his letter by saying, "Finding myself in this miserable condition . . . I appeal to your strong arm." He was so ill that his son had to sign for him (personal documents of the Salinas family, 1837). Other cases of resistance to state officials and tribute collection during the late eighteenth and early nineteenth centuries is well documented for neighboring regions (see, e.g., Salomon 1987; Marzal 1981; Millones 1978).

8. Entries in the books of the municipal council speak of water-related conflicts as early as the mid 1920s, and an 1882 document from the parish archive indicates that these were much earlier. It mentions a lack of "good organization and order in these waterings" (BPA 1882) as well as the usurpation of lands by a woman (presumably a powerful misti) who was defeated "when the townspeople denounced her."

9. When the names of the water mayors appear in the municipal council books, it is someone else who signs for them "at their request."

10. Saturnino Vásquez Fuentes, for example, became a priest around the turn of the century in the city of Arequipa, and he helped create the first school in Cabanaconde (BMC). Though he lived almost his entire life outside of the community, this man is a sign of the strength of the Spanish enclave found in Cabanaconde, and the connection this enclave had with the elite forces of the region. Mariano Apaza, a famed usurper of land in the upper Colca Valley (Manrique 1985), was apparently part of this group (BMC). Femenias documents part of the larger configuration of power in the region in the early part of this century (1997, 334–345).

11. The stories of Antonio Fuentes's abuses of power are legion. He is known, for example, to have forced people to sell land or animals cheaply, threatening to create problems if they did not. The following is a partial list of the offices he held: justice of the peace

1922, 1924, 1926, 1957; second councilman 1930; governor 1932, 1933, 1935, 1969, 1970; officer, Irrigators Council 1943, 1956; mayor 1945, 1946, 1947 (BMC, BIC).

12. Staffs of authority are clearly the "dominant symbol" of political authority in many Andean communities (Rasnake 1988, 215). In Cabanaconde the nature of this symbology varied depending on the office. Although the water mayors' authority is not tied to the church, they apparently had to physically irrigate church lands. In 1888, two old men "who were Mayors irrigated and had these fields plowed, sowed, and the potato harvest gathered for the *señores* priests" (BPA).

13. The first mention that I have found of eriazos being sold by the municipal council is from 1925. There were repeated sales over the next few decades. Although in 1928 it was declared that this eriazo land should be sold at fifteen soles a tupu by "anyone who wishes to buy them," it was the very members of the municipal council who did most of the buying.

14. Some of these fields were as large as fifteen hectares. This is a considerable size if we remember that the wealthier members of the community today have only five or so irrigated hectares.

15. In 1929, a state representative was already promising a telegraph line and electricity. In 1947, the community still had not given up hope and had even asked the neighboring town of Tapay to supply the wood posts. Until 1998, when two telephones were installed in town, there was still no way to communicate directly with the outside world (except for an unreliable shortwave radio in the police station).

16. In 1945, while Domínguez was in office, the government gave a motor, a radio, and 1,200 soles to the community. This generosity is probably a reflection of the boom period Peru experienced during the Second World War (Thorp and Bertram 1978). The municipal authorities decided to use the money to install a system for providing drinking water; twenty-three years later this dream was realized (BMC).

A 1948 entry in the municipal council books provides a sense of the community's remoteness from state affairs as well as the continued existence of an elite group of men who, crowded around the radio in the council, listen to the sounds of the "modern" world. "By means of the radio on the 27th of the month we have learned that the government has been overthrown [by Odria]. . . . If it is true that there has been a change of Presidents, we have decided to send a telegram of congratulations to the First Authority of the Nation." A sense of the cultural difference between this group and others within the community is revealed by an entry that states, "That which we sometimes observe, in which they [presumably the "indios"] dance during a baby's funeral is something that should be done away with." The authorities prohibited this dancing and the presence of musicians at these burials, assessing a fifty-sol fine "to moralize the town" (BMC 1948).

17. A state notary was present, and the meeting was held under the "Presidency of the Water Judge." Geraldo Domínguez became the new president and Antonio Fuentes, the officer (fiscal). Fifty-eight people signed the act. It appears that a separate room was accommodated for the new organization. The water administrator now coordinated with the heads or representatives of each quarter, the governor, and the mayor for the journey to Hualca-Hualca. They also organized the canal cleanings.

18. The content and tone of Gamero's speech, as well as the actions of Geraldo Domínguez, were probably influenced by the urban intellectual movement, *indigenismo*. See, among others, Kristal (1987) and Marzal (1981) for different perspectives on this movement.

19. The Water Tribunal and Irrigators Council in fact formed two separate entities. The lack of a clear agenda for these relatively new offices is evidenced by the fact that during the rainy season of 1948, the water was "abandoned" and the municipal council once again had to take charge. The tribunal soon after its creation became the office of the water administrator (*administrador de aguas*). The administrator was in charge of overseeing the water mayors and had his own secretary and two officers (vocales). The Irrigators Council (made up of a president, a vice president, a secretary and officers), however, was ostensibly in charge of organizing canal cleanings and other tasks.

20. The author goes on to say that "this causes the emigration of her children to the urban centers, in which they enlarge the already huge legions of the unemployed." The author states that Cabanaconde's 570 hectares of maize and other cereals make it the

granary of Caylloma province and part of the department of Puno; the fruit from its valleys are taken to the markets of Arequipa. "The urgent need for the State to help Cabanaconde increase its waters has been clearly demonstrated. . . . It is the duty of the State to cooperate economically to help solve this grave social problem . . . providing the clear imprint of its National Agro-Pastoral Program."

21. On January 23, 1945, communal authorities decided to allot lands in the areas of Joyas, Liway, and Ukru-Ukru "to each household or head of family *without favoring anybody*" (emphasis added). This was clearly a communal response to the land abuses of the Patriarchs, as many of the new lands were those that had been bought by the Patriarchs and others from the municipality. Three years later, on March 1, 1948, another allotment of lands occurred "because the [1945] allotment was badly done . . . the townspeople did not work the lands because they had no land titles to back up their ownership and to push forward agrarian progress."

In February 1953, there formed a "commission for the betterment of the agricultural fields" (BJP); Geraldo Domínguez was elected by the community to be president. The commission planned to recover abandoned terraces in the areas of Auqi, Liway, Ukru-Ukru, Pacclapata, Sincilcoma, Achachiwa, and Joyas, including lands being contested by Antonio Fuentes and others. Three hundred signatures at the bottom of the act show it to be a popular initiative. It was declared that the lands to be recovered were "our exclusive property" against the claims of "ignorant people who attempt to appropriate lands individually" (ibid.). One entry states that the united townspeople would "defend themselves for the true progress of this densely populated Cabanaconde" against those "elements which attempt to demoralize the civic and patriotic participation of the Community" (ibid.). This land recovery effort also failed, however.

22. In September 1949, for example, Geraldo Domínguez (still the school director) presented a land title of ten tupus sold to him by the municipal council in 1936 "with its respective allotment of water." There must have been great local opposition to his irrigating these lands, however, as he was forced to appeal to higher authorities. The administrator, from either Chivay or Arequipa, declared, "This Administration has ordered the Water Repartitioners to provide Mr. Domínguez the water for irrigating his fields" (BIC 1949). Meanwhile, Antonio Fuentes continued to irrigate his eriazo lands. In 1952, for example, Fuentes rerouted the irrigation water for several hours, and "the irrigators asked that he not be conceded water."

23. Attempts to achieve the status of Comunidad Indígena began in 1950; two soles were collected from each family to this purpose (BMC). The Patriarchs' arguments against such a move, such as "Why should we call ourselves 'indígenas' when we are more than that?" masked their fear of a competing power base. On June 6, 1969, a negotiator for the Comunidad Indígena was named, but only ten years later did the community achieve official recognition. See Rappaport's (1994) fine study of history-making and the creation of a resguardo, an officially recognized community, in the Colombian Andes.

24. In Cabanaconde there are thirty-three fields of the religious brotherhoods (chakras cofradías), which are communally held and directed to the festive sponsorship of the saints. Until the late 1970s these fields belonged to the church. The chakras cofradías, each of which range from one to three hectares, rotate for three-year periods among community members, often the poorest. Purposely misinterpreting the cry of the Velasco revolutionary military government (1968–1975), "The land belongs to those who work it!" many of the thirty-three temporary holders, known as "mayordomos," tried to permanently usurp these lands. This intrigue was instigated by the local priest, who, afraid that these lands would be expropriated by the military government, sold them to the mayordomos. The newly formed Peasant Community, supported by the majority of community members, engaged the mayordomos in a legal battle and finally took the chakras cofradías by force, destroying the crops. The priest and several mayordomos left town for good, and the chakras cofradías reverted to the community. Today they continue in rotation among the poorer peasants.

25. Each district is divided into sectors and subsectors and includes one or more river basins. Cabanaconde was designated as one of four "Irrigation Sectors" within the Colca irrigation district. In the provincial capital, Chivay (a two-hour drive from the community), a Ministry of Agriculture water engineer (ingeniero de aguas) represents the state

at the provincial level. He and an extension agent of the ministry oversee the Irrigators Commission.

As in other parts of Peru, the state's irrigation bureaucracy in this region is extremely understaffed and underfunded. Although the extension agent for the Cabanaconde "sector" is in charge of overseeing irrigation in seven communities in addition to Cabanaconde, he has no reliable vehicle and limited material support. Moreover, as Lynch has observed in the Cajamarca region, the extension agent "is unlikely to be able to adequately supervise irrigation within his sector. This very weakness, however, means that he is likely to respond to strongly expressed requests for assistance coming from the comites and comisiones rather than execute a preconceived program" (1988, 347). During my stay, the first extension agent in two years came to town and converted one of the rooms of the municipal council into his office and living quarters. The bureaucratic amenities he possessed were few: a typewriter, a desk, and the seals of his office.

26. Like its predecessors, the Velasco regime often issued contradictory resolutions. Although the regime sought to abolish many of the archaic semifeudal relations in the highlands, it also sought to extend its control for taxation purposes. But this was resisted by many Andean communities, including Cabanaconde. In 1988, unlike other communities of the Colca Valley (Treacy 1994a; Guillet 1994; Valderrama and Escalante 1988) and those of other highland areas that had experienced the "bureaucratic transition" (Lynch 1988), Cabanaconde had no list of water users and had not paid a water tariff since 1982.

27. As we saw in Zuñiga's 1945 decree, the unpaid services of the water mayors was supposed to cease. Although this did not happen, the newly formed Irrigators Council did appoint other individuals to assist with distribution. As early as 1948, these were called controllers and were paid a wage by the Irrigators Council or municipality. The controllers worked together with the water mayors during the rainy season.

28. When in 1955 attempts were made to rehabilitate the lands of Achachiwa, which had been "completely abandoned because of the scarcity of water," it was "not known which sectors belong to each parcialidad" (BIC), that is, saya. The Irrigators Council proceeded to distribute the land between the sayas, giving five sectors to anansaya and six to urinsaya. New lands assigned in other sectors, those of Liway and Auqi, were also to be divided by saya. A later entry, however, states that "water will be given in rotational form" to these. Although these lands were abandoned again and we do not know which system would have in fact been implemented, it is clear that new lands affect distribution patterns for the cultivated area as a whole.

29. In that year, the water mayors were appointed according to the list of irrigators because "they should be large landowners" (BIC). In May of the same year the water mayor of anansaya paid a peon to take his place, and another powerful peasant was appointed to be water mayor. These events coincided with the first year that the water mayor's tenure was reduced to one round.

30. Contradictory resolutions concerning distribution—sometimes defied by local irrigation authorities—have consistently been put forth since state officials took a more active role in the community's irrigation practices. For example, on March 14, 1978, in the middle of a drought year, a Ministry of Agriculture decree authorized eight hours of water for several of the pudientes. The Irrigators Commission protested "the abuse of false resolutions" and denounced the technical administrator of the Colca Valley for "hindering the advancement of water . . . a publication will be made in the newspapers of Lima and Arequipa." And on April 13, 1979, the Irrigators Commission decided "not to cede water to majuelos nor give preference to several people according to the decree of the Engineer in light of the fact that the water is in its round in the lower part of the fields." For the positive and negative effects of state intervention and different distribution regimes in other Colca Valley communities, see Paerregaard 1994; Guillet 1985, 1994; Valderrama and Escalante 1988; Treacy 1989, 1994a.

SIX. WATER POLITICS

1. These vignettes are taken from my field notes for the period February-March, 1988.
2. The abuses of Anaya had grown so extreme that one day the town's megaphone in the main plaza squealed noisily to life, denouncing the "bad management" of water by

Anaya and the extension agent. Before Anaya was removed from office, the small funds and the tools of the commission had disappeared. The problem of corruption in the Irrigation Commission is not new (BIC). Commission members have also been known to irrigate more than their share and to favor friends and family with water. When a good commission is installed, however, the water mayors and the distribution system benefit greatly. The efficacy of the commission varies from year to year.

3. This group declared that Achachiwa was classified as irrigated land, even though it was common knowledge that at best it was dry farmed and had no right to irrigation water. Others solicited water for potatoes in Liway, declaring that these crops would die if not watered soon. Another group argued for the area of Pampakunka. The Achachiwa group solicited water from the reservoir, which they declared would not interfere with the flow of water. Furthermore, they argued, they had loans from the Agrarian Bank, and these lands had been mortgaged against the loans. The extension agent agreed and signed papers that gave them the rights to a reservoir full of water and charged the group three hundred intis for that right.

4. This is not untypical for the first day of the rounds, be it that of the controllers or that of the water mayors. Individuals realize that water is about to enter the sequence (*estar en su corte*), and they jockey to water their fields the night before.

5. In cases such as this, those who have intercropped majuelos with maize will be able to irrigate both.

6. Another example of local belief found in local documents comes from a 1949 entry: "The Water Mayors of the agricultural fields who are repartitioners of Both Sexes, or in other words, of both Parcialidades" (BIC). So, too, in 1950, the Irrigators Council decided that the water mayors would each receive a can of kerosene and "money for the tinkachu." An entry from 1952 states that the water mayors "will continue in Suyos" (complementary and spatially divided activities). Another example of the strength of the local model of belief and practice is that Tomanta, the outlet of the Majes Canal, is often invoked in the q'apas of the yakutinkays.

CONCLUSION

1. The spatial and social dualisms that the Inka established mutated into a thousand different forms, as the political, economic, and cultural processes of the Spanish Colonial and Republican periods impacted the saya divisions in myriad ways. As in the case of Cabanaconde, the dual divisions were often reified by the new administrations. The anansaya/urinsaya division in one shape or another—and this takes many varied forms—structures countless hundreds of community-based agricultural and pastoral systems, encompassing hundreds of thousands of hectares of land in different Andean regions (see Gelles 1995).

2. Given the success of this system year after year, the rationality that it embodies is clearly "instrumental" as well. The classic formulation of the question of rationality is, of course, Weber's (1947). For overviews of this topic, see Hollis and Lukes 1984; Tambiah 1985, 1990; Ulin 1984; Wilson 1984. See also Gudeman 1986 for an insightful analysis of the ways in which different rationalities are modeled and the ways that they structure practice. My conceptual framework, while drawing on these and other interpretive perspectives (e.g., Geertz 1980; Maybury-Lewis 1989), is also inspired by political economy and practice theories (see, among others, Bourdieu 1977, 1990; Moore 1986; Leach 1954; Ortner 1984). It is through the practices of individuals and groups, pursuing strategies shaped by both material and cultural forces, that different irrigation models are produced, reproduced, and transformed.

3. This is not to say that Andean cultural production does not take place in the cities of Peru; it most certainly does. But the relationships, social and spiritual, which have come to define lo andino take place in rural community settings. While today over 20 percent of the Peruvian population lives in these communities, Ossio (1992) estimates that 45 percent or more of the Peruvian population traces its immediate origins to the Andean peasant community.

4. Irrigation bureaucracies exclude not only those with different cultural orientations but women as well, both in the field and in the irrigation bureaucracies themselves (Lynch

1993). While we should not exaggerate gender parity in the local model of irrigation, the tinkachu that women organize are instrumental to its successful implementation. Their social relationships, especially the munaqkuna that they are able to mobilize, underlie the smooth functioning of the system. So, too, the female principle is exalted through the worship of Mount Hualca-Hualca and her life-giving water. These elements are absent in the state model.

5. Criollo is a marked cultural style clearly identified in music, food, and dance. Criollo and its derivatives are often applied to cultural literacy and the ability to move in certain social spaces. If one is *bien criollo* or *acriollado* (criolized), one has adopted clever city ways. But these terms can have both positive and negative connotations. For example, *una criollada* and *la viveza criolla* signify behaviors that can be seen as both clever and treacherous, witty yet duplicitous.

6. Irrigation allows for the intensification of agricultural land by, among other things, recycling nutrients, making unnecessary the constant rotation of land, and expanding the vertical and horizontal limits of production. Wittfogel received a good deal of his inspiration from Marx's Asiatic mode of production (see, e.g., Lansing 1991; Valeri 1991; Palerm 1972), which also stressed the supposed material and social exigencies of large hydraulic works. Many authors, working in a wide range of historical and ethnographic settings, have refuted Wittfogel's central causal notion at various levels, ranging from small communities and chiefdoms to empires (see, e.g. Chang 1983; Earle 1978; Geertz 1980; Kelly 1983; Lansing 1991; Leach 1961; Mabry 1996; Lees 1973; Mitchell 1981).

7. Irrigation politics in Peru and other nation-states of the Americas must thus be understood in terms of a "long tradition of Western thought which holds that ethnic attachments are irrational and archaic and ought therefore to evaporate as the world moves toward greater modernization and rationality in the conduct of its affairs" (Maybury-Lewis 1982, 220). Modernism, important among elites in all countries that model themselves on the West, "is especially important among the upper classes and urbanized people of Latin America" (Norgaard 1994, 9).

EPILOGUE

1. Migrants now living in Washington have sponsored the annual Virgin of Carmen and Candelaria fiestas on various occasions (see Gelles and Martínez 1993); the list of sponsors for these fiestas over the next few years includes several more Washington-based Cabaneños. During one Candelaria fiesta, a conflict broke out between the transmigrant sponsors and some local residents—this culminated in a protest in the central plaza at which the residents burned the transmigrants in effigy (one wearing a jacket that had "U.S.A." written on it). Such an event signals new tensions, disjunctions as well as conjunctions, between the traditional and the transnational in highland society.

2. Just as a number of Cabaneños are joining the labor force, trying to establish residency, and are receiving different ethnic classifications in the United States, many people from other highland regions are doing the same in Cabanaconde. After five years of residence in town, these Puneños, Cuzqueños, and other outsiders are eligible for comunero status with the attendant rights and obligations. Some adopt Cabaneño-style dress, whereas others wear their own regional dress.

3. Since the early 1990s, the Cabaneños have been required to pay thirty-six soles a hectare per year to water their lands in the new irrigation sectors—this has led to the monetarization of the main fields. Until 1998, the payment was made in the office of the Irrigators Commission, which would then issue a ticket to be given to the repartitioner. As of 1998, irrigators pay him directly in the field.

4. In the new irrigation sectors, water is not divided by saya and only some individuals make q'apa offerings. The reason Hualca-Hualca's water is used for the Joyas sector is that the offtake for this sector is far above where the Majes Canal crosses the Hualca-Hualca River.

5. Future research is needed to determine the long-term cultural and economic consequences of the Majes Project and land recovery in Cabanaconde.

Glossary

Glossary words are italicized only on their first usage in the text (in the sections of italicized text, which indicate the use of ethnographic vignettes, the glossary words stand out by not being italicized). In addition to foreign words, some technical terms and institutions are also explained in this glossary. The origin of the word is marked by "Q." for Quechua, "S." for Spanish, and "A." for Aymara.

acriollado (S.): *see* criollo.

administrador de aguas (S.): water administrator. An office that was created in Cabanaconde in the 1940s to, among other things, oversee the water mayors.

alcalde de barrio (S.): barrio mayor; mayor of one of the four barrios.

alcalde envarado (S.): *see* alcalde de barrio.

alcaldes de agua (S.): *see* yaku alcaldes.

alcaldes de campo (S.): *see* yaku alcaldes.

allp'a (Q.): the earth; earth illness.

altamisayuq (S. and Q.): *see* karpayuq.

altares (S.): a colonial practice that lasted until the 1940s. The altares, which took place on Good Friday, consisted of each family giving fruit, maize, and other produce to the priest in exchange for his blessing. After Easter Mass, the priest and town authorities would be served a feast while the townspeople looked on.

anansaya (Q.): upper half; refers to the moiety division. *See* saya.

anaq (Q.): upper.

anaq altus (Q.): upper pastures.

anaq chakra (Q.): upper fields.

aphru (Q.?): gifts presented to the bride and groom during the marriage ritual.

aphrutinkay (Q.?): marriage rite; coming together of the *aphrus*, the gifts, on the third and last day of the marriage festivities, which symbolizes the merging of the two families.

apu (Q.): mountain deities; *see* cabildo.

asamblea comunal (S.): communal assembly held by the Peasant Community on a monthly basis or as the need arises; the communal assembly is, by law, "the maximum authority" in town.

Autodema (S.): administrative branch of the Majes Project.

awki (Q.): mountain deities.

ayni (Q.): a fundamental aspect of Andean social organization (e.g., in fiesta sponsorship; agricultural labor); generally refers to the equal exchange of a given good or service. In agricultural labor, it usually refers to the exchange of a day of work between two parties. Ayni is one of many different forms of mutual aid in the Andes.

barbecho (S.): turning and preparation of the earth before the sowing; the first of the water mayors' four irrigation rounds.

barrios (S.): fourfold division that eclipsed the saya division as a means of organizing community in the early twentieth century; also called cuarteles.

blanco (S.): white; overlaps with Spaniard and misti as a racialized category. As with other terms, such as *indio* and *cholo*, the term *blanco* is part of a racial idiom used to express class and ethnic differences.

boca de la gente (S.): malicious gossip.

bofedales (S.): boggy pastures in the high reaches that provide an especially luxuriant grass for cattle.

caballeritos (S.): "little fellows"; a term applied by Cabaneños to the herders they employ as migrant farmworkers during the harvest.

Cabanaconde City Association: a migrant association of the Cabaneños located in Washington, D.C., founded 1983.

cabanita maize (S.): *see* maíz cabanita.

cabildos (S.): "council of authority, town council"; refers to the sacred mountains who have authority over Cabanaconde.

caja (S.): ritual holding case; dug into the ground during the tomatinkay ritual, it is used to hold a camelid fetus and different kinds of liquor.

campiña agrícola (S.): main fields surrounding the town.

cargo (S.): religious or political office undertaken by a member of the community. Undertaking a certain number of cargos, whether these be religious or civil, is generally obligatory for individual members of a community. Religious cargos often involve the organization and sponsorship of a religious festival in honor of a particular saint in the Roman Catholic pantheon. Political cargos are often a type of civic duty or community service in which townspeople are appointed or volunteer to fulfill a town office.

centavo (S.): a monetary unit equivalent to one hundredth of a sol. *See* sol.

ceqe (Q.) system: a conceptual model that helped order the social, ritual, and political organization of the Inka empire. Forty-one sightlines were conceptually arranged into four suyus, and this fourfold division was bisected to form halves or moieties, anansaya and urinsaya.

chakras cofradías (Q. and S.): fields of the religious brotherhoods which are communally held and directed to the festive sponsorship of the saints.

champa (S.): grassy clods of earth used to build and repair dams, intakes, and canals.

champería (S.): *see* Fiesta de Agua.

chaupi (Q.): the center.

chicha (Q.): corn beer; also a type of music that combines rhythms and melodies from Andean musical traditions (e.g., huayno) and from other Latin American music (cumbia, salsa).

chimpanas (Q.): small bridges that form part of the hydraulic infrastructure.

cholo, chola (S.): A denigrating term sometimes translated as "half breed," "mestizo," or "civilized Indian," it often is applied to a transculturated "Indian." There is often a sense of liminality implied by the term, as if the person being so described is between cultures and somehow inauthentic. As with other terms, such as *indio* and *blanco*, the term *cholo* is part of a racial idiom used to express class and ethnic differences.

cochinilla (S.): small insects that grow on prickly pear cactus and contain a red colorant that is used in the manufacturing of lipstick and other cosmetics.

comisario de barrio (S.): *see* alcalde de barrio.

comisión de regantes (S.): Irrigators Commission; a village-wide water users association, usually made up of literate men, which has an elected governing board. The commission appoints the water mayors and controllers each year and organizes canal cleanings and irrigator assemblies. Although the Irrigators Commission should in theory enact state policies, the relationship between local and state officials is often characterized by conflict.

communal assembly: *see* asamblea comunal.

compadrazgo (S.): godparenthood ties. Compadrazgo is an important institution used throughout the Andes in a wide variety of social fields, and the most important instances of it are baptism and marriage.

compadre, comadre (S.): co-father, co-mother; name used to express the relationship between the godparents and parents of godchildren.

comunero (S.): community member. By fulfilling communal obligations such as cargos and faena work, the comunero gains access to the common property resources of the community, such as irrigation water, grazing lands, medicinal herbs, and firewood.

comunidad campesina (S.): Peasant Community. The most respected and democratic institution in communal life, the officially recognized institution of the Peasant Community can legally act as a corporate body to defend communal interests from internal or external threats.

comunidad indígena (S.): Indigenous Community; precursor to the Peasant Community.

consejo municipal (S.): municipal council.

controladores (S.): controllers; office in charge of water distribution during the period when the state's de canto model of distribution is in effect.

cortamonte (S.): a ritual tree-felling that takes place during Carnival.

costa (S.): coast.

costeños (S.): coastal-dwellers.

criollo (S.): The term *criollo*, which was originally used to designate people of Spanish descent born in the Americas, refers to the dominant coastally based "white" culture that has held power since independence. Today, popular and national cultural discourses present the Spanish-speaking, white, West-facing minority as the model of modernity, the embodiment of legitimate national culture, and the key to Peru's future. To be *acriollado* is to be creolized; *una criollada* and *la viveza criolla* signify behaviors which can be seen as both clever and treacherous, witty yet duplicitous.

cuarteles (S.): quadrapartite division of the town; same as barrio.

cultura andina (S.): Andean culture.

cultura criolla (S.): criollo culture.

curandero (S.): healer.

de canto (S.): the state's system of distributing water sequentially, from field to adjacent field.

de riego (S.): irrigated; refers to land that is authorized for irrigation water.

de secano (S.): dry-farmed; refers to land that can be dry-farmed and is not authorized for irrigation water.

despedida (S.): farewell send-off.

devotos (S.): sponsors of ritual events.

el que pueda (S.): "whoever's able"; *see* sistema informal.

encantos (S.): enchanted objects.

encomendero (S.): owner of an encomienda.

encomienda (S.): a grant of a kuraka, and the "Indian" labor and tribute that he commanded, which was given to powerful Spaniards by the Crown in the early colonial period.

entero cabildokuna (S. and Q.): all of the cabildos or mountain deities.

entero munaqkuna (S. and Q.): all of one's loved ones and admirers.

eriazo (S.): legally uncultivable; refers to land that is not authorized for any kind of cultivation, be it irrigated or dry-farmed.

español (S.): Spaniard. As with other terms, such as *indio* and *cholo*, the term *español* is part of a racial idiom used to express class and ethnic differences.

estancada (S.): a reservoir full of water. The water of the one small reservoir in town is sometimes a source of contention.

estancias (S.): herd steads; small, isolated herding stations in the high reaches where alpaca, llama, and other cattle are kept.

extension agent: *see* sectorista.

faena (S.): communal work service; a kind of labor tax required of community members.

fiesta (S.): festival, religious celebration.

Fiesta de Agua (S.): Water Fiesta; physical and spiritual renewal of irrigation systems that takes place in hundreds of Andean communities in Huarochirí, Ayacucho, Cuzco, Arequipa, and other highland regions.

filtración (S.): filtration; process wherein water filters down from the high mountains and lakes through subterranean layers to emerge as springs at lower altitudes.

gobernador (S.): governor.

gringo, gringa (S.): foreigner. While the term is often applied to Europeans and North Americans in colloquial Spanish, highlanders in Peru also apply it to "white" monolingual Spanish-speakers from Lima. As with other terms, such as *indio* and *cholo*, *gringo* is part of a racial idiom used to express class and ethnic differences.

hallmayu (Q.): a second reinforcing and weeding of the plants; the water mayors' fourth round of water.

hanpi (Q.): medicine; trago mixed with herbs that is proffered on social occasions.

hanpiq (Q.): curandero, healer.

hectare: a measurement equivalent to approximately 2.5 acres and to three tupus.

herd stead: *see* estancia.

hualina (Q.): songs that are composed and sung during the Water Fiesta in many communities of the Santa Eulalia Valley, Province of Huarochirí. They are dedicated to sources of water and to the ancestor heroes who built the canals and reservoirs.

huayno (Q.): a kind of Andean music.

huesero (S.): bone doctor.

indígena (S.): indigenous; indigenous person.

indio (S.): Indian; as with other terms, such as *blanco* and *cholo*, the term *indio* is part of a racial idiom used to express class and ethnic differences.

infractores (S.): lawbreakers.

ingeniero de aguas (S.): water engineer; the highest-ranking regional authority in the state's irrigation bureaucracy.

interesados (S.): the interested parties; refers to those who share a canal or sector of the agricultural fields.

inti (Q.): "the sun"; a monetary unit worth 1,000 soles. *See* sol.

irantas (Q.): burnt offering; *see also* q'apa.

Irrigators Commission: *see* comisión de regantes.

Irrigators Council: precursor to the Irrigators Commission. The Irrigators Council, an office that was created in Cabanaconde in the 1940s, was in charge of organizing canal cleanings and other tasks.

ista (Q.): coca bag.

kañiwa (Q.): plant used in q'apa offerings.

karpayuq (Q.): most revered and accomplished of ritual specialists; generally a person who has been struck by lightning (usually three times) and who can communicate directly with the mountain deities.

kunuka (Q.?): an aromatic plant used in q'apa offerings.

kuraka (Q.): ethnic chieftain; indigenous authorities who mediated between local polities and the state during Inka and Spanish colonial rule.

kuti sara (Q.): return corn; a special kind of maize, in which the teeth of the corn are turned down and which are used in healing rituals.

kuya (Q.): miracle, fortune.

lampeo (S.): weeding and reinforcing the stalks; the water mayors' third round of irrigation water.

la salida a Hualca-Hualca (S.): The annual sojourn to Hualca-Hualca. This ritualized communal work project in which the community cleaned out the upper tributaries of the Hualca-Hualca River was discontinued in 1983.

las autoridades de siempre (S.): the eternal authorities.

layqa (Q.): witch.

Ley General de Aguas (S.): general water law of Peru.

Limeño (S.): person from the city of Lima.

llamero (Q. and S.): llama herder; term sometimes used as an insult in Cabanaconde.

lo andino (S.): things Andean; Andean culture.

machuwayra (Q.): ill wind; a kind of sickness that is generated by malignant spirits.

madrina (S.): godmother.

maíz cabanita (S.): Cabanaconde's main export and a valuable commodity for subsistence and trade, maíz cabanita is famous throughout the southern Andes for its taste and quality.

Majes Consortium: a group of construction companies from England, Sweden, South Africa, Spain, and Canada in charge of building the Majes Canal.

Majes Project: a billion-dollar development project financed in part by the World Bank and constructed by companies from England, Sweden, South Africa, Spain, and Canada. This state-sponsored project was supposed to expand agriculture and promote regional development in southwestern Peru by channeling water from the upper Colca Valley to the dry coast for large-scale irrigation development and cash cropping.

majuelos (S.): recently sowed alfalfa.

maldición (S.): curse.

malignos (S.): malignant beings; evil spirits.

mamadera (S.): breast pump; milk bottle; thing from which one derives nourishment.

mama qucha (Q.): mother lake; refers to the ocean.

mayorista (S.): person with major land or cattle holdings.

mediano (S.): person with medium land or cattle holdings.

mestiza, mestizo (Sp.): "mixed race"; *see* misti.

minoristas (S.): person with minor land or cattle holdings.

misa sara (S. and Q.): ritual corn; maize that usually presents unusual color characteristics (e.g., a shock of red color in an otherwise white cob) and which is used in different rituals.

misti (Q.): Derived from the Spanish word *mestizo, misti* is the term used by indigenous peasants in the southern Peruvian highlands to refer to nonindigenous peoples. As with other terms, such as *indio* or *cholo, misti* is part of a racial idiom used to express class and ethnic differences.

misticitos (Q. and S.): "little mistis."

moiety: The word *moiety* derives from the French word *moitié,* which simply means "half." Refers to the organization of society and conceptual schemas along dual lines. *See also* saya.

mullu (Q.): seashells used in rituals.

munaqkuna (Q.): one's loved ones and admirers.

muyuq (Q.): patrollers used during the informal system, usually family members, hired day laborers, or irrigators taking turns among themselves. The muyuq walks the canals to secure smaller intakes and wave off other irrigators. *See also* tiyaq.

oficio (S.): official document.

oro pimiento (S.): gold powder sprinkled on q'apas.

pachamama (Q.): Earth Mother. Deity of native Andean religion who is associated with fertility and who resides in the earth.

padrino (S.): godfather.

padrón comunal (S.): Members List of the Peasant Community.

pagos (S.): payments; refers to q'apa payments to Earth Mother and cabildos.

paqu (Q.): spiritist, shaman, ritual specialist.

parcialidades (S.): partiality; refers to division in moieties, that is, the sayas.

parteras (S.): midwives.

Peasant Community: *see* Comunidad Campesina.

pechowira (S. and Q.): fat from a llama breast used in q'apa offerings.

pitu (Q.): corn beer mixed with corn flour.

pobre (S.): poor.

por voluntad (S.): willfully; refers to work that is not paid and is done without the expectation of ayni, that is, return service.

pozotinkay (S. and Q.): water hole rite.

pudientes (S.): a group of powerful peasants who acceded to positions of authority after the 1950s.

puna (Q.): the large grassy plains, sparsely forested ravines, and steep mountains of the high reaches. The puna region is perceived as uncivilized and possessing an almost unlimited amount of untamed natural energy.

q'ala (Q.): naked, plucked clean, totally poor.

qallqay (Q.): *see* lampeo.

qalqinchas (Q.): wreaths made of flowers, fruit, peppers, maize, bread, and other items; given to the sponsors of important ritual events.

q'apas (Q.): burnt offerings made to mountain deities and Earth Mother; also called despachos, irantas.

qayqa (Q.): bewitchment; illness caused by envy; the vapors of the deceased or the earth.

qhapaq (Q.): powerful.

qualifying commission: a commission created by the Peasant Community to evaluate and select comuneros eligible to receive rehabilitated agricultural land.

quechua (Q.): the warm valley.

qulqilibru (Q.): silver-colored paper used in q'apas.

q'uñi maki (Q.): warm hands; a thrifty quality that women have, which is conducive to a judicious use of maize and money.

qurilibru (Q.): gold-colored paper used in q'apas.

ramo (S.): palm given as a gift.

raza (S.): race. The concept of race in Peru and racialized categories, such as *indio, cholo,* and *blanco,* are used to express class and ethnic differences.

reducción (S.): nucleated settlements created by the Spaniards in the 1570s for religious indoctrination and labor extraction.

regidores (S.): those in charge of water; refers to the water mayor and controllers.

repartidores (S.): repartitioners of water; refers to the water mayor and controllers.

ricachón (S.): rich one.

sarastallaman (Q.): lifting of the corn; ritual in which women transport the harvested corn to the dispensary.

saya (Q.): division in halves; refers to the moiety division of anansaya/ urinsaya; conceptual dual grid that overlays the agricultural fields of Cabanaconde and which guides water distribution and management in the local model.

sectorista (S.): extension agent; representative of the state's irrigation bureaucracy who resides part-time at the local level.

serranos (S.): highlanders; people from the sierra.

Shining Path: a revolutionary movement that took up armed struggle in the Peruvian Andes in 1980.

sierra (S.): mountains, refers to the Andean highlands.

sistema informal (S.): anarchic informal system used during the rainy season; *see also* tiyaq, muyuq.

sol (S.): the "sun"; a monetary unit that is equal to one hundred centavos. Its value has changed tremendously over time. In 1986, a new currency, the inti (Quechua for "sun"), replaced the sol (1,000 soles to one inti). Both currencies were in circulation simultaneously. In 1990, because of hyperinflation and the continued devaluation of the inti, the inti was replaced by the "new" sol (one million intis to one "new" sol).

solay (?): sowing ritual; the water mayors' second round of irrigation water.

susto (S.): illness caused by a sudden movement or shock.

suyu (Q.): a spatial divisioning or apportionment of tasks.

tapados (S.): hidden treasures.

tapar seco (S.): to plug dry; to effectively seal the canals and plug leaks.

taypi (A.): the center.

tierra (S.): earth; also refers to earth illness.

tinkachu (Q.): major social event on first day of irrigation round that the water mayor and his family sponsors.

tinkay (Q.): a libation ritual in which corn beer, wine, or hard liquor is ceremonially dripped or sprinkled on the earth or in the direction of a given mountain.

tinku (Q.): a meeting or encounter; refers to the ritual battles often fought between moieties.

tinkunas (Q.): place where two canals come together; refers to the irrigation offtakes generally used to channel excess water back to the Hualca-Hualca River.

tiyaq (Q.): water guards used during the informal system by irrigators. Family members, hired day-laborers, or irrigators taking turns among themselves, the tiyaq guard the large intakes where the main canals meet the river or secondary canals, making sure that no one redirects the water. Works in concert with muyuq.

toma (S.): intake from river to system of canals.

tomatinkay (S. and Q.): major water ritual held above the uppermost intake on the first day of the irrigation round.

torotinkay (S. and Q.): cattle rite during the sowing; disappeared in the mid-1970s with the arrival of the Majes Project.

trago (S.): liquor; low-grade rum that is a central ingredient in many social gatherings and rituals.

trucos (S.): tricks; small performative actions carried out by the water mayors to increase the flow of their water or decrease that of their rival.

tupu (Q.): Agrarian measure of land which is approximately eighty-eight by forty-four yards. There are approximately three tupus to one hectare.

turista (S.): tourist.

uray (Q.): lower.

uray altus (Q.): lower pastures.

uray chakra (Q.): lower cultivated fields.

urinsaya (Q.): lower half; refers to the moiety division. *See* saya.

usutas (Q.): tire sandals.

vicuña (*lama vicugna*) (Q.): a type of fine-wooled, undomesticated camelid that lives in the high puna.

vocales (S.): aldermen.

wakcha (Q.): orphan, poor.

wamani (Q.): mountain deities; *see* cabildos.

Water Fiesta: *see* Fiesta de Agua.

water mayor: *see* yaku alcaldes.

wayra maki (Q.): wind hands; opposite of warm hands (q'uñi maki). Men have "wind hands," which make the dispensary empty quickly.

wikchas (A.): offtakes; *see* tinkunas.

wititi (Q.): formerly a kind of tinku in which the moieties of Cabanaconde faced off in a sling fight; now a competitive dance during Carnival.

yaku alcaldes (Q. and S.): peasant "water mayors"; the water mayors are local authorities who carry snake-headed staffs and who are in charge of physically and ritually managing water distribution during the longest and most crucial period of the yearly irrigation cycle, from June through December.

yaku mama (Q.): Water Mother; deity of native Andean religion who resides in lakes and rivers.

yakutinkay (Q.): water rite; major ritual on the first day of the new irrigation round; refers to both the tomatinkay and tinkachu.

yunga (Q.): warm lower climes that encompass the orchards.

yarq'a asp'iy (Q.): canal scraping; refers to the Water Fiesta.

zanjas (S.): small rivulets and channels through which water flows.

Bibliography

ARCHIVES

ADA Archivo Departamental de Arequipa
AAA Archivo Arzobispal de Arequipa
BMC Books of the Municipal Council, Cabanaconde
BIC Books of the Irrigators Commission, Cabanaconde
BJP Books of the Justice of the Peace, Cabanaconde
BPA Books of the Parish Archive, Cabanaconde
BPC Books of the Peasant Community, Cabanaconde

PUBLISHED SOURCES

Abercrombie, Thomas. 1991. "To Be Indian, to Be Bolivian." In *Nation-States and Indians in Latin America*, edited by Greg Urban and Joel Sherzer, 95–130. Austin: University of Texas Press.
———. 1998. *Pathways of Memory and Power: Ethnography and History among an Andean People*. Madison: University of Wisconsin Press.
Abril Benavides, Dionicio Nilo. 1979. "Estudio hidrogeológico de la cuenca del río Hualca-Hualca." B.A. thesis, Universidad Nacional San Agustín de Arequipa.
Ackerman, Raquel. 1991. "Clothes and Identity in the Central Andes: Province of Abancay, Peru." In *Textile Traditions of Mesoamerica and the Andes: An Anthology*, edited by Margot Blum Schevill, Janet Catherine Berlo, and Edward B. Dwyer, 231–260. New York: Garland Publishing.
Aguirre, Carlos, and Charles Walker, eds. 1990. *Bandoleros, abigeos y montoneros: Criminalidad y violencia en el Peru, Siglos XVII–XX*. Lima: Instituto de Apoyo Agrario.
Alberti, Giorgio, and Enrique Mayer, eds. 1974. *Reciprocidad e intercambio en los Andes peruanos*. Lima: Instituto de Estudios Peruanos.
Albó, Xavier. 1973. *El futuro de los idiomas oprimidos en los Andes*. La Paz: Centro de Investigación y Promoción del Campesinado.
———.1994. "And from Kataristas to MNRistas? The Surprising and Bold Alliance between Aymaras and Neoliberals in Bolivia." In *Indigenous Peoples and Democracy in Latin America*, edited by Donna Lee Van Cott, 55–82. New York: St. Martin's Press.

Allen, Katherine. 1988. *The Hold Life Has*. Washington, D.C.: Smithsonian Institution Press.

Altamirano, G. Jose Segura. 1992. *Organización campesina y manejo del agua: problemática y alternativas en la sierra de Salas—Lambayeque*. Cusco: Bartolomé de las Casas.

Altamirano, Teofilo. 1984. *Presencia Andina en Lima Metropolitana: Un estudio sobre migrantes y clubes de provincianos*. Lima: Pontificia Universidad Católica del Peru.

———. 1990. *Los que se fueron: Peruanos en Estados Unidos*. Lima: P.U.C. Press.

Altieri, Miguel A. 1987. *Agroecology: The Scientific Basis of Alternative Agriculture*. Boulder, Colo.: Westview Press.

Andaluz, Antonio, and Walter Valdéz. 1987. *Derecho ecológico peruano: inventario normativo*. Lima: Editorial Gredes.

Anderson, Benedict. 1983. *Imagined Communities: Reflections on the Origin and Spread of Nationalism*. London: Verso.

Anderson, E. N. 1996. *Ecologies of the Heart: Emotion, Belief, and the Environment*. New York: Oxford University Press.

Andreas, Carol. 1985. *When Women Rebel: The Rise of Popular Feminism in Peru*. Westport, Conn.: Lawrence Hill and Co.

Apffel-Marglin, Frederique, ed. 1998. *The Spirit of Regeneration: Andean Culture Confronting Notions of Development*. New York: Zed Books.

Arguedas, José María. 1964. "Puquio, una cultura en proceso de cambio." Lima: Universidad Nacional Mayor de San Marcos.

———. 1985. *Yawar Fiesta*. Translated by Frances Horning Barraclough. Austin: University of Texas Press.

Astete, Fernando. 1984. "Los sistemas hidráulicos del valle de Cuzco (pre-hispánicos)." B.A. thesis, Universidad Nacional San Antonio Abad de Cuzco.

Autodema (Autoridad Autónoma de Majes). n.d. "Esto es majes . . . un sueño hecho realidad." Arequipa: Autodema.

Babb, Florence E. 1989. *Between Field and Cooking Pot: The Political Economy of Marketwomen in Peru*. Austin: University of Texas Press.

Barriga, Victor M. 1955. *Documentos para la historia de Arequipa*. Vol. 3. Arequipa: Editorial La Colmena.

Bastien, Joseph. 1978. *The Mountain of the Condor*. New York: West Publishing Co.

———. 1985. "Qollahuaya-Andean Body Concepts: A Topographical-Hydraulic Model of Physiology." *American Anthropologist* 87: 595–611.

Bauer, Brian. 1992. *The Development of the Inca State*. Austin: University of Texas Press.

Belote, Linda, and Jim Belote. 1988. "Gender, Ethnicity, and Modernization: Saraguro Women in a Changing World." In *Multidisciplinary Studies in Andean Anthropology*, edited by Virginia J. Vitzthum, 101–117. Ann Arbor: University of Michigan Press.

Benavides, María. 1983. "Two Traditional Andean Peasant Communities under the Stress of Market Penetration: Yanque and Madrigal in the Colca Valley, Peru." Master's thesis, University of Texas at Austin.

———. 1987. "Análisis del uso de tierras registrado en las visitas de los siglos XVI y XVII a los Yanque Collaguas, Arequipa, Perú." Oxford: *B.A.R. International Series*.

———. 1988a. "La división social y geográfica Hanansaya/Hurinsaya en el valle de Colca y la provincia de Caylloma." In *The Cultural Ecology, Archeology, and History of Terracing and Terrace Abandonment in the Colca Valley of Southern Peru*, edited by William Denevan. Technical Report to the National Science Foundation. Vol. 2, 46–53. Madison: Department of Geography, University of Wisconsin at Madison.

———. 1988b. "Grupos de poder en el Valle del Colca (Arequipa): Siglos XVI–XX," In *Sociedad andina, pasado y presente: contribuciones en homenaje de Cesar Fonseca Martel*, edited by Ramiro Matos Mendieta, 153–177. Lima: Fomciencia.

———. 1991. "Dualidad social e ideologica en la Provincia de Collaguas: Peru: Siglos XVI y XVII." Paper presented to *Quintas Jornadas de Historiadores Americanistas*, Santa Fe, Granada.

Blakie, Piers M., and Harold Brookfield. 1987. *Land Degradation and Society*. New York: Methuen.

Boelens, Rutgerd. 1998. "Equity and Rule-Making." In *Searching for Equity: Conceptions of*

Justice and Equity in Peasant Irrigation, edited by Rutgerd Boelens and Gloria Dávila, 16–34. Amsterdam: Van Gorcum.

Boelens, Rutgerd and Gloria Dávila, eds. 1998. *Searching for Equity: Conceptions of Justice and Equity in Peasant Irrigation*. Amsterdam: Van Gorcum.

Bolin, Inge. 1994. "Levels of Autonomy in the Organization of Irrigation in the Highlands of Peru." In *Irrigation at High Altitudes: The Social Organization of Water Control in the Andes*, edited by William P. Mitchell and David Guillet, 141–166. Washington, D.C.: Society for Latin American Anthropology and the American Anthropological Association.

Bolton, Ralph, and Enrique Mayer, eds. 1977. *Andean Kinship and Marriage*. Washington, D.C.: American Anthropological Association.

Bourdieu, Pierre. 1977. *Outline of a Theory of Practice*. Cambridge: Cambridge University Press.

———. 1990. *The Logic of Practice*. Stanford: Stanford University Press.

Bourgois, Philippe. 1996. *In Search of Respect: Selling Crack in El Barrio*. Cambridge: Cambridge University Press.

Bourque, Susan, and Kay Warren. 1981. *Women of the Andes: Patriarchy and Social Change in Two Peruvian Towns*. Ann Arbor: University of Michigan Press.

———. 1989. "Democracy without Peace: The Cultural Politics of Terror in Peru." *Latin American Research Review* 24, no. 1: 7–34.

Bourricaud, Francois. 1975. "Indian, Mestizo, and Cholo As Symbols in the Peruvian System of Stratification." In *Ethnicity: Theory and Practice*, edited by Nathan Glazer and Daniel P. Moynihan, 350–387. Cambridge: Harvard University Press.

Bouysse-Cassagne, Therese, and Olivia Harris. 1987. "Pacha: en torno al pensamiento aymara." In *Tres reflexiones sobre el pensamiento andino*, edited by Therese Bouysse-Cassagne, Olivia Harris, Tristan Platt, and Veronica Cereceda, 11–60. La Paz, Bolivia: Hisbol.

Bridges, Marilyn. 1991. *Planet Peru: An Aerial Journey through a Timeless Land*. New York: Professional Photography Division of Eastman Kodak Company and Aperture Foundation.

Brush, Stephen. 1977. *Mountain, Field, and Family*. Philadelphia: University of Pennsylvania Press.

Brysk, Alison. 1994. "Acting Globally: Indian Rights and International Politics in Latin America." In *Indigenous Peoples and Democracy in Latin America*, edited by Donna Lee Van Cott, 29–54. New York: St. Martin's Press.

Bunker, Stephen. 1985. *Underdeveloping the Amazon*. Urbana: University of Illinois Press.

Bunker, Stephen, and Linda Seligman. 1986. "Organización social y visión ecológica de un sistema de riego andino." *Allpanchis* 28, no. 27: 149–178.

Caballero, José. 1980. *Agricultura, reforma agraria y pobreza campesina*. Lima: Instituto de Estudios Peruanos.

Camino, Alejandro. 1980. "Tiempo y espacio en la estrategia de subsistencia andina: Un caso en las vertientes orientales sud-peruanas." In *Senri Ethnological Studies*, edited by Luis Millones and Hiroyasu Tomoeda. No. 10, 11–38. Osaka, Japan: National Museum of Ethnology.

Candler, Kay. 1993. "Place and Thought in a Quechua Household Ritual." Ph.D. dissertation, University of Illinois at Urbana-Champaign.

Castelli, Amalia, Marcia Koth de Paredes, and Mariana Mould de Pease, eds. 1981. *Etnohistoria y antropología andina*. Lima: Aguarico.

Cavallero, Raffael. 1991. *Large Site Methodology. Architectural Analysis and Dual Organization in the Andes*. Calgary, Alberta: Occasional Papers No. 5, Department of Archaeology, University of Calgary.

Cereceda, Veronica. 1987. "Aproximaciones a una estética andina: de la belleza al Tinku." In *Tres reflexiones sobre el pensamiento andino*, edited by Therese Bouysse-Cassagne, Olivia Harris, Tristan Platt, and Veronica Cereceda, 133–231. La Paz, Bolivia: Hisbol.

Chang, K. C. 1983. *Art, Myth, and Ritual: The Path to Political Authority in Ancient China*. Cambridge: Harvard University Press.

Chungara de Barrios, Domitila, and Moema Viezzer. 1979. *Let Me Speak! Testimony of*

Domitila, a Woman of the Bolivian Mines. Translated by Victoria Ortiz. New York: Monthly Review Press.

Clifford, James, and George Marcus, eds. 1986. *Writing Culture.* Berkeley: University of California Press.

Cock, Guillermo. 1978. "Los kurakas de los Collaguas: poder político y poder económico." *Revista del Museo Nacional de Historia,* no. 10: 95–125.

Cohen, John. 1979. *Q'eros: the shape of survival.* Berkeley, Calif.: Center for Media and Independent Learning. Film.

Collins, Jane. 1986. "The Household and Relations of Production in Southern Peru." *Comparative Studies in Society and History* 28, no. 4: 651–671.

Colloredo-Mansfeld, Rudy. 1999. *The Native Leisure Class: Consumption and Cultural Creativity in the Andes.* Chicago: University of Chicago Press.

Comaroff, John, and Jean Comaroff. 1992. *Ethnography and the Historical Imagination.* Boulder, Colo.: Westview Press.

Conklin, William. 1990. "Architecture of the Chimu: Memory, Function, and Image." In *The Northern Dynasties: Kingship and Statecraft in Chimor,* edited by Michael E. Mosely and Alana Cordy-Collins, 43–74. Washington, D.C.: Dunbarton Oaks.

Cook, David N. 1982. *The People of the Colca Valley: A Population Study.* Boulder, Colo.: Westview Press.

COPASA (Cooperación Peruana Alemana de Seguridad Alimentaria). 1997. "Estrategia de Intervención en los Sistemas de Riego Del Valle Del Colca." In *Serie Documentos Memoria Interna.* Arequipa: PDR-COPASA.

Costa y Cavero, Ramón. 1939. *Legislación de aguas e irrigación.* Lima.

Crawford, Stanley. 1988. *Mayordomo: Chronicle of an Acequia in Northern New Mexico.* Albuquerque: University of New Mexico Press.

Cronon, William. 1983. *Changes in the Land: Indians, Colonists, and the Ecology of New England.* New York: Hill and Wang.

Cruz Torres, Maria. 1992. "Shrimp Mariculture in Mexico." *World Aquaculture* 23, no. 1: 49–53.

Cuba, Saúl. 1988. "Informe Médico." Cabanaconde.

Davies, Thomas M. 1974. *Indian Integration in Peru: A Half Century of Experience, 1900–1948.* Lincoln: University of Nebraska Press.

de la Cadena, Marisol. 1991. "'Las mujeres son más indias': Etnicidad y género en una comunidad de Cusco." *Revista Andina* 9, no. 1: 7–29.

de la Torre, Carlos, and Manuel Burga, eds. 1986. *Andenes y camellones en el Perú andino.* Lima: Concytec.

de la Vera Cruz, Pablo. 1987. "Cambios en los patrones de asentamiento y el uso y abandono de los andenes en Cabanaconde, Valle del Colca, Perú." In *Pre-Hispanic Agricultural Fields in the Andean Region,* edited by William Denevan, Kent Mathewson, and Gregory Knapp, 89–128. Oxford: B.A.R. International Series.

Delgado Bedoya, Enrique. 1988. "Informe final del trabajo de campo." Lima: Pontificia Universidad Católica.

Denevan, William. 1987. "Terrace Abandonment in the Colca Valley, Peru." In *Pre-Hispanic Agricultural Fields in the Andean Region,* edited by William Denevan, Kent Mathewson, and Gregory Knapp, 1–44. Oxford: B.A.R. International Series.

———, ed. 1986. *The Cultural Ecology, Archeology, and History of Terracing and Terrace Abandonment in the Colca Valley of Southern Peru.* Technical Report to the National Science Foundation. Vol. 1. Madison: Department of Geography, University of Wisconsin at Madison.

———. 1988. *The Cultural Ecology, Archeology, and History of Terracing and Terrace Abandonment in the Colca Valley of Southern Peru.* Technical Report to the National Science Foundation. Vol. 2. Madison: Department of Geography, University of Wisconsin at Madison.

Dillon, Mary, and Thomas Abercrombie. 1988. "The Destroying Christ: An Aymara Myth of Conquest." In *Rethinking Myth and History: Indigenous South American Perspectives on the Past,* edited by Jonathan D. Hill, 50–77. Urbana: University of Illinois Press.

Dover, Robert V. H., Katherine E. Seibold, and John H. McDowell, eds. 1992. *Andean Cosmologies through Time.* Bloomington: Indiana University Press.

Duvoils, Pierre. 1973. "Huari y Llacuaz: una relación prehispánica de oposición y complementaridad." *Revista del Museo Nacional* 39: 153–191.

Earle, Timothy. 1978. *Economic and Social Organization of a Complex Chiefdom: The Halelea District, Kaua'i, Hawaii.* Ann Arbor: Museum of Anthropology, University of Michigan.

Earls, John. 1971. "The Structure of Modern Andean Social Categories." *Journal of the Steward Anthropological Society* 3, no. 1: 69–106.

Echeandia, Juan. 1981. *Tecnología y cambios en San Pedro de Casta.* Lima: San Marcos.

Erasmus, Charles. 1977. *In Search of the Common Good: Utopian Experiments Past and Future.* New York: Free Press.

Erickson, Clark. 1988. "An Archaeological Investigation of Raised Field Agriculture in the Lake Titicaca Basin of Peru." Ph.D dissertation, University of Illinois, Urbana-Champaign.

Erickson, Clark, and Kay Candler. 1989. "Raised Fields and Sustainable Agriculture in the Lake Titicaca Basin of Peru." In *Fragile Lands of Latin America: Strategies for Sustainable Development*, edited by John Browder, 230–249. Boulder, Colo.: Westview Press.

Escobar, Arturo. 1995. *Encountering Development: The Making and Unmaking of the Third World.* Princeton: Princeton University Press.

Espinoza Soriano, Waldemar. 1971. "Agua y riego en tres ayllas de Huarochirí, Siglo XV y XVI." In *Actas y Memorias del 34 Congreso International de Americanistas.* Vol. 3, 147–166. Lima.

"Estudio de Huataq." 1985. Cabanaconde communal archives.

Femenias, Blenda B. 1991. "Regional Dress of the Colca Valley, Peru: A Dynamic Tradition." In *Textile Traditions of Mesoamerica and the Andes: An Anthology*, edited by Margot Blum Schevill, Janet Catherine Berlo, and Edward B. Dwyer, 179–204. New York: Garland Publishing.

———. 1997.$2Ambiguous Emblems: Gender, Clothing, and Representation in Contemporary Peru." Ph.D. dissertation, University of Wisconsin at Madison.

Flores Galindo, Alberto. 1977. *Arequipa y el sur andino: Siglos XVIII–XX.* Lima: Editoial Horizonte.

———. 1987a. *Buscando un Inca: Identidad y utopía en los Andes.* Lima: Instituto de Apoyo Agrario.

———. 1987b. "In Search of An Inca." In *Resistance, Rebellion, and Consciousness in the Andean Peasant World, Eighteenth to Twentieth Centuries*, edited by Steve J. Stern, 193–210. Madison: University of Wisconsin Press.

Flores Ochoa, Jorge A. 1977. *Pastores de Puna. Uywamichiq punarunakuna.* Lima: Instituto de Estudios Peruanos.

———. 1985. "Interaction and Complementarity in Three Zones of Cuzco." In *Andean Ecology and Civilization: An Interdisciplinary Perspective on Andean Ecological Complementarity*, edited by Shozo Masuda, Izumi Shimada, and Craig Morris, 251–276. Tokyo: University of Tokyo Press.

Fock, Niels. 1981. "Ecology and Mind in an Andean Irrigation Culture." *Folk* 23: 311–330.

Fonseca, César. 1976. "Organización dual del sistema en las comunidades de Chaupihuaranga, Peru." *Actas del Congreso Internacional de Americanistas* 3: 445–552.

———. 1983. "El control comunal del agua en la cuenca del río Cañete." *Allpanchis* 19, no. 22: 61–74.

Fonseca, César, and Enrique Mayer. 1979. "Sistemas agrarios en la cuenca del río Cañete, Departmento de Lima." Lima: Impreso ONERN (Oficina Nacional de Energía y Recursos Naturales).

Fortmann, Louise P. 1989. "Great Planting Disasters: Pitfalls in Technical Assistance in Forestry." *Agricultural and Human Values* 5: 49–60.

Fuenzalida, Fernando. 1970. "La matriz colonial." *Revista del Museo Nacional* 35: 91–123.

———. 1971. "Poder, etnia y estratificación en Perú rural." In *Perú: Hoy*, 8–86. Madrid: Siglo Veinte Uno.

Galdos, Guillermo. 1985. *Kuntisuyu.* Arequipa: Fundación M. J. Bustamante de la Fuente.

Gandarillas A., Humberto, Luis Salazar V., Loyda Sánchez B., Luis Carlos Sánchez E., and Pierre de Zutter, eds. 1994. *Dios da el Agua. Que Hacen los Proyectos? Manejo de Agua y Organización Campesina.* Bolivia: Proyecto de Riego Inter Valles.

Geertz, Clifford. 1980. *Negara*. Princeton: Princeton University Press.
———. 1998. "Deep Hanging Out." *New York Review of Books* 45, no. 16: 69–72.
Gelles, Paul H. 1984a. "Agua, faenas, y organización comunal en los Andes: el caso de San Pedro de Casta." Master's thesis, Pontificia Universidad Católica.
———. 1984b. "Agua, faenas y organización comunal: San Pedro de Casta." *Antropológica* 2, no. 2: 305–334.
———. 1986a. "Sociedades hidraúlicas en los Andes: algunas perspectivas desde Huarochiri." *Allpanchis* 27: 99–147.
———. 1986b. "Selected Aspects of Dual Organization in Protohistoric and Contemporary Andean Societies." Special Paper, Harvard University.
———. 1988. *Los Hijos de Hualca-Hualca: Historia de Cabanaconde*. Arequipa: CAPRODA (Centro de Apoyo y Promoción al Desarollo Agrario).
———. 1990. "Channels of Power, Fields of Contention: The Politics and Ideology of Irrigation in an Andean Peasant Community." Ph.D dissertation, Harvard University.
———. 1992. "'Caballeritos' and Maíz Cabanita: Colonial Categories and Andean Ethnicity in the Quincentennial Year." *Kroeber Anthropological Society Papers* 75–76: 14–27. Oakland, Calif.: GRT Press.
———. 1993. "Irrigation As a Cultural System: Introductory Remarks." In *Proceedings of the Chacmool Conference*, pp. 329–332. Calgary, Alberta: University of Calgary Archeological Association.
———. 1994. "Channels of Power, Fields of Contention: The Politics of Irrigation and Land Recovery in an Andean Peasant Community." In *Irrigation at High Altitudes: The Social Organization of Water Control in the Andes*, edited by William P. Mitchell and David Guillet, 233–273. Washington, D.C.: Society for Latin American Anthropology and the American Anthropological Association.
———. 1995. "Equilibrium and Extraction: Dual Organization in the Andes." *American Ethnologist* 22, no. 4: 710–742.
———. 1996a. "Introduction." In *Andean Lives: Gregorio Condori Mamani and Asunta Quispe Huamán*, edited by Ricardo Valderrama and Carmen Escalante, 1–13. Austin: University of Texas Press.
———. 1996b. "The Political Ecology of Irrigation in an Andean Peasant Community." In *Canals and Communities: Small-Scale Irrigation Systems*, edited by Jonathan Mabry, 88–115. Tucson: University of Arizona Press.
Gelles, Paul H., and Gabriela Martínez. 1996. "Glossary and Annotations." In *Andean Lives: Gregorio Condori Mamani and Asunta Quispe Huamán*, edited by Ricardo Valderrama and Carmen Escalante, 145–179. Austin: University of Texas Press.
Gelles, Paul H., and Wilton Martínez. 1993. *Transnational Fiesta: 1992*. Berkeley, Calif.: Center for Media and Independent Learning. Film.
Glick, Thomas. 1970. *Irrigation and Society in Medieval Valencia*. Cambridge: Harvard University Press.
Godoy, Ricardo. 1984. *Common Field Agriculture: The Andes and England Compared*. Cambridge: Harvard Institute for International Development Press.
Gose, Peter. 1994. *Deathly Waters and Hungry Mountains: Agrarian Ritual and Class Formation in an Andean Town*. Toronto: University of Toronto Press.
Gudeman, Stephen. 1986. *Economics as Culture: Models and Metaphors as Livelihood*. London: Routledge and Kegan Paul.
Guillet, David. 1985. "Irrigation Management Spheres, Systemic Linkages and Household Spheres in Southern Peru." Paper presented at the annual meeting of the American Anthropological Association, Washington, D.C.
———. 1987. "Terracing and Irrigation in the Peruvian Highlands." *Current Anthropology* 28, no. 4: 409–430.
———. 1992. *Covering Ground: Communal Water Management and the State in the Peruvian Highlands*. Ann Arbor: University of Michigan Press.
———. 1994. "Canal Irrigation and the State: The 1969 Water Law and Irrigation Systems of the Colca Valley of Southwestern Peru." In *Irrigation at High Altitudes: The Social Organization of Water Control Systems in the Andes*, edited by William P. Mitchell and David Guillet, 167–188. Washington, D.C.: Society for Latin American Anthropology and the American Anthropological Association.

Guillet, David, and William Mitchell. 1994. "Introduction: High Altitude Irrigation." In *Irrigation at High Altitudes: The Social Organization of Water Control Systems in the Andes*, edited by William P. Mitchell and David Guillet, 1–20, Washington, D.C.: Society for Latin American Anthropology and the American Anthropological Association.

Gutiérrez, Zulema, and Gerben Gerbrandy. 1998. "Water Distribution, Social Organization and Equity in the Andean Vision." In *Searching for Equity: Conceptions of Justice and Equity in Peasant Irrigation*, edited by Rutgerd Boelens and Gloria Dávila, 242–249. Amsterdam: Van Gorcum.

Harris, Olivia. 1985. "Ecological Duality and the Role of the Center: Northern Potosi." In *Andean Ecology and Civilization*, edited by Shozo Masuda, Izumi Shimada, and Craig Morris, 311–336. Tokyo: University of Tokyo Press.

Harrison, Regina. 1989. *Signs, Songs, and Memory in the Andes*. Austin: University of Texas Press.

Harvey, Penelope. 1994. "The Presence and Absence of Speech in the Communication of Gender." In *Bilingual Women: Anthropological Approaches to Second Language Use*, edited by Pauline Burton, Ketaki Kushari Dyson, and Shirley Ardener, 44–64. Oxford: Berg Press.

Hecht, Susanna, and Alexander Cockburn. 1990. *The Fate of the Forest: Developers, Destroyers, and Defenders of the Amazon*. New York: Harper.

Herzfeld, Michael. 1992. *The Social Production of Indifference: Exploring the Symbolic Roots of Western Bureaucracy*. Chicago: University of Chicago Press.

Hollis, Martin, and Steven Lukes, eds. 1984. *Rationality and Relativism*. Cambridge: MIT Press.

Hoogendam, Paul. 1998. "¿Hasta dónde llegamos en nuestro entendimiento de la Gestión campesina de sistemas de riego en los Andes?" Paper presented at the Seminario Internacional about "Gestión campesina de sistemas de riego," Cochabamba, Bolivia.

Hopkins, Diane. 1982. "Juego de enemigos." *Allpanchis* 20: 167–188.

Huallpa, Alberto Pilares. 1992. *Los proyectos de riego en las communidades de zonas altoandinas: Impacto socio-económico del riego en la communidad de Huichay-Jaran (Puno)*. Cuzco, Peru: Bartolomé de las Casas.

Hunt, Robert, and Eva Hunt. 1976. "Canal Irrigation and Local Social Organization." *Current Anthropology* 17: 389–411.

Hurley, William. 1978. "Highland Peasants and Rural Development in Southern Peru: The Colca Valley and the Majes Project." Ph.D. dissertation, Oxford University.

Isbell, Billy Jean. 1974. "Kuyaq: Those Who Love Me. An Analysis of Andean Kinship and Reciprocity within a Ritual." In *Reciprocidad e intercambio en los Andes peruanos*, edited by Giorgio Alberti and Enrique Mayer, 110–152. Lima: Instituto de Estudios Peruanos.

———. 1978. *To Defend Ourselves: Ritual and Ecology in an Andean Village*. Austin: University of Texas Press.

Ismodes, Amparo, and María Angélica Salinas. 1985. "Organización económico social de la comunidad campesina en Cabanaconde." B.A. thesis, Universidad Nacional San Agustín de Arequipa.

Julien, Catherine J. 1982. "Inca Decimal Administration in the Lake Titicaca Region." In *The Inca and Aztec States, 1400–1800*, edited by George Collier, Renato Rosaldo, and John Wirth, 121–151. New York: Academic Press.

———. 1983. *Hatunqolla: A View of Inca Rule from the Lake Titicaca Region*. Series Publications in Anthropology, vol. 15. Berkeley: University of California Press.

———. 1991. *Condesuyo: The Political Division of Territory under Inca and Spanish Rule*. Bonn, Germany: Estudios Americanistas de la Universidad de Bonn.

Kearney, Michael. 1996. *Reconceptualizing the Peasantry: Anthropology in Global Perspective*. Boulder, Colo.: Westview Press.

Kelly, William. 1983. "Concepts in the Anthropological Study of Irrigation." *American Anthropologist* 85: 880–886.

Kertzer, David I. 1988. *Ritual, Politics, and Power*. New Haven, Conn.: Yale University Press.

Kirk, Robin. 1992. *Untold Terror: Violence against Women in Peru's Armed Conflict*. New York: Human Rights Watch.

———. 1997. *The Monkey's Paw*. Amherst: University of Massachusetts Press.

Kondo, Dorinne K. 1990. *Crafting Selves: Power, Gender, and Discourses of Identity in a Japanese Workplace*. Chicago: University of Chicago Press.

Kosok, Paul. 1965. *Life, Land, and Water in Ancient Peru*. New York: Long Island University Press.

Kristal, Efraín. 1987. *The Andes Viewed from the City: Literary and Political Discourse on the Indian in Peru, 1848–1930*. New York: Lang Publishing.

Kus, James. 1980. "La agricultura en la costa norte del Perú." *América Indígena* 40, no. 4: 713–729.

Landau, Martin. 1990. "On Decision Strategies and Management Structures: With Special Reference to Experimentation." In *Social, Economic, and Institutional Issues in Third World Irrigation Managment*, edited by R. K. Sampath and Robert A. Young, 59–74. Studies in Water Policy and Managment, no. 15. Boulder, Colo.: Westview Press.

Langer, Erick D. 1993. "Native Cultural Retention and the Struggle for Land in Early Twentieth-Century Bolivia." In *The Indian in Latin American History: Resistance, Resilience, and Acculturation*, edited by John E. Kicza, 171–196. Wilmington, Del.: Jaguar Books.

Lansing, Stephen J. 1989. *The Goddess and the Computer*. Los Angeles: University of Southern California. Film.

———. 1991. *Priests and Programmers: Technologies of Power in the Engineered Landscape of Bali*. Princeton: Princeton University Press.

———. 1996. "Simulation Modeling of Balinese Irrigation." In *Canals and Communities: Small-Scale Irrigation Systems*, edited by Johatan Mabry, 139–156. Tucson: University of Arizona Press.

Leach, Edmund R. 1954. *Political Systems of Highland Burma: A Study of Kachin Social Structure*. London: Athlone Press.

———. 1961. *Pul Eliya*. Cambridge: Cambridge University Press.

Lees, Susan. 1973. *Sociopolitical Aspects of Canal Irrigation in the Valley of Oaxaco*. Ann Arbor: Museum of Anthropology, University of Michigan.

Lévi-Strauss, Claude. 1949 [1969]. *The Elementary Structures of Kinship*. Boston: Beacon Press.

———. 1963. *Structural Anthropology*. New York: Basic Books.

———. 1976. *Structural Anthropology II*. Chicago: University of Chicago Press.

Ley General de Aguas. 1969. Perú.

Lira, Jorge A. 1982. *Diccionario Kkechuwa-Español*. 2d. ed. Bogotá: Editora Guadalupe.

Lombardi, Francisco. 1988. *The Mouth of the Wolf*. New York: Cine Vista. Film.

Long, Norman, and Bryan Roberts, eds. 1978. *Peasant Cooperation and Capitalist Expansion in Central Peru*. Austin: University of Texas Press.

Lowenthal, Abraham F. 1975. *The Peruvian Experiment: Continuity and Change under Military Rule*. Princeton: Princeton University Press.

Lynch, Barbara. 1988. "The Bureaucratic Transition: Peruvian Government Intervention in Sierra Small Scale Irrigation." Ph.D. dissertation, Cornell University.

———. 1991. "Women and Irrigation in Highland Peru." *Society and Natural Resources* 4: 37–52.

———. 1993. "The Bureaucratic Tradition and Women's Invisibility in Irrigation." Proceedings of the 24th Chacmool Conference, 333–342. Calgary, Alberta: University of Calgary Archeological Association.

Mabry, Jonathan B. 1996. "The Ethnology of Local Irrigation." In *Canals and Communities: Small-Scale Irrigation Systems*, edited by Jonathan Mabry, 3–32. Tucson: University of Arizona Press.

Mabry, Jonathan B., and David A. Cleveland. 1996. "The Relevance of Indigenous Irrigation: A Comparative Analysis of Sustainability." In *Canals and Communities: Small-Scale Irrigation Systems*, edited by Jonathan Mabry, 227–260. Tucson: University of Arizona Press.

MacCormack, Sabine. 1991. *Religion in the Andes*. Princeton: Princeton University Press.

Málaga, Alejandro, Ramon Gutiérrez, and Cristina Esteras. 1987. *El valle del Colca: Cinco siglos de arquitectura y urbanismo*. Argentina: Libros de Hispanoamérica.

Mallon, Florencia E. 1983. *The Defense of Community in Peru's Central Highlands: Peasant Struggle and Capitalist Transition, 1860–1940*. Princeton: Princeton University Press.

———. 1995. *Peasant and Nation: The Making of Postcolonial Mexico and Peru*. Berkeley: University of California Press.

Malpass, Michael. 1986. "Prehistoric Agricultural Terracing at Chijra, Coporaque." In *The Cultural Ecology, Archeology, and History of Terracing and Terrace Abandonment in the Colca Valley of Southern Peru*, edited by William Denevan. Technical Report to the National Science Foundation. Vol. 1, 150–166. Madison: Department of Geography, University of Wisconsin at Madison.

Mannheim, Bruce. 1985. "Southern Peruvian Quechua." In *South American Indian Languages, Retrospect and Prospect*, edited by Harriet E. Manelis Cline and Louisa R. Stark, 481–515. Austin: University of Texas Press.

———. 1991. *The Language of the Inka Since the European Invasion*. Austin: University of Texas Press.

Manrique, Nelson. 1985. *Colonialismo y pobreza campesina: Caylloma y el valle del Colca, Siglos XVI–XX*. Lima: DESCO.

———. 1988. *Yawar mayu: sociedades terratenientes serranas, 1879–1910*. Lima: DESCO.

Marcus, George. 1997. "The Uses of Complicity in the Changing Mise-en-Scène of Anthropological Fieldwork." *Representations* 59: 85–108.

Marcus, George, and Michael Fisher. 1986. *Anthropology as Cultural Critique*. Chicago: University of Chicago Press.

Martínez Escobar, Gabriela. 1983. *Ch'ullacuy*. Berkeley, Calif.: Center for Media and Independent Learning. Film.

———. 1994. *Mamacoca: The Other Face of the Leaf*. Berkeley, Calif.: East Bay Media Center.

Marzal, Manuel. 1981. "Los ritos andinos en Andagua a fines de la Colonia." Paper presented at the Tercera Jornada de Ethnohistoria Andina, Lima.

Masson, Luis. 1982. "La recuperación de los andenes como alternativa ecológica para la ampliación de la frontera agrícola." Lima: ONERN (Oficina Nacional de Energía Recursos Naturales).

———. 1987. "La ocupación de andenes en Perú." *Pensamiento Iberoamericano* 12: 179–200.

Matienzo, Juan de. 1567 [1967]. *Gobierno del Perú*. Travaux de l'Institut Francais d'Etudes Andines, t.11. Lima: Institut Francais d'Etudes Andines.

Maybury-Lewis, David. 1960. "The Analysis of Dual Organization: A Methodological Critique." *Anthropologica. Bijdragen tot de Taal-, Land-, en Volkenkunde* 116, no. 1.

———. 1974. *Akwe-Shavante Society*. New York: Oxford University Press.

———. 1979. "Conclusion : Kinship, Ideology, and Culture." In *Dialectical Societies. The Ge and Bororo of Central Brazil*, edited by David Maybury-Lewis, 301–312. Cambridge: Harvard University Press.

———. 1982. "Living in Leviathan: Ethnic Groups and the State." In *The Prospects for Plural Societies*, edited by David Maybury-Lewis, 220–232. Washington, D.C.: American Ethnological Society.

———. 1989. "The Quest for Harmony." In *The Attraction of Opposites: Thought and Society in the Dualistic Mode*, edited by David Maybury-Lewis and Uri Almagor, 1–18. Ann Arbor: University of Michigan Press.

Mayer, Enrique. 1985. "Production Zones." In *Andean Ecology and Civilization*, edited by Shozo Masuda, Izumi Shimada, and Craig Morris, 45–84. Tokyo: University of Tokyo Press.

———. 1991. "Peru in Deep Trouble: Mario Vargas Llosa's 'Inquest in the Andes' Reexamined." *Cultural Anthropology* 6, no. 4: 466–504.

———. 1994. "Recursos naturales, medio ambiente, tecnología y desarrollo." In *Perú: El problema agrario en debate Sepia V*, edited by Oscar Dancourt, Enrique Mayer, and Carlos Monge, 479–534. Lima: Sepia.

McCay, Bonnie J., and James M. Acheson. 1990. *The Question of the Commons: The Culture and Ecology of Communal Resources*. Tucson: University of Arizona Press.

Melville, Roberto. 1994. "TVA y la comisión del Tepalatepec—una comparison tentativa." In *Sistemas hidráulicos, modernización de la agricultura y migración*, edited by Carmen Viqueira Landa and Lydia Torre Medinia Mora, 269–296. Mexico City: Universidad Iberoamericana.

Mendéz, Cecilia. 1991. "Los campesinos, la independencia y la iniciación de la república.

El caso de los iquichanos realistas: Ayacucho 1825–1828." In *Poder y violencia en los Andes*, edited by Henrique Urbano, 165–188. Cuzco: Centro Bartolomé de las Casas.

Mendoza-Walker, Zoila. 1993. "Shaping Society through Dance: Mestizo Ritual Performance in the Southern Peruvian Andes." Ph.D. dissertation, University of Chicago.

Millones, Luis. 1978. "Los ganados del Señor. Mecansimos de poder en las comunidades andinas. Arequipa, Siglos XVII–XIX." *Historia y Cultura* 11: 7–43.

Ministry of Agriculture, Perú. 1980. *Relación de recibos y tarifa de agua para el Distrito de Cabanaconde*.

———. 1987. *Diagnóstico de Cabanaconde*.

Mitchell, William P. 1981. "La agricultura hidraúlica en los Andes: implicaciones evolucionarias." In *Tecnología del mundo andino*, edited by Heather Lechtman and Ana Maria Soldi. Vol. 1, 145–167. Mexico City: Universidad Nacional Autonomo de Mexico.

———. 1991. *Peasants on the Edge: Crop, Cult, and Crisis in the Andes*. Austin: University of Texas Press.

———. 1994. "Dam the Water: The Ecology and Political Economy of Irrigation in the Ayacucho Valley, Peru." In *Irrigation at High Altitudes: The Social Organization of Water Control in the Andes*, edited by William P. Mitchell and David Guillet, 275–302. Washington, D.C: Society for Latin American Anthropology and the American Anthropological Association.

Mitchell, William P., and David Guillet, eds. 1994. *Irrigation at High Altitudes: The Social Organization of Water Control Systems in the Andes*. Washington, D.C: Society for Latin American Anthropology and the American Anthropological Association.

Molinié-Fioravanti, Antoinette. 1986. "The Andean Community Today." In *Anthropological History of Andean Polities*, edited by John V. Murra, Nathan Wachtel, and Jacques Revel, 342–358. Cambridge: Cambridge University Press.

Montoya, Rodrigo. 1987. *La cultura quechua hoy*. Lima: Hueso Húmero Ediciones.

Montoya, Rodrigo, M. J. Silveira, and F. J. Lindoso. 1979. *Producción parcelaria y universo ideológico: El caso de Puquio*. Lima: Mosca Azul Editores.

Moore, Sally. 1958. *Power and Property in Inca Peru*. New York: Columbia University Press.

———. 1986. *Social Facts and Fabrications: Customary Law on Kilimanjaro, 1880–1980*. Cambridge: Cambridge University Press.

Mosely, Michael. 1990. "Structure of History in the Dynastic Lore of Chimor." In *The Northern Dynasties: Kingship and Statecraft in Chimor*, edited by Michael E. Mosely and Alana Cordy-Collins, 1–41. Washington, D.C.: Dumbarton Oaks.

Murra, John. 1968. "An Aymara Kingdom in 1567." *Ethnohistory* 15: 115–151.

———. 1975. *Formaciones económicas y políticas del mundo andino*. Lima: Instituto de Estudios Peruanos.

———. 1980. *The Economic Organization of the Inca State*. Greenwich, Conn.: JAI Press.

———. 1982. "The Cultural Future of the Andean Majority." In *The Prospects for Plural Societies*, edited by David Maybury-Lewis, 30–39. Washington, D.C.: American Ethnological Society.

Murra, John, and Nathan Wachtel. 1986. "Introduction." In *Anthropological History of Andean Polities*, edited by John V. Murra, Nathan Wachtel, and Jacques Revel, 1–8. Cambridge: Cambridge University Press.

Neira, Máximo. 1961. "Los Collaguas." Ph.D. dissertation, Universidad Nacional San Agustín de Arequipa.

Netherly, Patricia. 1984. "The Management of Late Andean Irrigation Systems on the North Coast of Peru." *American Antiquity* 49, no. 2: 227–254.

———. 1990. "Out of Many, One: The Organization of Rule in the North Coast Polities." In *The Northern Dynasties: Kingship and Statecraft in Chimor*, edited by Michael E. Mosely and Alana Cordy-Collins, 461–487. Washington, D.C.: Dumbarton Oaks.

Norgaard, Richard B. 1994. *Development Betrayed: The End of Progress and the Coevolutionary Revisioning of the Future*. New York: Routledge.

Obando Aguirre, Marcos. *El proyecto Majes*. Arequipa: Universidad Nacional San Agustín.

ORDEA. 1980. "Diagnóstico del distrito de riego no. 49: Colca." Sub-dirección nacional de aguas y suelo. Mimeo, Arequipa.

Oré, María Teresa. 1998. "From Agrarian Reform to Privatisation of Land and Water: The

Case of the Peruvian Coast." In *Searching for Equity: Conceptions of Justice and Equity in Peasant Irrigation*, edited by Rutgerd Boelens and Gloria Dávila, 268–278. Amsterdam: Van Gorcum.

Orlove, Benjamin. 1980. "The Position of Rustlers in Regional Society: Social Banditry in the Andes." In *Land and Power in Latin America: Agrarian Economies and Social Processes in the Andes*, edited by Benjamin S. Orlove and Glynn Custred, 179–194. New York: Holmes and Meier Publishers.

———. 1991. "Mapping Reeds and Reading Maps: The Politics of Representation in Lake Titicaca." *American Ethnologist* 18, no. 1: 3–38.

Orlove, Benjamin, Michael Foley , and Thomas Love, eds. 1989. *State, Capital and Rural Society*. Boulder, Colo.: Westview Press.

Orlove, Benjamin, and Ricardo Godoy. 1986. "Sectorial Fallowing Systems in the Andes." *Journal of Ethnobiology* 6, no. 1: 169–204.

Ortiz, Alejandro. 1973. *De Adaneva a Inkarrí. Una visión indígena del Perú*. Lima: Ediciones Retablo de Papel.

Ortner, Sherry. 1984. "Anthropological Theory Since the Sixties." *Comparative Studies in Society and History* 26, no. 1: 126–166.

Ossio, Juan M. 1973. "Guamán Poma: nueva corónica o carta al Rey. Un intento de aproximación a las categorías del pensamiento del mundo andino." In *Ideología mesiánica del mundo andino*, edited by Juan Ossio, 153–215. Lima: Edición Ignacio Prado Pastor.

———. 1976. "El simbolismo del agua en la representación del tiempo y el espacio en la fiesta de la acequia en Andamarca." Mimeograph. Lima: Pontificia Universidad Católica.

———. 1980. "La estructura social de las comunidades andinas." In *Historia del Perú, Tomo II*. Lima: Editorial Mejía Baca.

———. 1992a. *Parentesco, reciprocidad y jerarquía en los Andes: Una aproximación a la organización social de la comunidad de Andamarca*. Lima: Pontificia Universidad Católica.

———. 1992b. *Los indios del Perú*. Madrid: Editorial MAPFRE.

Osterling, Jorge, and Olivera Llanos. 1981. "La Fiesta del Agua en San Pedro de Casta." Mimeograph. Lima: Pontificia Universidad Católica.

Outhwaite, William, and Tom Bottomore, eds. 1993. *The Blackwell Dictionary of Twentieth-Century Social Thought*. Oxford: Blackwell Publishers.

Paerregaard, Karsten. 1989. "Exchanging with Nature: T'inka in an Andean Village." *Folk* 31: 53–73.

———. 1992. "Complementarity and Duality: Oppositions between Agriculturalists and Herders in an Andean Village." *Ethnology* 31, no. 1: 15–25.

———. 1994. "Why Fight over Water? Power, Conflicts, and Irrigation in an Andean Village." In *Irrigation at High Altitudes: The Social Organization of Water Control in the Andes*, edited by William P. Mitchell and David Guillet, 189–202. Washington, D.C.: Society for Latin American Anthropology and the American Anthropological Association.

———. 1997. *Linking Separate Worlds: Urban Migrants and Rural Lives in Peru*. New York: Berg Press.

Palerm, Angel. 1972. *Agricultura y Sociedad en Mesoamérica*. Mexico City: Sepsententas.

Palerm, Juan. 1994. "La intersección del agua y el trabajo en la modern agricultura de California." In *Sistemas Hidráulicos, Modernización de la Agricultura y Migración*, edited by Carmen Viqueira Landa and Lydia Torre Medinia Mora, 41–88. Mexico City: Universidad Iberoamericana.

Palomino, Salvador. 1971. "Duality in the Socio-cultural Organization of Several Andean Populations." *Folk* 13: 65–88.

———. 1984. *El sistema de oposiciones en la comunidad de Sarhua*. Lima: Pueblo Indio.

Patterson, Thomas. 1991. *The Inka Empire: The Formation and Disintegration of a Precapitalist State*. New York: Berg Press.

Pease, Franklin, ed. 1977. *Collaguas I*. Lima: Pontificia Unversidad Católica.

———. 1981. "Ayllu y parcialidad: reflexiones sobre el caso de Collaguas." In *Etnohistoria y antropología andina*, edited by Amalia Castelli, Marcia Koth de Paredes and Mariana Mould de Pease, 19–34. Lima: Aguarico.

Peluso, Nancy Lee. 1992. *Rich Forests, Poor People: Resource Control and Resistance in Java.* Berkeley: University of California Press.

Pfaffenberger, Bryan. 1988. "Fetishised Objects and Humanised Nature: Towards an Anthropology of Technology." *Man* 23, no. 2: 236–252.

Philip, George D.E. 1978. *The Rise and Fall of the Peruvian Military Radicals, 1968–1976.* London: Athlone Press of the University of London.

Platt, Tristan. 1986. "Mirrors and Maize: The Concept of *Yanantin* among the Macha of Bolivia." In *Anthropological History of Andean Polities*, edited by John V. Murra, Nathan Wachtel, and Jacques Revel, 228–259. Cambridge: Cambridge University Press.

———. 1987. "Entre Ch'axwa y Muxsa. Para una historia del pensamiento político Aymara." In *Tres reflexiones sobre el pensamiento andino*, edited by Thérese Bouysse Cassagne, Olivia Harris, Tristan Platt, and Veronica Cereceda, 61–132. La Paz, Bolivia: Hisbol.

Poole, Deborah. 1987. "Landscapes of Power in a Cattle-Rustling Culture of Southern Andean Peru." *Dialectical Anthropology* 12, no. 4: 367–398.

———. 1990. "Ciencia, peligrosidad y represión en la criminología indigenista peruana." In *Bandoleros, abigeos y montoneros*, edited by Carlos Aguirre and Charles Walker, 335–368. Lima: Instituto de Apoyo Agrario.

Portocarrero, Javier, ed. 1986. *Andenería, conservación de suelos y desarollo rural de los Andes peruanos.* Lima: Tarea.

Pratt, Marie Louise. 1986. "Fieldwork in Common Places." In *Writing Culture: The Poetics and Politics of Ethnography*, edited by James Clifford and George Marcus, 27–50. Berkeley: University of California Press.

Pulgar Vidal, Javier. 1987. *Geografía del Perú.* Lima: Peisa.

Rappaport, Joanne. 1994. *Cumbe Reborn: An Andean Ethnography of History.* Chicago: University of Chicago Press.

Rasnake, Roger. 1988. *Domination and Cultural Resistance: Authority and Power among an Andean People.* Durham, N.C.: Duke University Press.

Reinhard, Johan. 1985. "Chavin and Tiahuanaco: A New Look at Two Andean Ceremonial Centers." *National Geographic Research Reports* 1, no. 3: 395–422.

———. 1986. *The Nazca Lines: A New Perspective on Their Origin and Meaning.* Lima: Editorial Los Pinos.

———. 1998. *Discovering the Ice Maiden: My Adventures on Ampato.* Washington, D.C.: National Geographic Society.

Remy, María Isabel. 1994. "The Indigenous Population and the Construction of Democracy in Peru." In *Indigenous Peoples and Democracy in Latin America*, Donna Lee Van Cott, 107–132. New York: St. Martin's Press.

Roddick, Jackie. 1988. *The Dance of the Millions: Latin American and the Debt Crisis.* London: Latin American Bureau.

Rosaldo, Renato. 1986. "From the Door of His Tent: The Fieldworker and the Inquisitor." In *Writing Culture: The Poetics and Politics of Ethnography*, edited by James Clifford and George Marcus, 77–97. Berkeley: University of California Press.

———. 1989. *Culture and Truth.* Boston: Beacon Press.

Roseberry, William. 1989. *Anthropologies and Histories.* New Brunswick: Rutgers University Press.

Rostworowski, María. 1977. *Etnia y sociedad.* Lima: Instituto de Estudios Peruanos.

———. 1978. *Estructuras andinas de poder.* Lima: Instituto de Estudios Peruanos.

———. 1981. "La voz parcialidad en su contexto en los siglos XVI y XVII." In *Etnohistoria y antropología andina*, edited by Amalia Castelli, Marcia Koth de Paredes, and Mariana Mould de Pease, 35–48. Lima: Aguarico.

———. 1983. *Estructuras andinas de poder.* Lima: Instituto de Estudios Peruanos.

———. 1990. "Ethnohistorical Considerations about the Chimor." In *The Northern Dynasties: Kingship and Statecraft in Chimor*, edited by Michael E. Mosely and Alana Cordy-Collins, 447–460. Washington, D.C.: Dumbarton Oaks.

Rowe, John. 1946. "Inca Culture at the Time of the Spanish Conquest." In *Handbook of South American Indians.* Bulletin 143, vol. 2: 183–330. Washington, D.C.: Bureau of American Ethnology.

———. 1982. "Inca Policies and Institutions Relating to the Cultural Unification of the

Empire." In *The Inca and Aztec States 1400–1800. Anthropology and History*, edited by George Collier, Renato Rosaldo, and John Wirth, 93–118. New York: Academic Press.

Rudolph, James D. 1992. *Peru: The Evolution of a Crisis*. New York: Praeger.

Said, Edward. 1978. *Orientalism*. New York: Vintage Books.

Sallnow, Michael. 1987. *Pilgrims of the Andes: Regional Cults in Cusco*. Washington, D.C.: Smithsonian Institution Press.

Salomon, Frank. 1986. *Native Lords of Quito in the Age of the Incas: The Political Economy of North Andean Chiefdoms*. Cambridge: Cambridge University Press.

———. 1987. "Ancestor Cults and Resistance to the State in Arequipa, ca. 1748–1754." In *Resistance, Rebellion, and Consciousness in the Andean Peasant World, Eighteenth to Twentieth Centuries*, edited by Steve J. Stern, 148–165. Madison: University of Wisconsin Press.

———. 1991. "Introduction." In *The Huarochirí Manuscript: A Testament of Ancient and Colonial Andean Religion*, edited by Frank Salomon and George Urioste, 1–38. Austin: University of Texas Press.

Salomon, Frank, and George Urioste. 1991. *The Huarochirí Manuscript: A Testament of Ancient and Colonial Andean Religion*. Austin: University of Texas Press.

Santillán, Hernando de. 1563–1564 [1968]. *Relación del origen, descendencia política, y gobierno de los incas*. Madrid: Biblioteca de Autores Españoles. Vol. 209, 97–149.

Scheper-Hughes, Nancy. 1992. *Death without Weeping: The Violence of Everyday Life in Brazil*. Berkeley: University of California Press.

Schmink, Marianne, and Charles D. Wood. 1992. "The 'Political Ecology' of Amazonia." In *Lands at Risk in the Third World*, edited by Peter D. Little and Michael Horowitz, 38–57. Boulder, Colo.: Westview Press.

Schreiber, Katharina J. 1992. *Wari Imperialism in Middle Horizon Peru*. Ann Arbor: Museum of Anthropology, University of Michigan.

Scott, James C. 1985. *Weapons of the Weak: Everyday Forms of Peasant Resistance*. New Haven, Conn.: Yale University Press.

Scott, Joan Wallach. 1988. *Gender and the Politics of History*. New York: Columbia University Press.

Seligmann, Linda J. 1987. "Land, Labor, and Power: Local Initiative and Land Reform in Huanoquite, Perú." Ph.D. dissertation, University of Illinois at Urbana-Champaign.

———. 1989. "To Be in Between: The *Cholas* as Market Women in Peru." *Comparative Studies in Society and History* 31, no. 4: 694–721.

———. 1995. *Between Reform and Revolution: Political Struggles in the Peruvian Andes, 1969–1991*. Stanford: Stanford University Press.

Seligmann, Linda J., and Stephen G. Bunker. 1994. "An Andean Irrigation System: Ecological Visions and Social Organization." In *Irrigation at High Altitudes: The Social Organization of Water Control in the Andes*, edited by William P. Mitchell and David Guillet, 203–232. Washington, D. C.: Society for Latin American Anthropology and the American Anthropological Association.

Selverston, Melina H. 1994. "The Politics of Culture: Indigenous Peoples and the State in Ecuador." In *Indigenous Peoples and Democracy in Latin America*, edited by Donna Lee Van Cott, 131–154. New York: St. Martin's Press.

Sherbondy, Jeanette E. 1982a. "The Canal Systems of Hanan Cuzco." Ph.D. dissertation, University of Illinois at Urbana-Champaign.

———. 1982b. "El regadío, los lagos y los mitos de origen." *Allpanchis* 17, no. 20: 3–32.

———. 1986. "Los ceques: Código de canales en el Cusco incaico." *Allpanchis* 27: 39–74.

———. 1994. "Water and Power: The Role of Irrigation Districts in the Transition from Inca to Spanish Cuzco." In *Irrigation at High Altitudes: The Social Organization of Water Control in the Andes*, edited by William P. Mitchell and David Guillet, 69–98. Washington, D.C.: Society for Latin American Anthropology and the American Anthropological Association.

Sheridan, Thomas E. 1988. *Where the Dove Calls: The Political Ecology of a Peasant Corporate Community in Northwestern Mexico*. Tucson: University of Arizona Press.

———. 1996. "*La gente es muy perra*: Conflict and Cooperation over Irrigation Water in Cucurpe, Sonora, Mexico." In *Canals and Communities: Small-Scale Irrigation Systems*, edited by Jonathan Mabry, 33–52. Tucson: University of Arizona Press.

Shimada, Izumi. 1985. "Introduction." In *Andean Ecology and Civilization*, edited by Shozo Masuda, Izumi Shimada, and Craig Morris, xi–xxxii. Tokyo: University of Tokyo Press.

Sikkink, Lyn. 1994. "House, Community, and Marketplace: Women as Managers of Exchange Relations and Resources on the Southern Altiplano of Bolivia." Ph.D. dissertation, University of Minnesota at Minneapolis.

Silverblatt, Irene. 1987. *Moon, Sun, and Witches: Gender Ideologies and Class in Inca and Colonial Peru*. Princeton: Princeton University Press.

Sindicato de Trabajadoras de Hogar. 1982. *Basta: Testimonios*. Cuzco: Centro de Estudios Rurales Andinos "Bartolomé de las Casas."

Skar, Harold. 1982. *The Warm Valley People: Duality and Land Reform among the Quechua Indians of Highland Peru*. New York: Columbia University Press.

Skar, Sarah. 1981. "Andean Women and the Concept of Space/Time." In *Women and Space*, edited by Shirley Ardener, 35–49. New York: St. Martin's Press.

Smith, Gavin. 1989. *Livelihood and Resistance: Peasants and the Politics of Land in Peru*. Berkeley: University of California Press.

Smith, M. G. 1982. "The Nature and Variety of Plural Units." In *The Prospects for Plural Societies*, edited by David Maybury-Lewis, 146–186. Washington, D.C.: American Ethnological Society.

Spalding, Karen. 1984. *Huarochirí*. Stanford: Stanford University Press.

Starn, Orin. 1991. "Missing the Revolution: Anthropologists and the War in Perú." *Cultural Anthropology* 6, no. 1: 13–38.

———. 1992. "I Dreamed of Foxes and Hawks: Reflections on Peasant Protest, New Social Movements, and the Rondas Campesinas of Northern Peru." In *The Making of Social Movements in Latin America: Identity, Strategy, and Democracy*, edited by Arturo Escobar and Sonia E. Alvarez, 89–111. Boulder, Colo.: Westview Press.

Starn, Orin, Carlos Iván Degregori, and Robin Kirk, eds. 1995. *The Peru Reader: History, Culture, and Politics*. Durham, N.C.: Duke University Press.

Stern, Steve J. 1987. "New Approaches to the Study of Peasant Rebellion and Consciousness: Implications of the Andean Experience." In *Resistance, Rebellion, and Consciousness in the Andean Peasant World, Eighteenth to Twentieth Centuries*, edited by Steve J. Stern, 3–25. Madison: University of Wisconsin Press.

———, ed. 1998. *Shining and Other Paths: War and Society in Peru, 1980–1995*. Durham, N.C.: Duke University Press.

Stoner, Bradley Philip. 1989. "Health Care Delivery and Health Resource Utilization in a Highland Andean Community of Southern Peru." Ph.D. dissertation, Indiana University.

Sven, Herman. 1986. "Tuteños, chacras, alpacas y Macones." Master's thesis, University of the Netherlands.

Tambiah, Stanley J. 1976. "The Galactic Polity: The Structure of Traditional Kingdoms in Southeast Asia." In *Anthropology and the Climate of Opinion*, edited by Stanley Freed, 69–97. New York: New York Academy of Sciences.

———. 1985. *Culture, Thought, and Social Action: An Anthropological Perspective*. Cambridge: Harvard University Press.

———. 1990. *Magic, Science, Religion, and the Scope of Rationality*. Cambridge: Cambridge University Press.

Taussig, Michael. 1987. *Shamanism, Colonialism, and the Wild Man: A Study in Terror and Healing*. Chicago: University of Chicago Press.

Tello, Julio C., and Próspero Miranda. 1923. "Wallallo: Ceremonias gentilicas realizadas en la región cisandina del Perú Central." *Revista Inca* 1, no. 2: 475–549.

Thorp, Rosemary, and Geoffrey Bertram. 1978. *Peru 1890–1977: Growth and Policy in an Open Economy*. New York: Columbia University Press.

Thurner, Mark. 1997. *From Two Republics to One Divided: Contradictions of Postcolonial Nationmaking in Andean Peru*. Durham, N.C.: Duke University Press.

Tord, Luis Enrique. 1983. *Templos coloniales del Colca, Arequipa*. Lima: Papelera Atlas.

Trawick, Paul. 1994. "The Struggle for Water in the Andes: A Study of Technological Change and Social Decline in the Cotahuasi Valley of Peru." Ph.D. dissertation, Yale University.

Treacy, John M. 1988. "Agricultural Terraces in the Colca Valley: Promises and Problems of an Ancient Technology." In *The Cultural Ecology, Archeology, and History of Terracing and Terrace Abandonment in the Colca Valley of Southern Peru,* edited by William Denevan. Technical Report to the National Science Foundation. Vol. 2, 186–203. Madison: Department of Geography, University of Wisconsin at Madison.

———. 1989. *The Fields of Coporaque: Agricultural Terracing and Water Management in the Colca Valley, Arequipa, Peru.* Ph.D. dissertation, University of Wisconsin, Madison.

———. 1994a. *Las chacras de Coporaque: Andenería y riego en el Valle del Colca.* Lima: Instituto de Estudios Peruanos.

———. 1994b. "Teaching Water: Hydraulic Management and Terracing in Coporaque, the Colca Valley, Peru." In *Irrigation at High Altitudes: The Social Organization of Water Control in the Andes,* edited by William P. Mitchell and David Guillet, 99–114. Washington, D.C.: Society for Latin American Anthropology and the American Anthropological Association.

Trelles, Efraín. 1983. *Lucas Martínez Vegazo: funcionamiento de una encomienda peruana inicial.* Lima: Pontificia Universidad Católica Press.

Turino, Thomas. 1991. "The State and Andean Musical Production in Peru." In *Nation-States and Indians in Latin America,* edited by Greg Urban and Joel Sherzer, 259–285. Austin: University of Texas Press.

Ulin, Robert. 1984. *Understanding Cultures: Perspectives in Anthropology and Social Theory.* Austin: University of Texas Press.

Ulloa Mogollón, Juan de. 1965 [1586]. "Relación de la Provincia de los Collaguas para la descripción de las Indias que Su Majestad manda hacer." In *Relaciones Geográficas de Indias,* edited by Marcos Jiménez de la Espada. Vol. 1, 326–333. Madrid: Biblioteca de Autores Españoles.

Urban, Greg, and Joel Sherzer. 1991. "Introduction: Indians, Nation-State, and Culture." In *Nation-States and Indians in Latin America,* edited by Greg Urban and Joel Sherzer, 1–18. Austin: University of Texas Press.

Urbano, Henrique. 1992. *Modernidad en los Andes.* Cuzco: Centro de Estudios Regionales Andinos "Bartolomé de las Casas."

Urton, Gary. 1981. *At the Crossroads of the Earth and the Sky.* Austin: University of Texas Press.

———. 1984. "Ch'uta: El espacio de la práctica social en Paqaritambo." *Revista Andina* 2, no. 1: 7–56.

———. 1990. *The History of a Myth: Paqaritambo and the Origin of the Inkas.* Austin: University of Texas Press.

Valderrama, Ricardo, and Carmen Escalante. 1976. "Pacha T'inka o la T'inka a la Madre Tierra en el Apurimac." *Allpanchis* 9: 177–192.

———. 1977. *Gregorio Condori Mamani: Autobiografía.* Edición bilingue Quechua-Castellano. Cuzco: Centro de Estudios Rurales Andinos "Bartolomé de las Casas."

———. 1988. *Del Tata Mallku a la MamaPacha: Riego, sociedad y ritos en los Andes peruanos.* Lima: DESCO.

———. 1992. *Nosotros los humanos (Ñuqanchik Runakuna): Testimonio de los quechuas del siglo XX.* Edición bilingue Quechua y Castellano. Cuzco: Centro de Estudios Regionales Andinos "Bartolomé de Las Casas."

Valderrama, Ricardo, and Carmen Escalante, eds. 1996. *Andean Lives: Gregorio Condori Mamani and Asunta Quispe Huamán.* Translated by Paul H. Gelles and Gabriela Martinez. Austin: University of Texas Press.

Valeri, Valerio. 1991. "Afterword." In *Priests and Programmers: Technologies of Power in the Engineered Landscape of Bali,* by Steve Lansing, 134–144, Princeton: Princeton University Press.

Van Cott, Donna Lee. 1994. "Indigenous Peoples and Democracy: Issues for Policymakers." In *Indigenous Peoples and Democracy in Latin America,* edited by Donna Lee Van Cott, 1–28. New York: St. Martin's Press.

Van Den Berghe, Pierre L., and George P. Primov. 1977. *Inequality in the Peruvian Andes: Class and Ethnicity in Cuzco.* Columbia: University of Missouri Press.

Vargas Llosa, Mario. 1987. "The Valley of Marvels." In *Discovering the Colca Valley,* edited by Mauricio de Romaña, Jaume Blassi, and Jordi Blassi, 23–29. Barcelona: Francis O. Pathey and Sons.

Vélez-Ibáñez, Carlos G. 1996. *Border Visions: Mexican Cultures of the Southwest United States.* Tucson: University of Arizona Press.

Viqueira Landa, Carmen, and Lydia Torre Medinia Mora, eds. 1994. *Sistemas hidráulicos, modernización de la agricultura y migración.* Mexico City: Universidad Iberoamericana.

Walker, Charles. 1988. "Los peruanos en los EE.UU.: El caso de Chicago." *Quehacer* (Lima).

———. 1992. "Peasants, Caudillos, and the State in Peru: Cusco in the Transition from Colony to Republic, 1780–1840." Ph.D. dissertation, University of Chicago.

Wasserstrom, Robert. 1985. "'Libertad de mujeres': A Savings and Loan Cooperative in the Bolivian Andes." In *Grassroots Development in Latin America and the Caribbean,* edited by Robert Wasserstrom, 42–68. New York: Praeger.

Weber, Max. 1947. *The Theory of Social and Economic Organization.* New York: Free Press.

Webster, Steven S. 1977. "Kinship and Affinity in a Native Quechua Community." In *Andean Kinship and Marriage,* edited by Ralph Bolton and Enrique Mayer, 28–42. Washington D.C.: American Anthropological Association.

Weismantel, Mary J. 1988. *Food, Gender, and Poverty in the Equadorian Andes.* Philadelphia: University of Pennsylvania Press.

Wheatley, Paul. 1971. *The Pivot of the Four Quarters.* Edinburgh: Edinburgh University Press.

Williams, Raymond. 1980. *Problems in Materialism and Culture.* London: New Left Books.

Wilson, Bryan, ed. 1984. *Rationality.* Worcester, England: Basil Blackwell.

Winterhalder, Bruce. 1994. "The Ecological Basis of Water Managment in the Central Andes: Rainfall and Temperature in Southern Peru." In *Irrigation at High Altitudes: The Social Organization of Water Control in the Andes,* edited by William P. Mitchell and David Guillet, 21–68. Washington, D. C.: Society for Latin American Anthropology and the American Anthropological Association.

Wittfogel, Karl A. 1957. *Oriental Despotism: A Comparative Study of Total Power.* New Haven, Conn.: Yale University Press.

Wolf, Eric. 1982. *Europe and the People without History.* Berkeley: University of California Press.

Zimmerer, Karl S. 1994. "Transforming Colquepata Wetlands: Landscapes of Knowledge and Practice in Andean Agriculture." In *Irrigation at High Altitudes: The Social Organization of Water Control in the Andes,* edited by William P. Mitchell and David Guillet, 99–114. Washington, D.C.: Society for Latin American Anthropology and the American Anthropological Association.

Zorn, Elayne. 1986. "Textiles in Herders' Ritual Bundles of Macusani, Peru." In *The Junius B. Bird Conference on Andean Textiles,* edited by Anne Rowe, 289–307. Washington, D.C.: Textile Museum.

———. 1987. "Encircling Meaning: Economics and Aesthetics in Taquile, Peru." In *Andean Aesthetics: Textiles of Peru and Bolivia,* edited by Blenda Femenias, 67–79. Exhibition catalogue. Madison: Elvehjem Museum of Art and Helen Allen Textile Collection, University of Wisconsin-Madison.

Zuidema, Tom R. 1964. "The Ceque System of Cuzco." Ph.D Dissertation, University of Leiden.

———. 1967. "El juego de los ayllus y el amaru." *Société des Américanistes* 51, no. 1: 41–51.

———. 1982. "Myth and History in Ancient Peru." In *The Logic of Culture,* edited by Ino Rossi, 150–175. South Hadley, Mass.: Bergin and Garvey Publishers.

———. 1986. "Inca Dynasty and Irrigation: Another Look at Andean Concepts of History." In *Anthropological History of Andean Polities,* edited by John V. Murra, Nathan Wachtel, and Jacques Revel, 177–200. Cambridge: Cambridge University Press.

———. 1989. "The Moieties of Cuzco." In *The Attraction of Opposites,* edited by David Maybury-Lewis and Uri Almagor, 255–276. Ann Arbor: University of Michigan Press.

———. 1990a. "Dynastic Structures in Andean Culture." In *The Northern Dynasties: Kingship and Statecraft in Chimor,* edited by Michael E. Mosely and Alana Cordy-Collins, 489–505. Washington, D.C.: Dumbarton Oaks.

———. 1990b. *Inca Civilization in Cuzco.* Translated by Jean-Jacques Decoster. Austin: University of Texas Press.

Index

About the Author

Paul H. Gelles is an associate professor of anthropology at the University of California at Riverside. Formerly a postdoctoral fellow in the College of Natural Resources at the University of California at Berkeley, he has carried out research on different aspects of highland society in the central and southern Peruvian Andes. He is the author of numerous articles on the history and cultural politics of Andean irrigation, and he is also the cotranslator of *Andean Lives: Gregorio Condori and Asunta Quispe Huamán* and the coproducer of *Transnational Fiesta: 1992*, a film about Cabanaconde.

Printed in the United States
20118LVS00005B/58-114